Women and the Constitution in Canada

edited by
Audrey Doerr and Micheline Carrier

Published by the
Canadian Advisory Council
on the Status of Women
151 Sparks Street
Box 1541, Station B
Ottawa, Ontario
K1P 5R5

©Minister of Supply and Services Canada 1981
Available in Canada through
Authorized Bookstore Agents and other bookstores
or by mail from

Canadian Government Publishing Centre
Supply and Services Canada

Hull, Quebec, Canada K1A 0S9

Catalogue No. LW31-8/1981E   Canada: **$2.95**
ISBN 0-660-10872-0   Other countries: **$3.55**

Price subject to change without notice.

Cette édition est aussi disponible en français.

Contents

Preface — Doris Anderson   V
Introduction — Audrey Doerr and Micheline Carrier   VII

I. Women and Constitutional Renewal   1
    — Mary Eberts, "Women and Constitutional Renewal"   3

II. Entrenchment of Rights for Women   29
    — Beverley Baines, "Women, Human Rights and the Constitution"   31
    — Statement by Native Women's Association of Canada on Native Women's Rights   64

III. Family Law   75
    — Myrna Bowman, "From Bad to Worse in One Easy Step: Proposed Transfer of Divorce Jurisdiction: An Assessment"   77
    — Carol Mahood Huddart, "Property Division on Marriage Breakdown in the Common Law Provinces"   94
    — Nicole Bénard, "Family Law and the Constitution"   113
    — Statement by the Fédération des femmes du Québec on Jurisdiction in Family Law   119

IV. Overlapping Jurisdictions and Women's Issues   121
    — Audrey Doerr, "Overlapping Jurisdictions and Women's Issues"   123
    — Statement by the National Action Committee on the Status of Women   149
    — Louise Dulude, "Women, Poverty and the Constitution"   165
    — Muriel Duckworth, "Social Services and Women"   172

V. Economic and Social Issues Facing Women   179
    — Micheline Carrier, "Women's Rights and 'National Interests'"   181
    — Lucienne Aubert, "Employment and Motherhood"   208
    — Statements by the Fédération des femmes du Québec on Women and Work   213

Postscript   221
List of Contributors   223

PREFACE

With the emergence of women's issues in the federal provincial constitutional discussions last year, the Canadian Advisory Council on the Status of Women scheduled a conference on "Women and the Constitution" to be held in September 1980. Unfortunately, the Conference had to be cancelled due to a translators' strike. It was then decided that the papers which had been prepared for the Conference should be made available in published form. This book presents an edited version of those papers and the several viewpoints to be represented. While the views contained herein represent the views of the respective authors and organizations and not those of the Canadian Advisory Council on the Status of Women, it is the hope of the Council that they will help to explain some of the major issues at stake for women in the process of constitutional change.

Women constitute 52 per cent of the population. It is *our* constitution, *our* lives that will be affected. It is, therefore, important that any new constitution reflects the realities and needs of our lives as workers, homemakers, mothers, wives and citizens. It is up to the women of Canada to make sure that the constitution gives all of us equality and good government for the next 100 years. Let the debate begin.

The preparation of this book involved the contributions and commitment of many people. The co-operation and responsiveness of the editors and the authors in revising material and meeting deadlines were commendable. The efforts of the Council staff also deserve acknowledgement. In particular, Julyan Reid, Director of Research deserves special mention for her part in getting the book underway and in seeing it through to completion. The assistance of Julie Woodsworth and Marcia Lalonde in the various stages of preparation and copy-editing of the text is gratefully acknowledged. A note of thanks is also extended to Joy Brown for the secretarial assistance she provided.

Doris Anderson

Introduction

Women's issues have received remarkably little attention in the current debate on constitutional reform in Canada. In fact, the absence of discussion on women's issues could be considered as a noteworthy feature of the debate. There is now evidence, however, that this situation may be changing.

The assumption that women's issues can be folded into general issues respecting "people" is valid only to the extent that women are indeed equal in status to men in law and in the practice of the laws especially by our governmental institutions. By and large, the articles in this volume challenge the assumption that women's concerns can be treated simply as "citizens' concerns." They are certainly citizens' concerns but they are also distinct in that equal status or equal opportunity in many areas of government activity cannot be presumed. The absence of equitable numbers of women in the boardrooms of the nation and the seats of political power is but one kind of evidence that women's status is not what it might be. The roots of discontent are deep within the social and cultural fabric of the country and are often perpetuated by weakly-worded legislation and curiously-argued judicial interpretations of the law. It has been fifty years since the Judicial Committee of the Privy Council in England upheld that women were persons under the British North America Act and yet today examples abound of cases in which the equality of women is not fully recognized.

The purpose of this book is to provide a reference source for women and men who wish to acquaint themselves with some of the key women's issues relevant to constitutional reform. Nevertheless, the collection of articles is not intended to be an exhaustive survey of all the issues or problems which might be considered. Rather it represents a starting point for discussion and investigation of these and other issues. The papers have been written from a number of perspectives. Some provide background and analysis; others deal with day-to-day problems as presented by women's organizations and concerned women. Thus, both theoretical issues and practical problems are put forward so the reader may assess the arguments on their several merits.

In the first section of the book, Mary Eberts provides an overview of the issues covered in subsequent chapters. She considers the question of women as "persons" and their special historical relationship to the constitution. The implications of the entrenchment of an equal rights clause in the constitution and the complexity of family law matters especially respecting divorce are also addressed. The representation of women in federal institutions and the impact of divided jurisdiction between federal and provincial governments on services for women are raised. Eberts emphasizes the need for a greater awareness of these issues among women and the importance of the participation of women in the constitutional debate. Complacency is not the road to reform.

In the second section, Beverley Baines provides a detailed consideration of the human rights of women in the context of a new Canadian constitution. She meticulously makes the argument that only a carefully worded "equality clause" in an entrenched Charter of Rights will protect women and guarantee equal treatment and status under the law. Judicial interpretations of the provisions in the present *Canadian Bill of Rights* legislation such as those provided in the *Lavell* and *Bliss* cases demonstrate the inadequacy of those provisions in protecting women's rights. While entrenchment of rights is important to women's interests, a major drawback to support of such entrenchment rests in the wording of the provision itself. As she concludes: "If the constitution-makers were to propose a clause which provided for the women's human right to equality in words that the Supreme Court of Canada could not emasculate, entrenchment would be appropriate." Beyond that, appointment of women to the Supreme Court itself would represent a positive and complementary action.

The lack of equality in the law affects native women in a doubly disadvantageous way. In its brief, the Native Women's Association of Canada laments the position of double jeopardy. Not only does the present constitution not recognize their rights as native people but also there is no guarantee of their rights as women. In sum, the position of native women is that a new constitution must recognize native rights and provide for the rights of native women and native people. Above all, these rights must be defined by the native peoples themselves.

The third section of the book focuses on the issue of family law. There are two main points of view contained in these chapters. On the one hand, lawyers from common law provinces support the exercise of federal authority in this area. Myrna Bowman argues that the federal government's proposed transfer of jurisdiction over divorce would undermine any basis for equal treatment on matters such as property settlement and child custody. Bowman challenges the proposition that divorce is a matter of a strictly local and private concern. She does not think that the transfer of jurisdiction from the federal government would enable provinces to make laws to conform more closely with the values of Canadians or that such a transfer would permit a more integrated approach to family law within provinces. In her view, there are three main types of problems which would be accentuated: jurisdiction shopping; rights based on marital status; and enforcement.

Carol Huddart provides a detailed comparison of current provincial legislation respecting property division on marriage breakdown. The existing system is highly complex and confusing and represents a high degree of balkanization of the legal process in this area. If citizens are guaranteed mobility rights in a new constitution, it would seem to follow that some degree of uniformity in laws respecting property settlement across the country should also exist. As she asks: "Should something so fundamental as our family rights and obligations, our marital status, or the status of the child be different depending on our choice of residence?" In answering this question, she offers several alternative approaches to the current system.

In contrast, the paper by Nicole Bénard, "Family Law and the Constitution," starts from a different set of assumptions. The civil law in Quebec has for centuries protected the rights and property of individuals. It is held that the provincial government is the only government over which Quebecers exert any real influence and, thus, matters of a local and private nature such as family law should be retained by the province. Recent amendments to the Civil Code and related statutes have served to modernize and update family law provisions. While further reforms are still needed, these are best done at the provincial level. The statement following this paper by the Fédération des femmes du Québec reasserts the position that the province of Quebec must exercise exclusive jurisdiction in the field of family law.

In the fourth section of the book, women's issues with respect to the division of powers and overlapping jurisdictions between federal and provincial governments are considered. Audrey Doerr discusses how the federal spending power has been used to promote the "national interest" in areas of provincial jurisdiction. She sets out three types of situations in which activities of provincial and federal governments overlap in the areas of employment, education and day care. On the one hand, the results may be beneficial for women in that an initiative by one level or the other can provide an impetus for improving women's position. On the other hand, they can be detrimental by leaving expectations unfulfilled in a labyrinth of federal-provincial joint funding agreements and programs that do not adequately take account of women's concerns.

In practical terms, overlapping jurisdictions have created serious problems for women's groups and individual women dependent on or desirous of developing services. In its statement, the National Action Committee on the Status of Women focuses on the problems of joint federal-provincial action in the provision of services. Funding arrangements have been found to be largely unsatisfactory. The particular types of problems that are created in respect of operating rape crisis centres and transition houses and providing child care, health care and pension and maternity benefits are considered. Louise Dulude's paper continues the discussion of the implications of joint responsibility particularly as they affect women on welfare. The inadequacy of support for low income mothers is a specific concern. In view of the positive effect that federal initiatives have had, she suggests that any effort to curb the federal spending power in the social service field will be detrimental to women. Muriel Duckworth expresses a similar concern but in a more direct and fundamental way. In her view, governments do not place a high enough priority on social problems; power not caring is their underlying motivation.

In the final section of the book, the discussion returns to continuing problems and concerns of women. In the chapter on "Women's Rights and 'National Interests'," Micheline Carrier describes the "three-sided cage of the status of women". She examines the problems of economic dependence and poverty of women, sexual exploitation and physical and moral violence. In her view, until women break out of their current bondage, they will have little real influence on affairs that affect them. The constitutional debate provides one opportunity to promote the rights of women. She recommends that women form committees at the community level to discuss and develop proposals for constitutional change which, in turn, could find expression in a nationally-constituted forum. Lucienne Aubert laments the problem of stereotyping women's issues. In her review of employment and motherhood, she examines critically the linkage of government unemployment policies with particular assumptions respecting women as child-bearers and mothers. The briefs by the Fédération des femmes du Québec demonstrate the prevalence of discrimination — overt and covert — against women in the workplace. In sum, there are many changes needed before the equality of women becomes a reality. Above all, a sustained commitment on the part of women to improve their status is a necessary prerequisite.

In conclusion, the following pages will take the reader down a largely uncharted road which has not been travelled by many. There is no pot of gold at the end, but there are many stark and revealing experiences to be met along the way.

Audrey Doerr
Micheline Carrier
December 1980

I. Women and Constitutional Renewal

Women and Constitutional Renewal

Mary Eberts

On July 4, 1980, the Prime Minister gave this brief but vivid description of the constitutional reform process:

> ... for 53 years, politicians have been trying to bring the Constitution back. Ten different and distinct attempts during the terms of six different prime ministers and politicians have always failed. And that's why it's up to you, the people, to decide that this matter must be done. So let us move![1]

Ordinary Canadians have been aware of discussions about "the Constitution" and "patriation" over the years. It is probably a safe guess, however, to say that few ordinary Canadians have believed this process to have much relevance to their lives. Constitutional discussion has seemed to be the specialty of governments and of specialists within governments. The prospect of returning our Constitution to Canada and of the changes that will attend that return should have much more meaning for Canadians than it does. Part of the reason for our lack of interest may well be the thick cloud of professional, and non-professional, terminology that hangs over the vital debate. We must try to decipher the differences between "constitutional review" and "constitutional renewal." Our options include "renewed federalism" and "restructured federalism." Special committees, task forces and continuing committees all figure in the deliberations. To the non-professional, outside of the constitutional-change bureaucracy, the picture is fuzzy indeed.

A more significant reason, perhaps, for Canadians' lack of zest for the constitutional review (or renewal) process is the difficulty of translating the abstractions of constitutional debate into terms that have real immediacy. Conditional and unconditional grants may seem remote topics. Few of us realize how vital the services funded by such grants may be to our well-being on a daily basis. It is crucial to begin putting the debate into this less grand, more concrete, perspective so that those whose lives, and whose children's lives, will be affected can see the whole process as one in which they have much at stake.

This paper is directed at one group of ordinary Canadians with a very special relationship to the Constitution: the women of Canada. It explores, briefly, the background of the constitutional debate and then moves to discuss some issues of particular interest to women in Canada. Not all such issues will be covered. Women are citizens and as such will have as wide a range of particular concerns as any other similarly large and diverse group of citizens. On the other hand, some issues can be expected to have impact on a large number of women, and these will be dealt with here. As other papers will treat particular issues in greater detail, only a general outline will be given. It is hoped, however, that the outline will be a sufficient point of departure for research and discussion that particular groups or individuals want to pursue.

The Constitution

A simple but satisfactory definition of a constitution has been provided by the Pepin-Robarts Task Force on Canadian Unity. In the report, *Coming to Terms:The Words of the Debate,* the Task Force states:

> A constitution is a set of fundamental laws, customs and conventions which provide the framework within which government is exercised in a state.
>
> A constitution contains essentially: (1) the basic principles, objectives and rules which command the political life of a society; (2) the definition of the principal organs of government in all four branches — the legislative, the executive, the judicial and the administrative — their composition, functions, powers and limitations; (3) the distribution and coordination of powers between the two orders of government if the form of government is a federal one; (4) the definition of relationship between the governors and the governed, particularly the rights of the latter.[2]

This definition, although simple, is a broad one. A narrower definition of a constitution is those rules which are embodied in a basic constitutional document.[3]

Our basic constitutional document is the *British North America Act,* passed in 1867 by the British Parliament to bring about Confederation, and amended a number of times since then.[4] This Act does not have a preamble that sets out our basic goals and understandings as Canadians. It lacks a Bill of Rights. It cannot be amended in Canada, except for those parts of it that affect only the federal government. The *British North America Act* does contain provisions about the organization of some of our basic institutions like the Senate, House of Commons and Supreme Court. There are many, however, who consider that these institutions need re-organization. The *British North America Act* also contains provisions that allocate legislative power to the federal and the provincial governments. Over some topics, like banking, the federal government has sole authority to pass laws. The provincial government has sole authority over certain other topics like property rights. In some fields, for example, both levels of government may pass laws. The need to re-evaluate the distribution of legislative power in light of contemporary problems and responsibilities is stressed again and again by governments.

Since the centennial of Confederation in 1967, there have been scores of meetings and many reports on the subject of constitutional review. In 1971, at the Constitutional Conference in Victoria, the federal and provincial governments narrowly failed to reach agreement on a charter of basic provisions for a new constitution. This "Victoria Charter" was reviewed, and a full proposal for a new constitution put forward in the 1972 *Report of the Special Joint Committee of the Senate and of the House of Commons on the Constitution of Canada* (Molgat-MacGuigan Report). The Pepin-Robarts Task Force on Canadian Unity was appointed in July 1977 not long after the Parti Québecois was elected to form the government of Quebec. Its main report, *A Future Together,* was published in 1979. Shortly before that, the federal government had tabled in Parliament Bill-60, the *Constitutional Amendment Bill,* its unsuccessful attempt to proceed unilaterally with reform of certain topics it considered to be within federal jurisdiction. Prior to the Quebec Referendum, the Government of Quebec published in November 1979 *Quebec-Canada: A New Deal — The Quebec Government's Proposal for a New Partnership Between Equals: Sovereignty Association.* In January 1980, the Constitutional Committee of the Liberal Party of Quebec issued its proposal: *A New Canadian Federation.* Other groups, public and private, have also prepared major position papers on the constitutional debate.

The first Constitutional Conference since Victoria was held in Ottawa from October 30 to November 1, 1978. At that meeting, it was agreed that study should go ahead on 14 items relating to the distribution of powers. The First Ministers also established a Continuing Committee of Ministers on the Constitution to meet to discuss these items and prepare a report for the next First Ministers' Conference, scheduled for February 1979. At the February Conference, a "best effort" draft of proposals on family law was discussed. This topic, quickly broached by the Prime Minister at the 1978 meeting, has since become a focal point for women's growing awareness of the constitutional debate. Governments' positions on it continue to evolve. Following the February 1979 conference, the Prime Minister made public a list of 11 subjects which he proposed for the second phase of constitutional review. In June 1980, the federal government announced its dedication to a full review of all constitutional measures now applying to the federation, singling out certain priority matters in a third list of topics. In July 1980, the Continuing Committee of Ministers on the Constitution resumed its meetings in preparation for another First Ministers' Conference scheduled for September 1980.

What Business Is This of Ours?

Anyone who has watched the televised meetings of the First Ministers will have noticed the total, or almost total, absence of women from the personnel of various governmental delegations. Constitutional review has been up to now a pursuit of men, as well as the business of specialists. It is time that women became more involved, and there are signs that this is beginning to happen.

In its May/June *NAC Memo,* the National Action Committee on the Status of Women announced that constitutional reform was its first priority of this year. It gave its tentative list of "Issues for Women in the Debate." The list included 15 items, and a warning that it was not all-inclusive! The items were:

1. Entrenchment of the human rights in the Constitution.
2. Indian rights as they relate to native women.
3. Family law — marriage, divorce, property and civil rights.
4. Economic — equal pay, maternity leave, child care, UIC, etc.
5. Education — retraining, skill training.
6. Political — representation of women in the Senate, on boards and commissions, courts, Lieutenant Governors, Crown.
7. Income security — pensions.
8. Health and welfare.
9. Criminal law — abortion.
10. Immigration.
11. Administration of justice.
12. Communications.
13. Cultural policy.
14. Housing.
15. Environment.

There is certainly some overlap between the topics on this list and those on the lists made public by government in connection with the constitutional review process. The topics agreed upon for study at the meeting of October-November 1978, for example, included communications, Senate, Supreme Court, family law, charter of rights and spending power. The Prime Minister's "second list," issued after the February 1979 meeting, proposed examination of the questions of the appointment of Superior Court judges and of Canada's native peoples and the Constitution. The "priority" list released in June 1980 lists among its 13 topics a statement of principles, a charter of rights, communications, family law, a new upper house and the Supreme Court.

Although there is this core of common interest in basic rights, government institutions and family law, there is some real divergence on the other matters. The National Action Committee list, for example, sees economic issues in terms of immediate impact on individuals: pensions, equal pay, child care, unemployment insurance. The "official" lists give priority to matters like resource ownership, interprovincial trade, general powers affecting the economy, and reduction of regional disparities through equalization or sharing. There is little doubt that these issues are significant for women, as for all Canadians. On the other hand, women may well wonder if there is a way of ensuring that they will share the economic well-being that governments hope will be generated by these measures. They also want to share in that economic well-being in a way that accords with their sense of priorities.

Some of the issues that women seem to have in common with the governments involved in constitutional review are: the preamble and charter of rights, government institutions and family law. Proposals affecting the spending power of governments are also important to women because control over that power — whether at the federal or the provincial level — is what determines what programs will be started, how much funding they will receive and how long they will live. It may well be here that we find the connection between the larger economic preoccupations of governments and the day-by-day economic interests of women.

Women's Special Relation to the Constitution

At one time, the Chief Justice of Canada stated that it would be a "vast" constitutional change to hold that women were "persons" who could be eligible to sit in the Senate.[5] Earlier, an English Law Lord had described as "momentous and far reaching" the constitutional change inherent in holding a woman eligible to vote in parliamentary elections.[6] Until the decision of the Privy Council in *Edwards v. A.G. Canada*,[7] the "Persons Case," women were regarded as incapable under the Constitution of taking part in public life. As Nellie McClung said, "That men are human beings, but women are women, with one reason for their existence, has long been the dictum of the world."[8]

In a long series of legal cases, in the British Isles as well as Canada, women had sought to assert that the enlightened reform legislation conferring political rights on "persons" or on "men" also applied to them. Until the "Persons Case," they were unsuccessful. For example, the New Brunswick Supreme Court held in 1905 that Mabel French was not a "person" who could become a barrister in that province. Once again, the personhood of women was described as a "radical" change.[9] In Quebec, with its civil law tradition, the same arguments of civil incapacity were met by a woman applicant for a call to the Bar. In a 1915 action by Annie Langstaff for admission to the Quebec Bar, Mr. Justice Saint-Pierre stated that for a woman to be admitted as a barrister "would be nothing short of a direct infringement upon public order and a manifest violation of the law of good morals and public decency."[10]

This, then, was the state of women's constitutional position as late as the 1920s in Canada. A series of statutes had secured some access to the franchise, but this was by no means universal, as women in some provinces were still subject to exclusions. In 1928, five women from Alberta petitioned the government to have the Supreme Court of Canada decide whether women were "qualified persons" who could be appointed to the Senate under section 24 of the *British North America Act*, 1867. The "Five Persons," as they came to be known, were Henrietta Muir Edwards, Irene Parlby, Louise Crummy MacKinney, Nellie McClung and Emily Murphy. The latter, a police magistrate, had often heard argued in her court the quaint proposition that "women are persons in matters of pain and penalties but not persons in the matter of rights and privileges."[11] The Supreme Court rejected the proposition that women are persons, but the case was appealed to the Judicial Committee of the Privy Council in England. The Privy Council accepted the idea, and it now forms part of the constitutional law of this country. As such it should be jealously guarded.

The difficulty of relying on neutral language like "person" or generic language like "man" to deal with women's rights has been demonstrated in the cases leading up to the "Persons Case." We still, however, have a provision in our *Interpretation Act* which states that "unless a contrary intention appears,"[12] words "importing male persons include female persons and corporations."[13] How easy it may still be for a "contrary intention" to be found!

Accordingly, it is probably more than wise — although somewhat tiresome — to scrutinize carefully the language employed in a new constitution for any sweeping declarations of principle. Examples abound. The *Declaration of the Rights of Man and of the Citizen* (France, 1789) states, "Men are born and remain free and equal in respect of rights." The *American Declaration of Independence* provides, "We hold these truths to be self evident, that all men are created equal . . ." In 1950, the Senate Special Committee on Human Rights wrote, "The brotherhood of man results from the fatherhood of God, and a fundamental equality among men necessarily follows."[14] The Canadian *Bill of Rights* affirms that:

> The Canadian nation is founded upon principles that acknowledge the supremacy of God, the dignity and worth of the human person and the

position of the family in a society of free men and free institutions . . . .[15]

The second important consequence of our constitutional "frailty" is that we can really take nothing for granted where basic rights are concerned. The basic political rights of voting and holding office depend on a combination of case law and statute. If a bill of rights were to be "entrenched" in a constitution, firmer safeguards could — and should — be given these fundamental rights. This sort of protection was proposed by the federal government prior to the Victoria Conference.[16] Article 5 of Part I of the Victoria Charter affirmed that no citizen shall, by reason of race, ethnic or national origin, colour, religion or sex be denied the right to vote in an election of members of the House of Commons or the Legislative Assembly of a province, or be disqualified from membership therein.[17] This sort of fundamental and unqualified guarantee should be looked for in any new constitution. The provincial governments are not uniformly in favour of an entrenched bill of rights. The federal government is, but its present proposal contained in Section 3 of the Charter of Rights and Freedom[18] would permit a "reasonable" distinction or limitation in the right to vote. Surely, there is little need for such qualification.

An Entrenched Bill of Rights

The former incapacity of women at common law gives them a special interest in the question of whether the Constitution of Canada should include an entrenched bill of rights. Briefly, a bill of rights is a safeguard of the rights which the citizen holds secure from invasion or curtailment by the state. "Entrenchment" means that those rights are preserved from legislative interference by the state as well as from administrative interference. The courts are to judge the propriety of government action according to the standards in the constitution. As will be outlined below, simply "entrenching" protections is not enough. It is also important to consider what an "entrenched" bill of rights should guarantee. Some types of protection are, unfortunately, next to meaningless.

The present *Canadian Bill of Rights*, passed in 1960, does set forth a number of fundamental rights and freedoms which, it says, have always been enjoyed by Canadians. The Bill, however, is expressly stated not to affect provincial actions. As an ordinary federal statute, it can affect only matters within federal jurisdiction under the *British North America Act*. An entrenched bill of rights would affect both federal and provincial spheres of activity.

Judicial interpretation of the *Canadian Bill of Rights* has been cautious, to say the least. It clearly reflects the view of the Supreme

Court of Canada that Parliament did not intend the *Bill of Rights* to apply to legislative activities of Parliament, as distinct from the simple "administration of the law."

A provision of particular significance for women is the provision in section 1(b) of the *Bill of Rights:*

> It is hereby recognized and declared that in Canada there have existed and shall continue to exist without discrimination by reason of race, national origin, colour, religion or sex, the following human rights and fundamental freedoms, namely . . . (b) the right of the individual to equality before the law and the protection of the law.

The phrase was immediately seen by women (and some men) as a way of achieving real equality by requiring removal of legislated differences between the sexes. This may have been a fond hope right from the outset. After all, the Justice Minister who proposed the Bill, Mr. Davie Fulton, stated in committee hearings on the Bill: "I do feel that the expression . . . would not be interpreted by the courts so as to say we are making men and women equal, because men and women are not equal: they are different."[19]

The far-reaching implications of these equality arguments were soon recognized. Judge Schultz of the British Columbia County Court bench stated in a 1970 case that if the *Bill of Rights* were

> interpreted to mean that there is 'discrimination by reason of . . . sex' unless every crime contained in the Criminal Code applies to both males and females, then a number of sections of the Criminal Code are inoperative and, indeed, the criminal law of Canada is now in an *emasculated*, chaotic state.[20] (emphasis supplied)

This remark perhaps indicates the lighter side of jurisprudence on the "equality-before-the-law" clause. The decisions of the Supreme Court are more serious. They reveal the inability, or unwillingness, of the Court to approach section 1(b) as a strong guarantee of equality.

In the well-known case of Indian woman Jeanette Lavell,[21] a majority of the Court rejected the claim that section 12(1)(b) of the *Indian Act* constitutes a denial of equality before the law. Section 12(1)(b) provides that an Indian woman who marries a non-Indian loses her Indian status. A similar "statutory excommunication" is not created for the male Indian who marries a non-Indian. The reasons of the majority stated that the equality before the law guarantee applied only to ensure equality in the administration of the law and not equality in the law itself.

In Manitoba, women distributed an announcement of mourning for the *Bill of Rights* after the Lavell decision. It stated that "its short valuable life was dedicated to the freedom of MAN; its sudden, untimely death occurred when women expected to be included."[22] In his dissenting reasons in the *Lavell* case, Mr. Justice Laskin, as he then was, doubted whether discrimination on account of sex, in the absence of biological or physiological rationale, "could be sustained as a reasonable classification even if the direction against it was not as explicit as it is in the Canadian Bill of Rights."[23] This language would be a strong guarantee of equal treatment if it were adopted by the Court. Unfortunately, there is little indication that it will be.

The current position with regard to "equality before the law" is that set out in the case of Vancouver woman Stella Bliss.[24] Stella Bliss was in the classic Catch-22 position. She had not worked long enough to qualify for maternity benefits under the *Unemployment Insurance Act*. She didn't really want them either: she was fit and wanted to work. But her employer dismissed her for maternity-related reasons. Being jobless and willing and able to work, she applied for regular unemployment insurance. She was advised that she was not entitled to regular benefits because she could have the special pregnancy benefits. But she was advised that she couldn't have the pregnancy benefits because she hadn't worked long enough. And so on.

The Supreme Court held that Bliss was not denied equality before the law with other unemployed workers. It stated that the distinction between her and other workers was made on the basis of pregnancy, not sex, and was, moreover, for a "valid federal object." The object of the legislation was considered to be the provision of benefits to pregnant women. The Court regarded the object as valid largely because it accepted the argument of government lawyers that it was "beneficial." "Validity" was made to depend on benevolence. The problem was that Sheila Bliss did not find the plan at all beneficial.

The "valid" or "beneficial" federal objects test seems to allow a Court to uphold any kind of sex-based distinction as long as the motives for it are good. When one considers that benevolent paternalism — the "gilded cage" or "pedestal" phenomenon — has been at the root of much of the restriction on women's roles, the dilemma becomes clear. The test for validity will uphold the very legislation which keeps women the most cloistered.

The need for a stronger constitutional stand against discrimination has been recognized. The 1968 federal government *Working Paper on a Canadian Charter of Human Rights* recognized the need to "entrench" guarantees of equaliy before the law, and to provide specific anti-discrimination measures in a new constitution. Other works, like the Molgat-MacGuigan Report, the Quebec Liberal Party's *A New Canadian Federation*, the Pepin-Robarts *A Future*

Together, and Bill C-60 also speak of "entrenching" an equality-before-the-law guarantee.

The *Canadian Charter of Rights and Freedoms* does contain an entrenched equality guarantee in section 15. It reads, in part: "Everyone has the right to equality before the law and to the equal protection of the law without discrimination because of race, national or ethnic origin, colour, religion, age or sex." The first phrase, "equality before the law" simply repeats the wording of the present *Bill of Rights*, which has been restrictively interpreted. It would not be realistic to expect our Supreme Court to enlarge the meaning of this phrase.

The second guarantee, the right "to the equal protection of the law" seems like an effort to incorporate into our Charter the language of the Fourteenth Amendment to the United States Constitution. The drafters of the Charter perhaps think that doing so will ensure that our section 15 will be interpreted in the same way as the Fourteenth Amendment. They may well think that such an interpretation will be a satisfactory guarantee of egalitarian rights.

There are, however, some real problems with the approach. To begin, there is no assurance that Canadian courts will see this phrase as their cue to import American interpretations. Even if they do, women should be aware that women's rights have not been as strongly protected under the Fourteenth Amendment as have the rights of those complaining of racial discrimination. There may well be a strong case for seeking some improvement in the language of section 15. A guarantee along the lines of "Every individual shall have equality of rights under the law without regard to. . ." the enumerated factors would be a stronger protection.

Women should be wary of other aspects of the "equality" guarantee. Section 29(2) of the Charter states that section 15 will not come into effect until three years after the passage of the Charter. It is suggested by some that this is provided to allow governments time to eliminate discrimination. Most women are aware, however, that the Royal Commission on the Status of Women pointed out, 10 years ago, what laws had to be changed to eliminate discrimination and many Advisory Councils on the Status of Women have, in the interval, up-dated this fundamental work. Three more years is not really necessary.

Section one of the Charter states that the guarantees of rights and freedoms are "subject only to such reasonable limits as are generally accepted in a free and democratic society with the parliamentary system of government." This sweeping clause makes "general acceptability" the test for validity of a limitation on our rights. This is foreign to the purposes of a Bill of Rights, which includes safeguarding the rights of unpopular, under-regarded or unknown groups and individuals. Given the general acceptability of sexual stereotyping, women have good reason to want a restriction of section one.

Some of the provinces believe, on the other hand, that basic rights are not best protected by an entrenched Bill of Rights. They argue that fundamental rights are well protected by our unwritten traditions of freedom and by the legislation of governments responsive to local goals and conditions. In my view, a Charter of Rights is a valuable and essential guarantee and governments committed to these principles should not hesitate to express them in a Charter.

Federal Institutions

Proposals for constitutional change quite commonly address the question of the composition of the Upper House. The desire to ensure greater representation from the provinces and territories is a common theme. The National Action Committee on the Status of Women has identified the issue of women's appointments generally as one deserving attention in the constitutional context. This should really come as no surprise. The efforts by the National Council of Women and many others to secure the appointment of a woman Senator precipitated the celebrated "Persons Case." Women's groups across Canada have repeatedly raised their concerns about appointments at both the federal and the provincial levels.

There have been many proposals for restructuring and renaming the Upper House. It has been suggested that we create a Council of the Federation (Pepin-Robarts), a House of the Federation (Bill C-60), and a Federal Council (Quebec Liberals). These proposals are all silent, however, on the question of women's presence in the Upper House. The question arises, therefore, whether women wish to make an issue out of their representation in any proposed new chamber. The reason why the issue can be suggested is quite simple. As long as the Upper House continues to be an appointed body, governments have control over who sits there. It may be the provincial and territorial governments rather than the federal government, or along with the federal government. Nonetheless, appointment of persons means that governments, and not the electoral process, influence who will be chosen.

Do Canadian women want to have a constitutional guarantee of equal representation in a new Upper House? Some Canadian women may want to see the Upper House abolished altogether, in common with others of this view. Should we merely reform the Senate, however, instead of abolishing it, the question may have to be met.

The issue of guaranteed equality in appointments is one that will prove controversial. In the United States, where affirmative action programs for minorities have been in existence for a considerable time, there is a re-evaluation of the justice of programs that promote the advancement of one group in compensation for past wrongs. A constitutionally-entrenched guarantee of equal representation in an appointed Upper House would be such a special measure, and would raise the same fundamental issues.

On the one hand, proponents of guaranteed representation might point to the slow progress in securing women's appointments since the "Persons Case" established their eligibility. Women do compose at least half the population. There are women of all political and religious beliefs, living in all parts of Canada, and deriving from all the national and cultural groups making up our country. And yet there are only 10 women in the Senate. It cannot be that lack of "qualifications" is keeping women out. Governments need some direction to redress the balance.

On the other hand, "quota systems" and affirmative action measures are seen by many to be artificial and unneeded. It is said that they would prevent the recognition of real talent or merit by creating the impression that all women were appointed only because of the requirement to appoint women. Moreover, the justice of requiring advancement for one group and not for another, or of "holding one group back" in favour of another, has been questioned most strenuously.

The fact is that a time of constitutional change may be the best time to require all governments to reaffirm their commitment to equal opportunity for women. The vigour with which they do this may be the guide by which women will decide how hard they must work for better representation in the Upper House, and what sort of guarantees they will consider requiring.

One reason why the issue of compostion of the Upper House becomes important is that a number of reform proposals suggest a greater role for a reformed Upper House in the selection or approval of Supreme Court justices. The concept of Senate approval of justices is familiar to Canadians who follow American politics. The very cautious performance of our Supreme Court in human rights areas may be, in part, attributable to the fact that the judges are drawn from a very narrow group: successful middle-aged, white, male lawyers. Having a more representative composition in the approving group may ensure over the years that potential judges with different backgrounds are sought out.

There may be other, more direct, ways of affecting the characteristics of the group from which our Supreme Court justices are chosen. Once again, the question of direct requirements arises. Regional representation and rules relating to the legal background of appointees have already found wide acceptance. Perhaps another stipulation requiring a certain number of women justices should be added. Against this is the problem that the stipulation may prevent the best from being chosen, or make the "lady judge" feel like a token, or prejudice the chance for more women than required by the constitutional guarantee.

These issues, deceptively so simple, are difficult. Yet it is imperative that a Court with greater responsibilities under an entrenched Charter of Rights and Freedoms must be drawn from a wider group of society than is now the case.

Family Law

Under section 91 of the *British North America Act*, 1867, Head 26, the federal government has jurisdiction over "Marriage and Divorce." Head 12 of section 92 gives to the provinces "The Solemnization of Marriage in the Province," and the provinces also have jurisdiction over "Property and Civil Rights in The Province." The federal jurisdiction under the *British North America Act* allows the federal Parliament to stipulate what would be necessary to establish a valid marriage. Not much use has been made of this power. The provincial governments are also able to make provisions related to the validity of marriage because of their power over solemnization of marriage. This present division of power means that both governments can impose requirements for validity. In the past, these requirements have related to matters like the degree of relationship between the parties (federal) and the requirement of parental consent where the parties are below a certain age (provincial).

The most current reform proposal in this area is the "best effort" draft of the February 1979 First Ministers Meeting, affirmed in July 1980. It would transfer all jurisdiction over the requirements for valid marriages to the provincial governments. This suggestion probably does not seriously change the present position, given the small degree of federal government activity in the field.

The more controversial area of the current constitutional debate is the proposal to transfer a large part of the federal power over divorce to the provinces. Initially, the federal government proposed in October/November 1978 that all jurisdiction over divorce be transferred to the provinces. A series of discussions in February 1979 and July 1980 have both elaborated and cut back this proposal.

The plan as it now stands has a number of features. First of all, jurisdiction over divorce would be transferred to whichever provinces want it. Those which do not would continue to have in effect the federal *Divorce Act*. Secondly, the federal government would continue to keep control over the jurisdictional bases upon which divorce can be granted, and over the recognition of divorce decrees. This means that the federal government would stipulate for all the provinces certain minimum requirements which must be met before a person could get a divorce. It is also designed to allow the federal government to set uniform standards about when one province should recognize as legal a divorce obtained in another. These two provisions are aimed at reducing concern about "divorce havens" and at preventing a situation where a person might be regarded as divorced by one part of Canada but married by another. However, this proposal does not ensure uniformity in the grounds for divorce across Canada. At the present time, grounds are uniform throughout the country, set out in the 1968 *Divorce Act*. This has not always been the case.

Prior to the 1968 *Divorce Act*, there was "a patchwork of laws derived from pre-Confederation, English and federal statutes."[25] For persons domiciled in Quebec and Newfoundland, the only way to obtain a divorce was by a private act of the federal Parliament. In New Brunswick, Nova Scotia and Prince Edward Island, divorce was available on the grounds of adultery or of marriage within the prohibited degrees of kinship. Cruelty and impotence were additional grounds in Nova Scotia, whereas frigidity or impotence were additional grounds in New Brunswick and Prince Edward Island. In Ontario until 1930, divorce was by Act of the federal Parliament. Until 1925, a husband could obtain a divorce on the ground of his wife's adultery. The wife was obliged to prove one of incestuous adultery, bigamy with adultery, adultery with cruelty, adultery with desertion without reasonable excuse for two years and upwards, or rape, sodomy or bestiality. After 1925, either spouse could petition on simple adultery. There are doubtless many who fear a return to this sort of patchwork and the problems caused by having one spouse in a province with "liberal" grounds for divorce and one in a province where divorce is harder to obtain.[26]

Before the passage of the 1968 *Divorce Act*, it was clear that the provinces had the constitutional power to pass laws dealing with the custody of children and the support of spouses. The 1968 federal *Divorce Act* also dealt with these topics, empowering a court to make an order of maintenance or custody in a divorce action.[27] It was affirmed by the courts that the federal government's power over divorce in the *British North America Act* enabled it to include these matters in its *Divorce Act*.[28] They are called "corollary relief" in the Act itself, and sometimes also referred to as being "ancillary" to divorce. The point of the terminology is that the federal government can legally deal with custody and maintenance only when these issues come up in the context of divorce. If there is no divorce power at the federal level, there would be no power to legislate on support and custody.

In February 1979, the "best effort" proposal about family law, which received support from governments, was prepared to let all the federal jurisdiction over these "ancillary" matters go to the provinces. This, as much as any other detail of the proposals, caused a storm of reaction from women's groups. In essence, the arguments in favour of shifting divorce and all its "ancillary" matters to the provinces are straightforward. For example, the Molgat-MacGuigan Report of 1972 recommended transfer of marriage and divorce to the provinces, because social policy ought to be within provincial jurisdiction where possible; because it would allow for a more integrated approach to family law within provincial jurisdictions; and, because it would allow for a more integrated approach within the civil and common law systems.[29] The report of the Pepin-Robarts Task Force on Canadian Unity, *A Future Together,* recommended provincial jurisdiction over marriage and divorce because the essential role of the provinces is to take the main responsibility for the social and cultural well-being and development of their communities.[30] The Lévèsque government's summary of the position is that the "recovery of all powers over marriage, divorce and the courts will allow us to create true family courts, to update our family law and to recognize the equality of Quebec women in all areas."[31]

It has been pointed out by both the federal government and the Quebec Liberal Party that federal jurisdiction over divorce at all is an exception to the general principle that control over local and private matters is in provincial hands. As the reasons for the exception related to religious differences existing at Confederation, but no longer, it is argued that a "return" to local control is desirable.

The problem with "returning" the ancillary matters of custody and support to the provinces is the already woeful state of enforcement of such orders. Even where all parties are within one province it has been demonstrated time and again that support orders are difficult for a spouse in need to enforce against one with no desire to pay. The problems of settling custody orders, and then making them work, are all too familiar. Where one spouse moves away from the jurisdiction where the order was made, enforcement problems can go from bad to worse.

Observers point out that the problem is serious even with a federal presence in the divorce field. Although the *Divorce Act* allows a spouse to file an order in a court anywhere in Canada and enforce it like an order of that court, problems of distance remain, and variation of an order when circumstances of the parties have changed must still be done in the province where it was first made, even though neither of the former spouses still lives there. Without a federal presence in the area, matters would arguably be much worse.

Similarly, the federal *Divorce Act* now provides certain standards in the support and custody areas which are uniform across the country and some protection against a more conservative local approach. Both parents are equally entitled to apply for custody in a divorce; the standards applied to measure fitness for custody are the same for both. Both spouses are entitled to apply for maintenance. Where local variations in laws applicable to the couple after they separate and before they divorce may still perpetuate differentiation between the sexes according to their stereotyped roles, the federal divorce standard offers a "last chance" to secure equal treatment.

The serious issues raised by women's groups did cause some re-evaluation in the position on family law in July 1980. Particularly, the federal government stated that the aspect of the proposal dealing with the enforcement of maintenance and custody orders must be reconsidered. Formerly, the proposal was simply to let jurisdiction pass to the provinces. In July, the federal government said that if such a transfer would not improve the enforcement of such orders, there was a clear obligation to search for better ways to secure enforcement.

It was proposed that the governments explore a number of options to improve enforcement. These included (1) federal jurisdiction over enforcement of extra-provincial orders; and (2) a constitutional provision requiring that one province enforce the orders made in another province. At this stage in the discussions, it is certain that women will want to see serious commitment to exploring these devices further. Even women who favour a strong local voice in family law, or exclusive provincial jurisdiction, may be concerned about inter-provincial problems.

The solution to the enforcement problem does not lie solely in constitutional change. Moreover, it may take a while to bring about such change. The federal government proposed in July that, to assist the constitutional discussion, governments might explore the possibility of establishing a joint federal-provincial registry of family law orders to improve the enforcement process.

The latest proposals are responsive to some of the concerns raised by women's groups. The recognition that both constitutional and non-constitutional means are necessary to solve the enforcement problem is a breakthrough. It will be important to see if non-constitutional means are explored with real seriousness, or whether governments are simply speaking "off the top of their heads." Regardless of the outcome of the constitutional talks, some better co-ordinating legislation and enforcement machinery between provinces is crucial.[32]

The proposals so far do not say anything about ensuring the maintenance of minimum standards of equality in divorce law once it is wholly in provincial hands. As the law stands now, nothing would prevent a province from making it easier for a man than for a woman to get a divorce. We are all familiar with the sex discrimination which, historically, was embedded in family law. We have probably all worked in our own provinces to change the law. Nothing now exists to stop a province from enacting new, discriminatory legislation.

Once again, the issue of a strong bill of rights emerges. An entrenched bill of rights is one way of securing a minimum standard in all government action, including that of the provinces. A strong guarantee of equality before the law would be very important. Any guarantee allowing discrimination for "benevolent objects" might well perpetuate benevolent paternalism in family law.

To be sure, this is just one way of discussing the question of standards. The discussion is necessary even where jurisdiction over marriage and divorce remains in federal hands. The necessity deepens when the activities of 12 or 13 jurisdictions start affecting us. Once again, women with a strong interest in local autonomy will nonetheless feel concern about the best way to ensure that their local governments affirm or strengthen their egalitarian treatment.

Another element of the current family law proposals is one which strengthens the unified family court concept. The proposed amendment would permit a province to transfer to provincially-appointed judges any of the traditional powers in the family law area of federally-appointed judges. This would facilitate the creation and staffing of unified family courts by the provinces. On their own initiative, they could appoint more judges, without having to seek federal appointments. They could also see that these judges performed wholly family law functions: most federally-appointed judges in Canada now hear a variety of different sorts of cases.

This provision is doubtless a welcome one. The careful observer might, however, wonder once again about representation of women's interests. Where, in our new Constitution, if at all, can we look to see if the provinces will be required to appoint women to these new unified family courts? How will we ensure, by constitutional or other means, that there will be adequate funding to provide the necessary judicial and administrative services?

There may be many now who feel that the crisis in the family law area has passed. There may be many, eager to see full provincial autonomy in family law, who never saw this set of proposals in crisis terms. There may well be others who will not be satisfied with the current proposals. These proposals are certainly not responsive to all of the concerns raised by women's groups: they ignore completely the problem of standards preventing discrimination on the basis of sex. A major achievement may well have been the recognition that non-constitutional, as well as constitutional, measures are needed to solve the enforcement dilemma. Whichever position one takes on the question of transfer, following up this initiative must be seen as an important priority.

The Spending Power

Canadian women are affected by a host of programs and services which might loosely be termed social welfare services. Some of them provide for the payment of an income to the person affected; some fund services to which they seek access. Even a cursory description of such measures shows how diverse they are. They include education, training and direct job creation. There are health and welfare services, like hospitalization and medicare. Income insurance measures include unemployment insurance, workmen's compensation and retirement provisions like the Canada and Quebec pension plans. Income support measures include family allowances, old age security, guaranteed income supplement, veterans' pensions and allowances, allowances for blind and disabled persons. Some of these programs are under the Canada Assistance Plan, a federal statute authorizing contributions by the government of Canada toward the cost of programs for the provision of assistance and welfare services "to and in respect of persons in need."

There are other types of services used by women which are not, by any objective standard, "welfare" for needy people. Rape crisis centres, day care services, and interval houses for battered women and their children are the sorts of programs needed by women of all socio-economic backgrounds. The Canada Assistance Plan being one of the few available sources of funding, however, day care and interval houses come under its aegis. They are, as a result, styled and treated as services for a welfare type of clientele, or as "income support" meaures. To complicate matters further, it is difficult to see where, if at all, rape crisis centres are placed for funding purposes. The harm in doing this is enormous: women needing services are deprived of them, either because they do not exist, or because they cannot accept anyone who does not fit the "welfare" label.

This array of women's services *does* have some connection with the ongoing constitutional debate. The issues are difficult and important. Any woman who has ever been given the run-around on funding by one or the other level of government has a good basic idea of what the issues are. Firstly, which level of government is responsible for initiating and developing services like this? What level of control over the services should the power of the purse bring with it? Lastly, how do ordinary people get into this process and ensure that the many governments pay attention to peoples' needs, not just government priorities?

The constitution has provisions relating to the raising of revenue by taxation. It has some, but not many, provisions about which level of government is responsible for a particular area like unemployment insurance or health care. However, vast areas of the present practice in these fields are not covered by any existing constitutional provision. Federal-provincial fiscal agreements, negotiated periodically, are the regulating mechanism. They are based on two premises: that the federal government's capacity to raise revenue is greater than that of the provinces and, that the provinces have responsibilities in health and social fields that outstrip their revenues. Getting federal money into provincial hands, with or without strings attached, is the basic purpose of these fiscal arrangements. When this money moves, and what strings should be attached are key questions for individual women as well as for groups seeking funding. Proposals for control of this federal spending power have come up in constitutional studies over the past few years. Should there be constitutional entrenchment of a method of control over the spending power, to replace or guide federal-provincial negotiation, the scheme adopted will affect us all for years.

Let us turn now to the first question mentioned above. Which level of government is responsible for services like those described?

With respect to some of them, the federal government has constitutional jurisdiction. A 1940 amendment to the *British North America Act,* 1867 gave the federal government exclusive jurisdiction in the field of unemployment insurance. Section 94A of the *British North America Act,* 1867 gives the federal government and the provincial governments a joint role with regard to some types of payments. It says that the federal government may "make laws in relation to old age pensions and supplementary benefits, including survivors' and disability benefits irrespective of age, but no such law shall affect the operation of any law present or future of a provincial legislature in relation to any such matters." With regard to veterans' allowances, the federal government would have jurisdiction by reason of its power over military and naval service and defence.

The provincial governments have constitutional authority over most of the others under section 92(13), property and civil rights in the province, and section 92(16), matters of a local and private nature. A number of considerations bear on whether we consider this provincial preponderance desirable, or whether women wish to argue for greater centralism or more nation-wide standards.

The opportunity to meet local needs, and respond to local interests is clearly a factor in favour of retained or enhanced provincial control. Local desires to develop a cohesive and comprehensive social policy will be promoted by stronger local control over the existence and content of assistance programs. Particularly if provincial governments win in the constitutional review process a greater power to raise money by taxation, the provinces could conceivably plan and fund an array of services designed to meet local priorities.

On the other hand are the historical arguments in favour of centralism. Portability from province to province is desirable in some areas of income insurance. Ensuring a uniform level of essential services in all areas of Canada, perhaps pursuant to international commitments, is another significant factor. Each individual who considers the question may well have personal preferences, based on the level of government she trusts or feels most able to influence.

The question of the appropriate government to have jurisdiction over a particular subject matter is bound to be influenced by fiscal considerations. These, in turn, have their roots in the *British North America Act* distribution of powers. Section 92(2) of the *Act* restricts the provinces to the levying of direct taxes, but there is no comparable limitation on the power of the federal government. As a result, the federal government has a greater capacity to fund these services and programs, but does not have the constitutional power to determine their content. The government which does have the power to determine content may well not have the revenue.

The traditional responsibilities of the provinces are in the areas where costs have escalated in the post-war years. To the extent that a "fiscal gap" exists between revenues and necessary expenditures, there have been various devices developed to transfer revenue from the federal government to the provinces. Those of primary interest are the federal-provincial grants, both conditional and unconditional. The unconditional grants are the carefully calculated "equalization payments" which are paid by the federal government to provinces with a below-average tax capacity. A number of constitutional reform proposals deal with the fate of the equalization grants, regarded as critical to well-being in less prosperous areas. In a significant respect, these transfers from the wealthier areas are an essential part of an overall national "equality" strategy for Canada.

It is conditional grants from the federal government to the provinces which fund a great number of the programs of significance to women. The largest intergovernmental transfer payments are made in the areas of hospital insurance, medicare, assistance to post-secondary education, the Canada Assistance Plan and regional development.[33] A number of constitutional issues emerge in these areas. The federal government may desire to control the use to which "its" money is put to ensure the achievement of social objectives. On the other hand, the provinces may chafe at the establishment of any program because it disrupts local priorities especially budgetary priorities. The provinces may, for example, wish to have unconditional grants or "block funding" from the federal government. Under this type of scheme, the federal government just transfers a sum to the province with no strings attached and lets the province decide how to spend it. Thus, these plans may let provinces build roads instead of day care centres. The safeguard of a federal check on the use of these funds may appeal to some women for, although there is a real loss of local autonomy, the goals of an autonomous locality may not be sympathetic to women's interests.[34]

Various proposals have been put forward to limit the control the federal government can exercise by way of its conditional grants. The Pepin-Robarts Task Force suggests that the way to limit the federal government's spending power would be to submit federal shared cost programs in areas of provincial competence to the consent of the provinces, or to a vote in a reformed Upper House.[35] The Molgat-MacGuigan Report endorses a federal proposal that a national consensus should be arrived at before a shared cost program is launched. It goes further, however, proposing that the national consensus rule apply every 10 years for each joint program, including existing programs, so as to prevent the undue perpetuation of certain joint programs.[36]

The individual woman — or group — may well doubt her/its ability to influence a game that is played on such a large scale. For example, the Royal Commission on the Status of Women in Canada recommended in its 1970 Report that the federal government "immediately" take steps to enter into an agreement with the provinces leading to a *National Day Care Act* under which federal funds would be made available to build and run centres. Nothing has been achieved to date, while the need for day care grows at an alarming rate. If a statutory reform relating to a federal-provincial joint program is this difficult to achieve, one can imagine the problems attending constitutional change.

Provisions for a "national consensus" may also seem daunting to women affected. The use by Ontario of what amounts to a veto to prevent the implementation of the proposed "drop-out" amendment of the Canada Pension Plan will come to the minds of many. National consensus in some cases means that women must convince all governments to care about women's issues. Convincing the federal government and one's province of residence is often quite hard enough.

Similarly, when these cost-sharing schemes provide that a province may "opt out" and receive an equivalent grant there are raised issues with which some women are already familiar. Is it the individual who receives directly the benefit the government has foregone on her behalf, or is it the government? Women certainly need to evaluate whether there are any mechanisms to safeguard the individual and her right to be heard when these large power games are played by governments.

Reform of the spending power is not an immediate priority with governments. It is, however, within the second category of the five "Powers Over the Economy" proposed for study by the federal government. This second category, "Redistribution of Income" should be a focus of women's study in the immediate future. Women have real influence here if they act in time.

Conclusions

A conference of the First Ministers on the Constitution convened in Ottawa on September 8. We have seen that the process of seeking agreement among governments was going on before that in the October 1978 and February 1979 meetings as well as in the Continuing Committee of Ministers on the Constitution. On October 2, the federal government published its "Proposed Resolution for a Joint Address to Her Majesty the Queen respecting the Constitution of Canada." The text was tabled in the House of Commons on

October 6. The rapid pace of events means that, on some matters of interest to women, we do not have a lot of leisure to make up our minds. If we linger, the choices will be made for us. In particular, we must determine where we stand on the question of entrenching a Bill of Rights and give serious thought to the proposed Charter of Human Rights and Freedoms which could become our entrenched Bill of Rights.

Thus, part of the task facing women awakened to our real stake in the constitutional debate is immediate and pressing. Part, however, is more long term. We know that discussions over taxation, particularly resource taxation, are unlikely to be easily resolved. The problems of arriving at any consensus on the large economic issues of a "common market" or economic union in Canada are formidable: the *British North America Act* deals with customs duties between the provinces, and all of the crucial economic issues raised by sovereignty-association proposals, labour mobility, government investment, and spending, remain to be thoroughly discussed. We are not yet in the economic mainstream of Canada. We are still out of positions of economic power and still seeking the basic individualized justice of day care so that we can work outside the home, and equal pay for work of equal value when we do. The government-shaking larger issues do, however, affect us daily. It is clearly in our interests to become more familiar with them, and to make our own values known. In the crucial area of services for women, our voice is essential to see that an equitable way of assessing spending priorities is developed — particularly if it is to be enshrined in a constitution.

As far as government institutions are concerned, our voice has long been heard, advocating fairer representation of women in decision-making bodies. The ambitious plans put forward by governments and others for reform have not yet addressed this aim. A famous revolution was once fought because of taxation without representation! If governments do not see our place and our voice in their assemblies, it is up to women to bring the point home. It is up to us to make sure that we are included in the constitutional review process, and that the perspectives and goals of women are taken seriously. We have a special, historical relationship to the constitution, as we had to fight so hard for so long to be included in even its minimal provisions. Let us not stop now.

Notes

[1] Pierre Elliot Trudeau, "The Prime Minister's Speech to the National Convention of the Liberal Party of Canada," Winnipeg, July 4, 1980 (Ottawa: Prime Minister's Office, 1980), p. 10.

[2]Task Force on Canadian Unity, *Coming to Terms: The Words of The Debate* (Ottawa: Supply and Services Canada, 1979), p. 29.

[3]Peter Hogg, *Constitutional Law of Canada* (Toronto: Carswell, 1977), p. 1.

[4]1871, 1886, 1907, 1915, 1930, 1940, 1943, 1946, 1949, 1949 (No. 2), 1951, 1952, 1960, 1964, 1965. See R.S.C., 1970, Appendix. See also Canadian amendments, *Representation Act, 1974*, S.C. 1974-75-76, c.13; *Northwest Territories Representation Act, 1975*, S.C. 1974-75-76, c.28; *British North America Act. (No. 2), 1975*, S.C. 1974-75-76, c.53.

[5]Anglin, C.J.C. in *Reference as to the Meaning of The Word 'Persons' in Section 24 of The British North America Act, 1867*, [1928] S.C.R. 276, 287.

[6]*Nairn* v. *University of St. Andrews*, [1909] A.C. 147 (H.L.)

[7][1930] A.C. 124.

[8]Nellie McClung, *In Times Like These* (Toronto: University of Toronto Press, 1972), p. 22.

[9](1905) 37, N.B.R. 359, at 371. A statute was required to provide for her entry to the bar. See S.N.B. 1906, s.5. In British Columbia, she met the same resistance. See *Re Mabel French* (1912), 1 WWR 488 (B.C.C.A.) and S.B.C. 1912, c.18

[10](1915), 47 Q.S.C. 131, at 142. Affirmed at (1915) 16 Q.K.B. 11.

[11]Grant MacEwan, *. . . and mighty women too* (Saskatoon: Western Producer Prairie Books, 1975). p. 133. See also *Rv. Cyr (alias Waters)*, [1917] 3 W.W.R. 849 (Alta. S.C.)

[12]R.S.C. 1970, c.I-23, s.3(1).

[13]R.S.C. 1970, c-I-23, s.26(6).

[14]Canada, Senate, "Official Report of Debates", 1950, Second Session, Twenty-first Parliament, 14 Geo. VI (Ottawa: King's Printer, 1950), Appendix, *Special Report of the Committee on Human Rights*, 585, at 587.

[15]S.C. 1960, c.44, R.S.C. 1970, Appendix III.

[16]Canada, Constitutional Conference 1968. Working Paper No. 3. *A Canadian Charter of Human Rights*. (Ottawa: Queen's Printer, 1968) p. 25.

[17]Canada, Parliament Special Joint Committee of the Senate and of the House of Commons on the Constitution of Canada, *Report* (Ottawa: Queen's Printer, 1972), p. 106.

[18]The Charter is Part I of *The Constitutional Act, 1980*, which forms Schedule B to the "Proposed Resolution for a Joint Address to Her Majesty the Queen respecting the Constitution of Canada", published on October 2, 1980 and tabled in the House of Commons on October 6, 1980

[19]Canada Special Committee on Human Rights and Fundamental Freedoms, *Minutes of Proceedings and Evidence*, Numbers 1 to 12 (July 12-29, 1960), p. 643.

[20]*R.* v. *Lavoie*, (1970), 16 D.L.R. (3d) 647, at p. 652.

[21]*A. G. of Canada* v. *Lavell; Isaac et al* v. *Bedard*, (1973) 38 D.L.R. (3d) 481 (S.C.C.).

[22]*Status of Women News*, Vol. 1, No. 2 (Winter 1974), cover and pages 2, 3.

[23](1973) 38 D.L.R. (3d) 481, at 510.

[24]*Bliss* v. *Attorney General of Canada*, (1978) 23 N.R. 527 (S.C.C.).

[25]Derek Mendes da Costa, "Divorce," *Studies in Canadian Family Law* (Toronto: Butterworths, 1972), p. 362.

[26]*Ibid.*, pp. 362-364.

[27]*Divorce Act*, R.S.C. 1970, CD-8, ss.

[28]*Zacks* v. *Zacks*, [1973] S.C.R. 891, (1973) 10 R.F.L. 53 (S.C.C.)

[29]Special Joint Committee Report (1972), p. 77.

[30]Canada Task Force on Canadian Unity, *A Future Together* (Ottawa: Supply and Services Canada, 1979), p. 85.

[31]Gouvernement du Québec, Conseil executif, *Quebec-Canada: A New Deal* (Quebec: Editeur officiel, 1979), p. 92.

[32] In 1974, the Uniform Law Conference of Canada adopted a uniform act dealing with the extra-provincial enforcement of custody orders for the guidance of the provinces. If all provinces adopt it, a coherent nation-wide system might emerge. Ontario and Quebec are the only provinces that have not adopted the uniform legislation. Manitoba provides a locating service and a lawyer at no cost to someone with a custody order from another province whose children have been abducted and moved to Manitoba, to help in enforcing the extra-provincial order.

[33] Robin W. Boadway, *Intergovernmental Transfers in Canada* (Toronto:Canadian Tax Foundation, 1980), p. 19.

[34] A wide range of social services are financed by matching grants under the Canada Assistance Plan. These include crisis intervention services, information and referral services, family planning services, children's services, rehabilitation services, day care, home support, transportation for the disabled, counselling, employment-related services, social integration services. In 1978 welfare ministers from the federal government and the provinces agreed in principle to replace the current 50:50 cost-sharing arrangement with a two-part scheme. The cost-sharing approach would continue to apply to basic income maintenance programs like welfare. Block funding, though, would apply to other existing programs and to any new ones. Part of the block funding is a "basic cash contribution" and part a "levelling payment." The basic cash contribution is a lump sum grant of equal per capita amounts to each province. As Boadway observes, "since the basic cash contribution is based on the national average federal transfer for social services, some provinces would gain and others lose." *Boadway*, p. 30. The foregoing description is taken from pp. 29 and 20 of *Boadway*. A bill to incorporate these changes was given first reading on May 12, 1978 (Bill C-55), but died on the order paper.

[35] Task Force on Canadian Unity, *Coming to Terms: The Words of the Debate* (Ottawa: Supply and Services Canada, 1979), p. 51.

[36] Special Joint Committee Report (1972), pp. 50-53.

II. Entrenchment of Rights for Women

Women, Human Rights and the Constitution

Beverley Baines

The current constitutional debate presents an opportunity to reconsider our human rights. The lack of an immediate threat to those rights may leave us more complacent than we should be. Unfortunately, discussions about human rights can seem intimidating if people feel constrained by a lack of knowledge about the issues. In this paper, I propose to provide the information and analysis which I consider pertinent to a discussion of the human rights of women in the context of a new Canadian constitution. I believe that this information will shatter any tendency toward complacency.

The first step in considering human rights is to delineate the boundaries of the discussion. A "right" is any claim which is protected by law. The phrase "human rights" will be used to designate those claims which people make against the state by virtue of their membership in the state. There are other terms such as "civil liberties" or "fundamental freedoms and rights" which might be used interchangeably with "human rights." Generally speaking, these terms focus on the distinction between what a citizen is entitled to do or not do and what a government can do or not do. If the normal function of government is to make and enforce rules, then a human, or citizen's, right imposes limitations on that rule-making ability. There is nevertheless a wide variety of expectations about what those limitations should be.

One way to illustrate the breadth of such expectations is to refer to the ways in which human rights have been legislated in Canada. There are four statutes in Canada in which the essential, or one of the essential, purposes is to serve as the basis for the claims that people can make against the state by virtue of their membership in the state. They are the Canadian[1] and Alberta bills of rights,[2] and certain sections of the *Quebec Charter of Human Rights and Freedoms*[3] and the *Saskatchewan Human Rights Code*.[4] The two bills of rights provide for similar types of claims which can be classified under four headings: political rights — the freedoms of religion, speech, assembly, association and press; legal rights — the right not to be deprived of life, liberty and security of the person except by due process of law[5]; egalitarian rights — the right to equality before the law without discrimination by reason of race, national origin, colour, religion or sex; and economic or property rights — the right not to be deprived of the enjoyment of property except by due process of law. The *Saskatchewan Human Rights Code* provides for the freedoms of conscience, expression and association; the freedom from arbitrary arrest; and the right to the franchise at least every five years. The *Quebec Charter of Human Rights and Freedoms* is probably the most innovative with provision for such rights as the right to assistance if a person's life is in peril; the right to the safeguard of a person's dignity, honour and reputation; the right to respect for a person's private life; the right to nondisclosure of confidential information; the right of every child to protection, security and attention by his or her family; the right, with some qualifications, to free public education; and so on.

The Manitoba Law Reform Commission has proposed a bill of rights for Manitoba that contains provisions similar to the Canadian and Alberta bills of rights, supplemented by provisions for the right to vote and be a candidate for public office, the right of ethnic or linguistic groups to enjoy and promote their own culture and language (Quebec has a similar provision), and the right of reasonable access to all public information.[6] Since the Second Constitutional Conference in 1969, the federal government has proposed the inclusion of language rights in any new charter of human rights.[7] In the 1978 Constitutional Amendment Bill the federal government supplemented freedom of religion with thought and conscience, and changed freedom of speech to freedom of opinion and expression. Both in 1978 and in the July 1980 draft of the Canadian Charter of Rights and Freedoms, the federal government proposed to create "mobility rights" including the right to pursue a livelihood in any province or territory.

All of these existing and proposed human rights are relevant to women. Many do, and will, serve as the basis for our claims for protection against governmental actions. However, one of these human rights is particularly important when women have to make claims based on the fact that they are women. Historically our legal system has treated women differently from men, with its treatment of men constituting the norm for legal personality. The goal of feminist claims is to ensure that women are treated as persons. The claim for legal personhood made by women is based on the principle which, in the words of the Royal Commission on the Status of

Women, "emphasizes the common status of women and men rather than a separate status for each sex."[8]

When expressed in traditional human rights terminology, the convention has arisen that women's claims for personhood are treated as claims for equality. The equality approach is based on female-to-male comparisons. There is always the risk that comparison will not produce a concept of legal personhood which is founded on the Royal Commission's principle of a common status of men and women. However, it is probably less feasible to propose a new approach which inevitably would have to contain details of the projected new common personhood status if it were to be substituted successfully for equality. It is more difficult to design and to implement a perfect system than to work within the existing framework. The equality approach could produce more immediate results, which hopefully would serve as the basis for an acceptable, if not utopian, personhood.

Women's human right to equality has some weak antecedents in the British and Canadian common law tradition. In one of the earliest British cases,[9] the court held that where a township contained only three houses, the inhabitants of all three could be appointed overseers of the poor, notwithstanding that two of them were labourers and relatively poor, and one was a woman. Five reasons were given for accepting the appointment of the woman, Alice Stubbs. These reasons were directed as much at precluding similar claims as at justifying this appointment. First Alice Stubbs, as a widow whose estate occupied the greatest part of land in the township, was a substantial landholder and therefore met the qualifications to be an overseer of the poor. Second, the position of overseer was not an "office of a higher nature." Third, the appointment was only for one year. Fourth, there was no danger that the appointment of a woman would become a common practice because judges had the discretion to refuse to make such appointments. Finally, it was necessary to appoint Alice Stubbs to the third overseer position because, aside from the other two appointees, there were no men in the parish qualified to fill the position.

From the time of this decision in 1788 until 1929 the British courts, when asked, consistently refused to allow women to vote in various electoral constituencies,[10] to hold elected or appointed public offices,[11] and to enter into training for various professional occupations,[12] especially the legal ones. In many of these cases, the women's claims were based on statutes which provided that "persons" were entitled to participate in the various activities. The grounds used by the courts for exclusion from personhood were expressed in terms of women's legal incapacity at common law to undertake public life, an incapacity which could only be removed by the most explicit legislative provisions. The use of the word "person" in legislation was not considered explicit enough to overcome their common law incapacity.

Since there were only two classifications at issue — the haves and the have-nots — equality terminology can be super-imposed on these "persons" decisions without distortion. This was recognized as early as 1868 when Mr. Justice Willes referred to women's separate but allegedly equal status:

> . . . women are under a legal incapacity to vote at elections. What was the cause of it, it is not necessary to go into: but, admitting that fickleness of judgement and liability to influence have sometimes been suggested as the ground of exclusion, I must protest against its being supposed to arise in this country from any underrating of the sex either in point of intellect or worth. That would be quite inconsistent with one of the glories of our civilization, — the respect and honour in which women are held.[13]

The impotence of this separate but equal status was demonstrated only five years later when Sophia Jex-Blake and nine other women brought an action against the Senate of the University of Edinburgh.[14] The women had been admitted to medical studies at the university with the provision that they were to attend special classes separate from the male students. However some of the professors refused to teach separate classes. When the eight man court divided four to four on the women's claim, four more judges were added to the bench. Thus a total of seven judges was found to deny that the women were entitled to complete their medical studies even in segregated classes. They dispelled the notion that a separate status for women could be seen as an equal status.

In Canada, courts in New Brunswick, Quebec and British Columbia refused to order the admission of women to the study and practice of law.[15] In 1917 Lizzie Cyr of Calgary appealed her conviction for vagrancy on the ground that the convicting police magistrate, Alice Jamieson, was a woman and thereby incapacitated from holding that position.[16] The appellant argued that the statute under which Alice Jamieson was appointed did not directly declare that women were eligible to be police magistrates; therefore she was incapacitated from holding that position according to the common law tradition.

Mr. Justice Stuart of the Alberta Supreme Court reached back 129 years to the Alice Stubbs case to hold that Alice Jamieson was not incapacitated. He reasoned that the Alice Stubbs case was the last case about a woman holding public office that was decided on general common law principles. All of the subsequent cases could be distinguished because their decisions were based on the interpretation of words, such as "person" or "man," in the pertinent statutes. Insofar as those cases referred to the common law, the references were not binding because they were incidental to the real basis for the decisions. Furthermore, he doubted that there was any decision that laid down as an absolute general rule that under the English common law a woman was disqualified from holding public office. This enabled him to conclude

> that applying the general principle upon which the common law rests, namely, that of reason and good sense as applied to new conditions, this Court ought to declare that in this Province, and at this time in our presently existing conditions, there is at common law no legal disqualification for holding public office in the government of the country arising from any distinction of sex.[17]

Mr. Justice Stuart's decision is significant for two reasons. First, it provides an illustration of creative judicial decision-making in the context of women's rights that is unparalleled in any subsequent Canadian decision. Secondly, it raises the question whether women's human right to equality would be better protected if left to the common law rather than codified. Unfortunately, history seems to weigh against reliance on the common law tradition as a source for women's rights. It is obvious that the number of earlier decisions rejecting women's claims far outweighed those supporting women. The significance of the *Cyr* decision has been diminished by the fact that it was not even mentioned in the next Canadian case, the "Persons Case."

When interpreting the word "persons" in section 24 of the *British North America Act*, the Supreme Court of Canada followed the traditional British precedent that women were under a legal incapacity which the word "persons" could not overcome.[18] The Judicial Committee of the Privy Council[19] overruled the Supreme Court of Canada on the ground that the word "persons" was sufficiently ambiguous that it could, and did, include women when the surrounding circumstances favoured that interpretation. Since the determinative circumstance was the constitutional significance of the *British North America Act*, the decision may not sustain support for reliance on the common law tradition in cases involving ordinary legislation.[20]

When assessing the value of the common law tradition, it is worth noting that the combined record of the Supreme Court of Canada and the Judicial Committee of the Privy Council showed at best ambivalence in deciding cases that today would be viewed as raising parallel claims for racial or ethnic equality. In 1899 the Judicial Committee of the Privy Council held that a British Columbia statute prohibiting women, children and Chinese men from working underground in mines was *ultra vires* insofar as it related to Chinese men.[21] (The exclusion of women was not challenged and therefore prevailed.) The Judicial Committee decided that the legislation was really directed towards those Chinese men who were either aliens or naturalized subjects. Thus, only the federal government could enact the legislation under the division of powers set out in the *British North America Act*. The court expressly stated that it had no right to consider whether prohibiting Chinese mine workers was a wise exercise of legislative jurisdiction. Therefore, although the effect of the decision was that Chinese men could continue to be employed in mines, they would not be able to look to the court for protection of their right not to be subject to discrimination. If the proper jurisdiction passed a discriminatory law, presumably it would stand. Thus, four years later the Judicial Committee held that British Columbia could deny the right to vote to men who were Chinese, Japanese or Indian.[22] (In 1902 women could not vote.) Not surprisingly, the Judicial Committee reiterated the view that it was not entitled to consider "the policy or impolicy of such an enactment as that which excludes a particular race from the franchise."[23]

In 1914 the Supreme Court of Canada followed the decisions of the Judicial Committee in holding that it was within the jurisdiction of the Saskatchewan government to pass a statute that prohibited Chinese men from employing white women.[24] Although each judge referred to the racial nature of the legislation, all used the division of powers approach as the basis for deciding to uphold the statute.

It was not until 1940 that a racial case was decided by the Supreme Court of Canada on grounds other than the federal-provincial division of powers.[25] The case involved a black man who was denied service in a Quebec tavern on the ground of his colour. The Court dismissed his claim for damages by referring to the general principle of freedom of commerce. This meant that any merchant was free to deal as he might choose with any individual member of the public. The effect of this decision was as devastating for the human right to equality as the earlier division of powers approach had been. It meant that discrimination on the ground of race could exist because freedom of commerce was to prevail.

In 1951 the Supreme Court of Canada did place a limited restriction on freedom of commerce when it decided that a restrictive covenant prohibiting the sale of land to Jews and blacks was unenforceable because it did not involve the use of the land.[26] The judges did not express any opinion about the discriminatory effect of the restrictive covenant.

The existence of these five racial or ethnic equality cases, by their omissions, reinforces the conclusion of the women's rights cases that the common law tradition provides little support for such claims. The highest courts in Canadian decision-making, by their words, do not establish themselves as proponents of egalitarian values. In fact, the "Persons Case," by openly referring to the history and effects of distinctions based on sex, came closer to acknowledging egalitarian values than any of the other cases with the possible exception of the dissenting judge in the 1914 Saskatchewan decision. However, the outcome in that Saskatchewan decision was the antithesis of equality.

The lesson to be learned is the absolute necessity of effectively worded legislation if women expect legal protection of their human right to equality. Even if the Supreme Court of Canada were to approve the very recent decision of the Ontario Court of Appeal by Madame Justice Bertha Wilson that there is a common law right not to be discriminated against on the grounds of ethnic origin,[27] women would not be assured the same right. Furthermore, if a common law right against discrimination on the ground of sex were to be sustained, it does not necessarily follow that it would have the status of a human right, that is, a claim against the government. In *Bhadauria,* the Ontario Court of Appeal was asked only whether the right existed in an employment situation. For now, the significance of the court's answer lies in the fact of recognition rather than in the specifics of what was recognized.

During the last 30 years in Canada, right to equality provisions for women and for other groups have been enacted primarily in bills of rights and human rights codes. This right is set out in the Canadian and Alberta bills of rights as "the right of the individual to equality before the law and the protection of the law ... without discrimination by reason of race, national origin, colour, religion or sex." There is no equivalent provision in the *Saskatchewan Human Rights Code.* The preamble to the *Quebec Charter of Human Rights and Freedoms* contains a reference to the "equal protection of the law," but as a preamble it may not have the same protective impact as the other independent statutory provisions. Moreover, there is no specific reference to sex as a proscribed classification.[28] In the remaining provinces which have not legislated the right to equality, the only recourse for women would be to the common law tradition, the limitations of which have been discussed above, or to international law which introduces new complexities, not the least of which includes a lack of effective sanctions.

Since all of the provinces and the federal government have enacted legislation which in nine of the 11 jurisdictions are called

37

"human rights" codes or acts (in Alberta, the *Individual's Rights Protection Act;* and in Quebec, the *Charter of Human Rights and Freedoms*), I will label these as "conventional" human rights codes to distinguish them from the kind of human rights provisions defined as the focus of this report, which I will call the "fundamental" human rights provisions. The conventional human rights codes enacted by all 11 jurisdictions, despite their variations, exist to forbid discriminatory practices in selected relationships such as between employer or employee, between tenants and lessors, between advertisers and the public. Obviously, conventional human rights codes are important because they regulate our everyday relationships with other people (including the government when it is acting as employer, lessor, advertiser, etc.). However, they do not deal with issues of the same magnitude as those raised when we claim our fundamental human right to equality against government. If an individual feels powerless in a fight with an employer or a lessor, that is, in voluntary relationships, this sense of vulnerability is even greater when the fight is the fundamental one of asserting our rights as citizens against a government which by its very nature is expected to exercise control over people.

There is a second important distinction between fundamental and conventional human rights legislation. Conventional human rights codes generally adopt non-discrimination terminology in contrast with the equality terminology of fundamental human rights legislation. In theory, both approaches have the same objective: the promotion of equality. However, in some cases the discrimination terminology of conventional human rights codes has been so narrowly interpreted by the courts that it is impossible to understand how equality has been promoted.

A case in point is the decision by the Ontario Court of Appeal that the Ontario Rural Softball Association had not offended the *Ontario Human Rights Code* when it refused to allow Debbie Bazso to play baseball.[29] If Ontario had provided for women's fundamental human right to equality, it would have been possible to use it as the basis for challenging the court's decision and the *Ontario Human Rights Code* provision. However, since Ontario does not provide for women's fundamental human right to equality, the legislature of Ontario cannot be compelled to revise the words of the *Ontario Human Rights Code* to ensure the inclusion of sports programs and facilities provided in public parks and arenas as Madame Justice Bertha Wilson had argued in her dissenting opinion in the *Bazso* case.

Unfortunately, the discrimination terminology of conventional human rights legislation, narrowly interpreted, also has been used to strike down two affirmative action programs in Alberta. A University of Calgary special program for native students was challenged by a non-native woman who had been refused admission to the program.[30] In the second case the Athabasca Tribal Council sought to make it a condition of the Energy Resources Conservation Board's approval of a new tar sands development that a special employment program for native people be established.[31] In both cases the affirmative action programs were held to have violated the non-discrimination provisions of the *Individual's Rights Protection Act*. The Alberta Court of Appeal said that

> the establishment of affirmative action programs would require amendments to the *Individual's Rights Protection Act* similar to those in a number of other provinces expressly exempting such programs from the operation of the statute.[32]

Alberta,[33] Newfoundland,[34] and Quebec[35] are the three jurisdictions which have not provided in their legislation for affirmative action programs. Since these decisions, Alberta has introduced an amendment that would allow Cabinet approval of such programs.[36] The remaining eight jurisdictions have legislated their approvals in their conventional human rights codes in a variety of ways. Five of those provinces — British Columbia,[37] Saskatchewan,[38] New Brunswick,[39] Prince Edward Island,[40] and Nova Scotia[41] — and the federal government[42] have specifically stated in their legislation that affirmative action programs, if approved, cannot be construed as discriminatory.

It is debatable, however, whether this type of legislation is sufficient to withstand challenge. A conventional human rights code which contains both non-discrimination provisions and an affirmative action provision communicates both the negative instruction — do not discriminate with respect to sex, and the positive instruction — discriminate with respect to sex. At least one of the conventional codes is expressed in this kind of converse language.[43]

Other conventional human rights codes have attempted to resolve this ambiguity by permitting affirmative action programs for "disadvantaged" groups.[44] If a group is defined as disadvantaged, discrimination is permissible to "even-up" the group's status in society. Therefore, the justification for affirmative action is the promotion of equality. It is equality that is sufficiently comprehensive to encompass both prohibition of discrimination and permission for affirmative action. However, this equality justification is speculative until or unless the legislatures and/or the courts approve it. In view of their past records in human rights, it is likely that the higher courts would be reluctant to define equality. Then, given the ambiguity of the negative and positive instructions, the most comfortable judicial resolution might be to prefer the more familiar non-discrimination approach with the consequence that most of the effective types of affirmative action programs would be defeated. In this event, the only instruction that the legislators might give successfully to intransigent courts would have to take the form of legislating the women's human right to equality so that it could serve as an explicit authorization of both the negative and positive discrimination instructions in conventional human rights codes.

Another argument used to challenge affirmative action programs would accept the decision of Ontario Court of Appeal judge Bertha Wilson that there is a common law right not to be subject to discrimination[45] and would extend this right to include sex discrimination. Again, such a non-discrimination right could be construed narrowly as exclusive of affirmative action programs. Then the question is whether this common law right of non-discrimination could be altered by legislating the more general fundamental human right to equality. On balance, it is probably more likely that the higher courts, traditionally so predisposed to defer to the legislature on questions of human rights, might accept a legislated definition of equality provided that the legislature underlined the significance of its intention by making the right fundamental.

At this point it is relevant to acknowledge the fact that Alberta is one of the two Canadian jurisdictions that has expressly legislated the provision for equality before the law without discrimination by reason of sex in its Bill of Rights. Yet it was an Alberta court which denied that affirmative action programs were acceptable. The American courts have wrestled with the equivalent problem without producing a majority opinion as to whether the affirmative action provisions in their Civil Rights Act violate their Bill of Rights equal-protection-of-the-law clause. Since the American Supreme Court has evaded this ruling for over a decade, it would not be surprising for the Supreme Court of Canada to adopt the same approach when confronted with this issue.

Women, whose interests lie in supporting affirmative action programs, may have to bear the cost of litigation either to procure or to uphold them. Therefore, they should seek the best protection possible, that is, legislation defining their fundamental human right to equality as including both positive and negative instructions about discrimination.

In sum, the common law is not a reliable source of women's human right to equality. Conventional human rights legislation, containing both non-discrimination and affirmative action provisions, is best safeguarded by the existence of a comprehensive and fundamental human right to equality. Therefore, the next question is whether our present equality-before-the-law clause can meet these requirements. The simple answer is that it does not.

In 1960, during House committee discussion of the clause respecting equality before the law without discrimination by reason of sex[46] in the *Canadian Bill of Rights,* the then Minister of Justice Davie Fulton expressed the view that men and women were different, not equal.[47] Although Canadian courts are not supposed to consider statements made by legislators when statutes are being passed, it is not hard to agree with Mary Eberts' conclusion that "This was not, however, a very auspicious beginning for a term that was soon to be used to attack incidents of the status of womanhood."[48]

The real test of the meaning and value of statutory statements of human rights arises when the courts, in particular the Supreme Court of Canada, the final court of appeal, are asked to apply them to actual confrontations between claimants and a government which in the case of the *Canadian Bill of Rights* is restricted to the jurisdiction of the federal government. If the court will not sustain the human right, then the statutory statement is without value. For women, the existence of the sex equality clause has engendered expectations of equality which have not been supported by the Supreme Court of Canada. The Supreme Court does not have a record of favouring the litigant who argues that an alleged inequality violates the equality-before-the-law clause, not only in the sex equality cases, but also in the general equality cases.

During the seventies the Supreme Court of Canada delivered 10 judgments that involved their interpretation of the equality-before-the-law clause of the *Canadian Bill of Rights.* Two of these cases alleged inequalities by reason of sex (*Lavell*[49] and *Bliss*[50]); two, by reason of race (*Drybones*[51] and *Canard*[52]); and the remaining six (*Smythe,*[53] *Curr,*[54] *Burnshine,*[55] *Prata,*[56] *Morgentaler,*[57] and *Hatchwell*[58]) alleged inequalities based on grounds other than the proscribed categories contained in the non-discrimination clause.

Of these ten cases, only one, *Drybones,* resulted in the decision that there was an inequality created by the federal statute. In that case, the section of the *Indian Act* that made it an offence for Indians to be intoxicated off a reserve was held to be inoperative. Mr. Justice Ritchie concluded his opinion by narrowly circumscribing the reason for his decision as follows:

> It appears to me to be desirable to make it plain that these reasons for judgment are limited to a situation in which, under the laws of Canada, it is made an offence punishable at law on account of race, for a person to do something which all Canadians who are not members of that race

may do with impunity; in my opinion the same considerations do not by any means apply to all the provisions of the Indian Act.[59]

The remaining nine decisions were decided after *Drybones* and in every case the Supreme Court of Canada denied that inequality existed. From the viewpoint of the persons alleging the inequalities from which they expect to be protected, this record is dismal. If these cases are seen as appropriate vehicles for the assertion of the human right to equality, then the dismal record in equality litigation must derive from inadequacies either of the Supreme Court of Canada or of the wording of the *Canadian Bill of Rights* equality-before-the-law clause, or of both, relative to what is expected of them.

Both race and sex are characteristics which, with a very few exceptions, are permanently ascribed at birth. As such, these involuntary characteristics should not serve as the basis for making distinctions among people when the law is being used to distribute the benefits and burdens of living in Canada. The *Canadian Bill of Rights* has recognized this invidiousness by proscribing race, sex, religion, colour and national origin, in the non-discrimination clause which introduces the various human rights clauses. Therefore, the race and sex cases were appropriate vehicles for raising inequality questions. Furthermore, it was analytically appropriate to raise the inequality issue in the race cases because they involved the comparison between the two classifications, Indians and non-Indians, the totality of which constituted the whole category of persons who might legally be punished for being intoxicated or might legally be permitted to administer a deceased's estate in Canada. Similarly inequality was an appropriate issue in the *Lavell* and *Bliss* cases because sex is the paradigm category containing as it does, only two classifications.

Six cases dealt with categories which were not proscribed. Since most laws only apply to some people — consumers, automobile drivers, and so on — it is normal for legislation to use categories or classifications. When the Supreme Court of Canada has to decide whether some categories are invidious or acceptable it has no standards on which to base that conclusion, other than the race, national origin, colour, religion or sex proscriptions in the non-discrimination clause. Perhaps the court should have refused to look beyond these proscribed categories, however, it has not accepted that limitation. Unfortunately, the consequence of extending the reach of the equality-before-the-law clause to categories other than the proscribed ones is that the court has then detrimentally applied the tests for invidiousness which it used in those cases to the cases involving race and sex. In fact the process should have been reversed. By virtue of their legislated status, the race and sex cases should have been analyzed to provide the standards for invidiousness required in the non-proscribed categories.

Without legislative standards, it is impossible to state conclusively whether it was appropriate to allege inequality in the six cases. Since they raise such a significantly different initial issue — the standard for ascribing invidiousness — from the race and sex cases which derive their invidiousness from the non-discrimination clause, consideration of the six should be restricted.

Assuming, therefore, that the race and sex cases were appropriate vehicles for the assertion of the human right to equality; the dismal record remains. In both of the sex cases and in one of the two race cases, the women who went to the Supreme Court of Canada expected that the equality-before-the-law clause of the *Canadian Bill of Rights* would protect their human right to equality. Their expectations were denied. Is there a relationship between those denials and the composition of the Supreme Court of Canada bench?

Since its origin in 1875, there has been an absolute male preference in the 59 appointments which have been made. The first woman in the British Empire to be admitted to the practice of law was Clara Brett Martin in Ontario in 1897. Since that time no woman lawyer has been appointed to the Supreme Court of Canada. In February 1970, the Royal Commission on the Status of Women recommended "that the federal government name more women judges to all courts within its jurisdiction."[60] Since this recommendation was made, there have been eight men appointed by the federal government to the Supreme Court of Canada. In the face of such intransigence, the only effective alternative is to demand legislation providing for the appointment of women to the Supreme Court of Canada.

Legislating the appointment of women judges to the Supreme Court of Canada is comparable with the present practice of appointing francophones to three out of the nine positions. The federal government's proposed *Constitutional Amendment Bill, 1978*, provided for an 11-member Supreme Court of Canada bench, four of whom would have been appointed from Quebec.[61] This was justified in terms of the importance of ensuring that questions relating to the civil law of Quebec were determined by judges trained in that law. If judges who are not admitted to the bar of Quebec may lack the requisite skill and expertise required to decide civil law cases, can it not also be argued that male judges may lack what Paul Weiler has called "the essential trait of judicial attitude" namely, "impartial and impersonal judgment,"[62] when deciding cases where sex inequality has been alleged by women?

There are two reasons why men may lack impartiality in sex equality cases. First, men never experience the deprivations from "personhood" which women face during their lifetime. Nor is it sufficient for a male judge to experience vicariously the deprivations of the women with whom he is intimate. The distance between being and perceiving can never be completely bridged even by the most sympathetic male judge.

A study of American cases carried out in 1971 by two middle-aged, white, male, law professors (their own self-characterization) is a case in point.[63] They analyzed a representative selection of American judicial opinions in which the judges were responding to allegations of sex discrimination. Their conclusion was that the performance of American judges in sex discrimination decisions ranged "from poor to abominable."[64] The judges "failed to bring to sex discrimination cases those judicial virtues of detachment, reflection and critical analysis which have served them so well with respect to other sensitive social issues."[65] The authors found particularly noteworthy the contrast between judicial attitudes in the sex discrimination cases and those in the race discrimination cases. They reported that:

> Judges have largely freed themselves from patterns of thought that can be stigmatized as "racist" — at least their opinions in that area exhibit a conscious attempt to free themselves from habits of stereotypical thought with regard to discrimination based on color. With respect to sex discrimination, however, the story is different. "Sexism" — the making of unjustified (or at least unsupported) assumptions about individual capabilities, interests, goals and social roles solely on the basis of sex differences — is as easily discernible in contemporary judicial opinions as racism ever was.[66]

The American study proceeded to offer "intuitive suggestions" as to the reasons why American male judges should have difficulty perceiving the harmful effects of sex discrimination. The initial reason was the judges' lack of knowledge and awareness of the injurious effects of sex discrimination; a lacuna which might be compounded if the judges over-generalized from their personal experiences because those women with whom the judges were in daily contact were likely to appear happy and satisfied.

The American study went on to suggest that even if male judges could understand the harmful effects of sex discrimination, their personal attitudes might deter them from granting the appropriate relief. It is the likelihood that these personal attitudes might consciously or unconsciously intrude that provides the second reason why male judges may lack impartiality in sex equality cases. A person is conditioned to conform to the social role expected of her or his sex. The process starts at birth with the question: Is it a girl or boy? It sometimes seems as if the nine months before birth is the only period in which it is really acceptable to ignore the dictates of social sex roles in favour of at least a female/male duality kind of personhood, if not a common status of personhood.

The conditioning process for one sex role is tantamount to rejection of the other sex role for any one peson. If the impartiality expected of judges includes empathizing with both parties, then in sex equality cases, judges would be required to fight their own sex role conditioning in order to empathize with female complainants. When the issue concerns not the secondary sex role differences of equal pay and equal opportunity, but the inherent sex differences of the sexual activity of marriage as in the *Lavell* case and of pregnancy as in the *Bliss* case, then the barriers to male judicial empathy may be insurmountable.

A recent study of British and American judicial decision-making entitled *Sexism and the Law* adopted the approach that "judicial pronouncements about females masked specific and discoverable material interests..."[67] and that such hidden material interests provided a better explanation of the survival of values of masculine supremacy "than the mere cultural inertia suggested by socialization theory."[68]

The specific material interest which caused men to resist equality between the sexes was "an interest in keeping women as head servants at home and keeping them out of the ranks of competitors at work."[69] The implication of this conflict of material interest explanation (the so-called sex war explanation) for the judiciary is that changing the situation would require more than re-educating the male judges. It would require the appointment of women to the bench, particularly to the Supreme Court of Canada as the court of final appeal, in such numbers that they would be representative of the number of women in Canada.

In the final analysis, changing the composition of the court cannot alter the existence of the precedent cases inimical to the women's human right to equality. As a general, if not absolute, rule, the Supreme Court considers that it must be guided by its prior decisions when deciding cases. The most reliable way to ensure that the Supreme Court would not consider itself bound by the unsatisfactory equality precedents is to change the wording of the legislation that provides for women's human right to equality. Since it also can be demonstrated that the existing legislation, the *Canadian Bill of Rights* equality-before-the-law clause, is inadequate, a change in wording becomes even more necessary if the clause is to have its expected legal impact.

The Supreme Court of Canada has taken the position that the meaning of the equality-before-the-law clause is not self-evident, but requires the intervention of a principle to give it substance. The range of judicial opinions as to the proper principle by which to explain the meaning of the equality-before-the-law clause is wide. At least five principles have been used. This creates uncertainty as to which one, if any, will be decisive in a case. Since too much uncertainty is an anathema to the rule of law, the present clause must be seen as inadequate because it does not give enough guidance to the court. Furthermore, each of the five principles which have been referred to in the equality cases has a serious shortcoming. It would not be constructive to wait and see if the court eventually were able to reduce the uncertainty by selecting one of them.

The two sex equality cases demonstrate the inadequacies of the equality-before-the-law clause. The judicial statements about equality before the law in the *Lavell* and *Bliss* cases make sufficient reference to what was said and decided about the equality-before-the-law clause in the other eight cases to obviate detailed references to the non-sex cases. These cases have very simple fact situations.

Jeanette Lavell was a registered Indian and band member who had married a non-Indian man. She was married in April 1970, and on December 7, 1970, her name was removed from her band's membership list by the Registrar pursuant to section 12(1) (b) of the *Indian Act*. She protested unsuccessfully to the Registrar and then to the York County Court. In his decision, York County Court Judge B.W. Grossberg said section 12(1) (b) of the *Indian Act* did not violate the equality-before-the-law clause of the *Canadian Bill of Rights* because when Jeanette Lavell married she had equality in status with all other married Canadian women.[70] The Federal Court of Appeal[71] recognized the ineptness of the County Court comparison of Indian married women with non-Indian married women and held that the appropriate comparison was between Indian women and Indian men when they married non-Indians. In a unanimous decision of the three-man bench, the Federal Court of Appeal ruled that section 12(1) (b) of the *Indian Act* was inoperative because it offended the *Canadian Bill of Rights* equality-before-the-law clause since "the consequences of the marriage of an Indian woman to a person who is not an Indian are worse for her than for other Indians who marry non-Indians..."[72] The Attorney General of Canada appealed the Federal Court of Appeal decision to the Supreme Court of Canada.

In Yvonne Bedard's case she had married in 1964 but subsequently returned to the reserve when she separated from her husband in 1970. She lived in a house which her mother had bequeathed to her and which she signed over to her brother. Her brother permitted her to continue living in the house, but the Band Council took action to have her evicted. Yvonne Bedard sought a court injunction to prevent her eviction. After she started the injunction proceeding, her name was removed from the band membership list, despite the fact that she was then separated from her non-Indian husband. Since she was merely separated, she could not qualify under the narrow relieving categories of a widow or a woman who had remarried an Indian as contained in section 12(1)(b). In the Ontario Supreme Court decision, Mr. Justice Osler ruled that he was bound by the Federal Court of Appeal decision given two months earlier in Jeanette Lavell's case.[73] In this case it was the defendants, the members of the Six Nations Band Council who appealed to the Supreme Court of Canada.

Since both the Attorney General and the Six Nations Band Council were appealing the decision that section 12(1)(b) was inoperative under the equality-before-the-law clause, the *Lavell* and *Bedard* cases were heard together and reported as one decision.[74] Up to the time that the Supreme Court appeal was heard, four of the five judges who had heard these cases had agreed to Jeanette Lavell and Yvonne Bedard's argument that section 12(1)(b) was invalid because it created inequality on the basis of sex. In a five-to-four decision, the Supreme Court of Canada reversed these decisions, thereby upholding the validity of section 12(1)(b). One of the five Supreme Court judges, Mr. Justice Pigeon, expressed no opinion on whether section 12(1)(b) created an inequality for Indian women. He said that he was prepared to uphold the validity of section 12(1)(b) because he did not believe that the *Canadian Bill of Rights* had the power to cause another federal law to be invalid. He had held the same view in *Drybones*, where he was in a minority. However, in the *Lavell* and *Bedard* decision, his opinion provided the majority needed to uphold the validity of section 12(1)(b). The numerical tally in this case underlines the importance of appointing women to the Supreme Court of Canada, where the infamous five prevailed.

The decision also emphasizes the need for a better legislative expression of the women's human right to equality. However, any proposed provision must be drafted to prevent the application of the principles used to deny that inequality existed. One must, therefore, understand those principles.

Mr. Justice Ritchie wrote the majority opinion in the *Lavell* and *Bedard* decision. He used what is known as the "rule of law" principle to explain why no inequality was created by section 12(1)(b) of the *Indian Act*. He derived the "rule of law" principle from the writings of a nineteenth century British constitutional lawyer, Dicey. According to Dicey, the "rule of law" was a fundamental principle of British government and it had three meanings. One of these meanings was "equality before the law or the equal subjection of all classes to the ordinary law of the land administered by the ordinary courts."[75] Therefore, Mr. Justice Ritchie said:

> in my opinion the phrase "equality before the law" as employed in section 1(b) of the Bill of Rights is to be treated as meaning equality in the administration or application of the law by the law enforcement authorities and the ordinary Courts of the land.[76]

In 1885, Dicey was concerned with denying the claims of officials for privilege or exemption from the ordinary law. However, the claims made by Drybones, Lavell and Bedard were not claims for exemption. On the contrary, Drybones claimed that he was entitled to be treated the way any intoxicated person who was not an Indian would be treated. Lavell and Bedard did not want to be excluded from the *Indian Act*; they claimed that s. 12(1) (b) excluded them when they wanted to continue to be included as Indians. Significantly, when Drybones was successful in his claim for inclusion, the "rule of law" principle of equality was never mentioned. This omission suggests that the "rule of law" principle should be confined to cases where an exemption is claimed. According to the *Drybones* decision, claims for inclusion involve a different principle of equality.[77]

Mr. Justice Ritchie referred to this rule-of-law principle in his opinion in the *Bliss* case and again it was inappropriate because Stella Bliss was not claiming an exemption. She argued against her exemption from unemployment insurance benefits. Stella Bliss claimed for ordinary unemployment insurance benefits under the *Unemployment Insurance Act* on the ground that she was capable of and available for work after she had given birth to her child.

The *Unemployment Insurance Act* provides for payment of three kinds of benefits[78]: ordinary benefits for those who are "capable of and available for" work; sickness benefits payable to those who are incapable of work because of illness, injury and quarantine; and pregnancy benefits during 14 weeks of pregnancy. To qualify for pregnancy benefits a woman must have been employed for a longer period that Stella Bliss had been employed, so she did not claim pregnancy benefits. She met the requirements for normal unemployment benefits except for section 46 of the *Unemployment Insurance Act* which states that during the 14-week pregnancy benefit period, no pregnant woman may claim other benefits under the *Act*. When Stella Bliss applied for the normal unemployment benefits, both the Unemployment Insurance Commission and the

Board of Referees to whom she appealed dismissed her claim that section 46 of the *Unemployment Insurance Act* created an inequality on the ground of sex.

She appealed again and Judge J. Collier of the Federal Court of Canada, sitting as Umpire under the *Unemployment Insurance Act*, supported her argument:

> I do not know the purpose of the legislators in injecting s. 46 into the 1971 legislation. It was suggested that, pre-1971, there was an assumption that women eight weeks before giving birth and for six weeks after, were, generally speaking, not capable of nor available for work; this, somehow gave rise to administrative difficulties or abuses; section 46 was enacted to make it quite clear that, in the 14-week period, pregnant women and women who had produced children, were, for the purpose of the statute, not capable of nor available for work, and therefore not entitled to benefits. All that may be. Nevertheless, I am driven to the inescapable conclusion that the impugned section, accidentally perhaps, authorizes discrimination by reason of sex, and as a consequence, abridges the right of equality of all claimants in respect of the Unemployment Insurance legislation.[79]

As in the case of Jeanette Lavell, it was the Attorney General who sought the next appeal to the Federal Court of Appeal. The three-man Federal Court of Appeal reversed Judge Collier's decision and held that section 46 was valid.

Mr. Justice Pratte wrote the decision. He said that the question was "not whether the Respondent has been the victim of discrimination by reason of sex but whether she has been deprived of 'the right to equality before the law' declared by s. 1(b) of the *Canadian Bill of Rights*."[80] He did not elaborate on his distinction between discrimination and deprivation of the right to equality before the law. However, there was no indication that he subscribed to the view adopted earlier in this paper that equality is the general concept which includes both nondiscrimination and affirmative action instructions.

Furthermore, Mr. Justice Pratte said, if there was discrimination arising from section 46, it was not discrimination by reason of sex:

> If section 46 treats unemployed pregnant women differently from other unemployed persons, be they male or female, it is, it seems to me, because they are pregnant and not because they are women.[81]

It seems that he refused to relate pregnancy to being a woman because not all unemployed women were, or ever would be, pregnant. But surely it could have been said in the *Drybones* case that not all Indians would become intoxicated. The issue is not whether all Indians or women are penalized; it is whether only Indians or only women can be penalized.

49

Having disposed of discrimination on the basis of sex as a way of explaining the equality-before-the-law clause, Mr. Justice Pratte adopted the "relevant distinction" principle to give meaning to the equality-before-the-law clause. According to this principle, statutes make distinctions between individuals. If there is "a logical connection between the basis for the distinction and the consequences that flow from it,"[82] the distinction is "relevant." Therefore,

> a person could be deprived of his right to equality before the law if he were treated more harshly than others by reasons of an irrelevant distinction made between himself and those other persons. If, however, the difference of treatment were based on a relevant distinction (or, even on a distinction that could be conceived as possibly relevant) the right to equality before the law would not be offended.[83]

Recognizing that his principle was not the rule of law principle of Mr. Justice Ritchie in *Lavell*, Mr. Justice Pratte stated that his own "wider definition" of the equality clause could be used because Mr. Justice Ritchie was not speaking for a majority of the *Lavell* court (Mr. Justice Pigeon, the "swing" judge, had remained silent about the meaning of equality).

The "relevant distinction," or logical connection, between the basis of the distinction (pregnancy) and the consequences that flow from it (denial of normal unemployment benefits) was twofold for Mr. Justice Pratte. First, he characterized pregnancy as the result of a voluntary act; his unstated implication being that women who became pregnant should bear the cost of any unemployment caused by their pregnancy. Second, he said that "Parliament possibly considered desirable that pregnant women refrain from work for 14 weeks on the occasion of their confinement."[84] In other words, it was perfectly logical to refuse pregnant women normal unemployment benefits during the "confinement" period because Parliament did not want women to work during that period of time. Either we are to assume that a logical connection is provided whenever Parliament desires something (pregnant women should not work), which in turn renders the principle useless; or Mr. Justice Pratte should have sought and evaluated Parliament's reasons for concluding that women should not work. Since he had already stigmatized pregnancy as voluntary, presumably he would not have found it difficult to assume that a policy that women should not work during the "confinement" period was for their own good and/or for the good of their co-workers.

The point which must be made is that Mr. Justice Pratte's application of the "relevant distinction" principle produced conclusions which were precisely what such a principle might be expected to produce. The principle rests on an assessment of what is logical or relevant. These are very wide and usually subjective categories. For example, if the state wanted to increase its population by having more babies born, it could justify the imposition of an annual tax on all women, or at least all women of child-bearing age who were not pregnant, on the ground that since only women get pregnant, taxing those who aren't will encourage them to get pregnant.

Since governments can give reasons for virtually all their legislation, the effect of linking inequality to irrelevance is that inequality will be defined out of the courts while still existing in real life. From the standpoint of the individual person, there is no protection against governmental action when inequality is defined in terms of irrelevance. The shocking problem is that the federal government has proposed in its constitutional discussions to do precisely this.

In the *Constitutional Amendment Bill, 1978,* the federal government sought to improve the equality-before-the-law clause by adding the word "equal" to the "protection of the law" clause, such that the two clauses would read "the right of the individual to equality before the law and to the equal protection of the law."[85] Otto Lang, then Minister of Justice, explained that "equality before the law" could be interpreted by the rule-of-law principle. Then "equal protection of the law" could mean that a law cannot apply in a discriminatory manner unless such discrimination is found to be justifiable in the community's interest on the basis of a reasonable classification test. Hence, a law requiring separate restroom facilities for men and women would be a reasonably justified discrimination. On the other hand, a law which denied public access to a park on the basis of colour or language would be found to be unjustifiable discrimination.[86] That is, by using language similar to that in the United States Bill of Rights, Mr. Lang wanted to tell Canadian courts to adopt the "reasonable classification" principle.[87] "Reasonable classification" is merely another way of expressing what Mr. Justice Pratte meant in *Bliss* by his "relevant distinction" principle.

Unfortunately, federal Justice Minister Chretien proposed a more perniciously expressed version of this "reasonable/relevant" principle in his July 1980 draft of the Canadian Charter of Rights and Freedoms:

> 7.(1) Everyone has the right to equality before the law and to equal protection of the law without distinction or restriction other than any distinction or restriction provided by law that is fair and reasonable having regard to the object of the law.[88]

How much more clearly can he say that any law that discriminates on the basis of sex, such as section 12(1)(b) of the *Indian Act* or section 46 of the *Unemployment Insurance Commission Act,* would be valid if it could be shown to have a reasonable purpose, such as being a mechanism to determine who is eligible for Indian status or being a mechanism to ensure that women are not available for and capable of working shortly after giving birth, respectively.

Insofar as the Supreme Court of Canada is concerned, Mr. Chrétien's proposal provides a ready-made principle, reasonableness, by which the Court could achieve precisely the same conclusions that it has been drawing from a variety of other principles. Interestingly enough in *Lavell*, Mr. Justice Ritchie rejected "the equalitarian concept exemplified by the 14th Amendment of the U.S. Constitution as interpreted by the Courts of that country"[89] which means he rejected the "reasonable classification" principle. Mr. Justice Laskin, expressing the view of the four dissenting judges that section 12(1)(b) of the *Indian Act* did create inequality for Indian women, said that the American cases had

> at best a marginal relevance because the Canadian Bill of Rights itself enumerates prohibited classifications which the judiciary is bound to respect; and, moreover, I doubt whether discrimination on account of sex, where as here it has no biological or physiological rationale, could be sustained as a reasonable classification even if the direction against it was not as explicit as it is in the Canadian Bill of Rights.[90]

Here Mr. Justice Laskin was espousing a third principle, the "prohibited classification" principle, to give meaning to the equality clause. This principle has two possible interpretations. By referring to "prohibited classifications," he may have meant that he preferred the "suspect classification" principle which the American Supreme Court has sporadically and unpredictably engrafted upon the "reasonable classification" principle. Sex has sometimes been given the status of a "suspect classification" and when it has the American Supreme Court has required a state to give a compelling reason, not merely a reasonable reason, for using the male or female classification in the law in question. The "suspect classification" principle was developed to answer the criticism that it was too easy for a government to comply with the "reasonable classification" principle by giving a reasonable purpose and thereby continuing to have discriminatory legislation. If sex were defined so as to remove any doubt that it was a suspect classification, the women's human right to equality would be better protected than under the Canadian federal government's present "reasonableness" proposal. At least the court would be under a duty to declare invalid legislation which created inequality and for which a government could not produce a compelling purpose. However, there is always the danger that the court's assessment of a compelling purpose might continue to be as superficial as its assessment of reasonableness/relevance.

It is not clear whether Mr. Justice Laskin intended to advocate the American "suspect classification" principle when he referred to the "prohibited classification" principle in *Lavell*. A second possible meaning for the "prohibited classification" principle is that laws can never use or make distinctions based on the proscribed categories of race, national origin, colour, religion or sex. Two obvious difficulties arise from such an interpretation of the "prohibited classification" principle. First, it would be impossible to continue to have any kind of *Indian Act;* and secondly, affirmative action programs geared to minority racial groups or women would be forbidden. There is no indication that Mr. Justice Laskin intended these consequences. Even if he had, affirmative action programs are sufficiently necessary for women's human right to equality under present social, economic and political conditions to suggest that this meaning of the "prohibited classification" principle should be rejected.

When Stella Bliss appealed the Federal Court of Appeal decision to the Supreme Court of Canada, she lost there as well. Mr. Justice Ritchie gave judgment for the seven-man court; there was no dissent. It has been suggested that Mr. Justice Laskin would have written a judgment had illness not prevented him from sitting on the case. In his decision, Mr. Justice Ritchie agreed with Mr. Justice Pratte that there was no discrimination based on sex because "Any inequality between the sexes in this area is not created by legislation but by nature."[91] By his statement it would appear that Mr. Justice Ritchie was unable to accept the possibility that legislation might compound natural differences. The cumulative impact of the two views, that being pregnant was not relevant to being a woman (Pratte, J.) and that legislation could not affect natural differences (Ritchie, J.), conveys a complete inability to comprehend the impact of legislating with respect to pregnancy.

In the course of his judgment Mr. Justice Ritchie referred to four of the principles that have been used to give meaning to equality, omitting only the "prohibited classification" principle. He applied his own rule of law principle developed in *Lavell* and held, without further explanation, that section 46 did "not involve denial of equality of treatment in the administration and enforcement of the law before the ordinary courts of the land . . ."[92]

Next, referring to Mr. Justice Pratte's "somewhat different" principle (the relevant distinction), he said, again without further explanation, that he had no doubt that "the period mentioned in s.46 is a relevant one for consideration in determining the conditions entitling pregnant women to benefits under a scheme of unemployment insurance . . ."[93] It is impossible to know whether the "benefits" referred to as relevant to the confinement period were pregnancy benefits or normal unemployment benefits. The confinement period was relevant for pregnancy benefits. However, once it was clear that Stella Bliss was not eligible for pregnancy benefits, the confinement period was irrelevant. By blurring this distinction throughout this judgment, Mr. Justice Ritchie created the illusion that pregnancy benefits rather than normal unemployment benefits were in issue.

Unfortunately, as a consequence of his blurred benefits approach, Mr. Justice Ritchie was unable to characterize section 46 as part of a legislative scheme to provide "additional benefits." This might have been an appropriate characterization if the provision of pregnancy benefits had been challenged on the ground that such benefits were not available to men.

However, in construing the legislation as beneficial rather than harmful to women, Mr. Justice Ritchie totally ignored the facts before him. Stella Bliss was not eligible for pregnancy benefits; she could not benefit from these "additional benefits." On the contrary, in her case there was no danger of double collection; there was only the reality of section 46 which meant she was disentitled to any benefits. In actual fact she was being treated more harshly.

Mr. Justice Ritchie used the "additional benefits" argument in the context of applying the fourth principle of equality. This is the "worse consequences" or "harsher treatment" principle which he originally applied in his *Drybones* decision.[94] The dangers of this principle can be illustrated by Mr. Justice Ritchie's own decision in *Burnshine*.[95] He held that incarcerating a young offender in British Columbia for a longer period than for a similar offender in any other province was not "harsher" treatment because the offender from British Columbia would benefit from the longer incarceration.

Women are as vulnerable to the vicissitudes of paternalism as young offenders. Whether the consequences of specific legislation should be construed as harmful or beneficial depends very much on the perspective of the viewer, as Mr. Justice Ritchie's *Burnshine* and *Bliss* opinions well illustrate. Furthermore, while the inequity of legislating harsher consequences for the same activity may be self-evident, the invidiousness of legislating some "benefits" historically has not been acknowledged. For example, legislation forbidding women to work underground in mines "for their protection" actually may have the effect of denying women employment in one-industry towns.

Realistically, it is impossible to avoid evaluative terms. This is the inevitable result of seeking a principle that will encompass both the non-discrimination and the affirmative action instructions. To reconcile these instructions some inequalities must be seen as invidious and some as necessary. Therefore, there must be a common evaluation mechanism that both describes and legitimates the reconciliation. Thus far the courts have not provided any such explanation for the "worse consequences" principle, or its beneficial corollary; the resulting applications have appeared arbitrary and sometimes irrational.

The fifth principle of equality is the "valid federal objectives" principle. This principle was first expounded by Mr. Justice Martland in the *Burnshine* case.[96] According to Mr. Justice Martland "Legislation dealing with a particular class of people is valid if it is enacted for the purpose of achieving a valid federal objective."[97] In other words, the "valid federal objective" principle is the old common law division-of-powers approach that was used in the early twentieth century human rights cases. As applied under the *Canadian Bill of Rights*, inequality could only exist when the federal government passed a law dealing with a matter assigned to the provinces in the *British North America Act*. The use of this priniple in *Bliss* enabled Mr. Justice Ritchie to uphold section 46 because he was "of the opinion that section 46 forms an integral part of a valid scheme of legislation enacted by Parliament in discharge of its legislative authority under the *British North America Act* . . ."[98]

It may be appropriate in a federal system to establish the legislative competence of the enacting government. However, competence and equality are two distinct issues. The "valid federal objective" principle must be supplemented by another principle which can give meaning to the human right to equality.

The analysis of the sex equality cases shows the uncertainty of the Supreme Court of Canada as to the appropriate principle to give meaning to the equality-before-the-law clause of the *Canadian Bill of Rights*. The inadequacy of each of the principles has been noted. The Court will not be able to alleviate the situation unilaterally. What is needed is a legislative expression which unambiguously speaks both to women and to the courts about women's human right to equality.

The experience of judicial interpretation of the present sex equality clause shows that any new expression will have to contain at least three components. First, the proscribed classification, women, should be used to emphasize that it is women who have been traditionally, and who continue to be, disadvantaged with respect to the legal status of personhood because of gender. In view of the startling inability of the courts to recognize when a gender classification has been used, it seems to be necessary also to provide that a law would be construed as classifying on the basis of womanhood when only, but not necessarily all, women and no men are included in or excluded from the law in question.

Second, as at present in the *Canadian Bill of Rights,* equality should remain as the positive value sought. In the federal government's July 1980 draft Charter of Rights and Freedoms for the first time the equality section has been entitled "Non-discrimination Rights." Expressing the generic value negatively could diminish its potential for encompassing both non-discrimination and affirmative action instructions. The negative terminology is neither historically nor logically necessary and should be rejected. Use of the negative terminology is particularly surprising in this draft because for the first time provision has also been made for affirmative action legislation: "7.(2) Nothing in this section precludes any programme or activity authorized by or pursuant to law that has as its object the amelioration of conditions of disadvantaged persons or groups."[99]

It is difficult to understand why the federal government is not prepared to specify the disadvantaged groups, at least by category such as race or colour, and by classification in the case of women since the category of sex has only two classifications one of which, women, is presently disadvantaged relative to the other. Failure to specify increases uncertainty and the likelihood of expensive and time-consuming litigation. Legislating the disadvantaged status of women in the affirmative action provision would necessitate an amendment when the disadvantaged status is overcome; but a single amendment is a less cumbersome and costly process than the alternative of having to respond to litigated challenges to affirmative action programs.

Furthermore, while section 7(2) legitimates affirmative action legislation under the specified conditions, it does not provide that women, or any other disadvantaged group, could require a government to pass affirmative action legislation. It would be unprecedented for government to place itself in a position where legally it could be forced to enact legislation. Nevertheless, that is a logical consequence of the human right to equality. The McRuer Royal Commission Inquiry into Civil Rights distinguished rights from freedoms. The freedoms — speech, assembly, religion, press and so on — were characterized as areas of option and opportunity in which individuals were free to act or not without being subject to legal regulation.[100] On the other hand, rights, such as life, property or equality, were characterized as having "specific and definite obligatory content" and therefore as depending on legal regulation.

If the specific obligatory content of the right to equality is "evening-up" the legal positions of disadvantaged groups relative to advantaged groups, then affirmative action legislation should be mandatory and not merely permissive.

The third and most important component is the provision of a new principle which gives meaning to equality in both of its non-discrimination and affirmative action guises. The defect in the American Equal Rights Amendment, which provides "Equality of rights under the law shall not be denied or abridged by the United States or by any State on account of sex" is the lack of a legislatively specified principle to give meaning to "equality." If this legislation were to be enacted in Canada, the Supreme Court of Canada would not have to vary its present negative approach to claims for women's human right to equality. Only if the legislature provides a principle for the interpretation of equality would a change on the part of the Court be required and expected.

There is no indication that any of the present Canadian constitution-makers have raised this issue, let alone tried to resolve it. There is no reason for leaving the response solely to the courts. Both judges and legislators make decisions which can be labelled "political" in the sense that both types of decisions involve important value choices. The distinction between judicial and legislative decisions lies not in the subject matter but in the process whereby each is expected to arrive at their respective decision. Judges are expected to make decisions based on reasoning from or to principles; legislators are free to use principles, history, intuition, self-interest, public opinion, and so on as the basis for their reasoning. The application of principles in judicial decisions does not mean that judges have a monopoly over the choice of principles that will be used to give meaning to fundamental values. This is particularly so in the case of women's human right to equality where the judicial record is one of confusion and discord.

If the constitution-makers were to assume the responsibility of providing a principle, it would have to be sufficiently general and flexible that the courts could apply it to the wide range of individual cases which might arise. At the same time, there would be the danger that too much generality and flexibility could invite a repetition of the present process where the unexplained conclusions appear to reflect the inadequacy of the guidelines. To compound these difficulties, it is unlikely that a model principle could be found in any other jurisdiction.

Nevertheless, the inequity of the present situation requires that an effort be made to suggest what the principle must do. It would then be the task of legislative draftspersons to convert the proposed policy into effective statutory words. The essential function which the principle must perform is to facilitate the process of "evening-up" the legal status of the disadvantaged group, women, relative to the legal status of the advantaged group, men. There is no simple way to recognize whether equality of legal status has been achieved. Equality is a goal-defining term the end product of which can only be described by words of relativity, such as "evening-up." However, what is significant about equality is that it is a positive goal to be sought, hence necessitating both the non-discrimination and affirmative action instructions. Put quite simply, the process of "evening-up" the legal status of a disadvantaged group relative to an advantaged group means that laws must not classify on the basis of the characteristic of the disadvantaged group, unless *that disadvantaged group* (not the courts, not the advantaged group, and not the government) is prepared to agree that such classification is necessary for this process. The final point to be made about the choice of a new principle to infuse meaning into women's human right to equality is that there must always be a "law," whether legislative or judicial and whether as worded or as applied, which serves as the mechanism for triggering a claim for women's human right to equality. On the other hand, questions in the future about the impact of a law, about whether women remain disadvantaged, about affirmative action programs, ultimately must depend for answers on the factual position of women in society as persons who work, marry, bear children, and so on. That factual position will reflect and guide their legal status, a circularity of life and law that is unescapable. As such, a caveat about the purpose of equality law is germane. It is foolish and unacceptable to expect that the purpose of equality law is sameness in the sense that individual differences and structural hierarchies would be abolished. Insofar as equality law would affect our lives in an ultimately equalitarian society, it should be through the neutralization of legal, not individual, differences.

If, and only if, the constitution-makers agree to legislate an equality clause that is sufficiently detailed to convey to the judges a meaning for equality that corresponds to women's expectations, then the question of whether to entrench human rights in the constitution becomes pertinent. First, entrenching human rights in the constitution, rather than leaving them in an ordinary law like the *Canadian Bill of Rights,* is seen as providing more protection for individual claimants because the courts will treat a constitutional law as more important and therefore more binding. If what is being discussed is entrenching the present clause, or a variant thereon, the effect of entrenchment would do nothing whatsoever to change the present negative response of the courts to women's claims for equality. The record in *Lavell* and *Bliss* makes this clear. Of all the Supreme Court of Canada judges who sat on these two cases, only one, Mr. Justice Pigeon in *Lavell*, based his decision on the conclusion that the wording of the *Canadian Bill of Rights* did not have the effect of overruling or invalidating another federal statute. No other judge was prepared to limit the effect of the *Canadian Bill of Rights* to the provision of a canon of construction rather than of invalidation. Every other judge who rejected the claims of Jeannette Lavell, Yvonne Bedard and Stella Bliss did so because he did not believe that any inequality was created by the laws in question. It is obvious that the courts are prepared to accept the binding nature of the present law; entrenchment to increase the binding nature of human rights claims is superfluous. It may be appropriate, as Walter Tarnopolsky has suggested,[101] to improve the terminology of the invalidation section, but as an ordinary law it was sufficiently binding to produce the *Drybones* decision.

The second reason for entrenchment, the achievement of uniform fundamental human rights legislation throughout Canada, is a good reason for supporting entrenchment given the present gaps in coverage. It has already been pointed out that only the federal and Alberta governments have legislated about the human right to equality. Human rights are so important that their existence should not be left to the vicissitudes of local politics. Some of the provinces have tried to argue that local conditions justify locally-defined human rights. This argument ignores the generality with which human rights must be expressed in order to cover the myriad of fact situations which may arise. It is this very generality which protects people under, and where necessary from, local conditions.

The more important argument against entrenchment has been expressed in terms of the inappropriateness of giving the courts the final say in human rights questions. In view of the courts' past record, women may have considerable sympathy with this view. Governments should be responsible for passing human rights laws of general application. On the other hand, it does not make any sense to ask a government to act as judge in a conflict in which it is one of the parties to the action. Resort to court adjudication will always be a part of the process of protecting human rights. However, even with entrenched human rights the legislature has the final say.[102] Entrenchment only makes changing the entrenched provisions more difficult, but not impossible. Walter Tarnopolsky has suggested that no government would find it politically feasible to repeal or amend any provisions of the present *Canadian Bill of Rights*.[103]

In conclusion, the argument for uniformity of protection is the one which compels women to support entrenchment, given the present gaps in protection. The present consitutional negotiations hold out the only possibility for uniformity and that appears in the guise of federal proposals for entrenchment of human rights. There are no serious disadvantages to entrenchment for women, save one — that of continuing to use the equality-before-the-law clause. If the constitution-makers were to propose a clause that provided for women's human right to equality in the words that the Supreme Court of Canada could not emasculate, entrenchment would be appropriate. The appointment of women to the Supreme Court of Canada bench would provide the balanced perspective currently lacking when women's claims to equality are adjudicated.

Notes

[1] *Canadian Bill of Rights*, R.S.C. 1970, Appendix III.

[2] *Alberta Bill of Rights*, S.A. 1972, c. 1.

[3] *Charter of Human Rights and Freedoms*, R.S.Q. 1977, c-12.

[4] *The Saskatchewan Human Rights Code*, S.S. 1979, c. S-24.1.

[5] This right also includes freedom from arbitrary arrest, the right not to receive cruel or unusual punishment, the right to be informed of the reasons for arrest, the right to retain counsel, the right of habeas corpus, the right not to be compelled to give evidence under certain circumstances, the right to a fair hearing, the right to be presumed innocent until proven guilty, the right to make reasonable bail except for just cause, and the right to an interpreter.

[6] Manitoba Law Reform Commission, *The Case for a Provincial Bill of Rights*, 1976, Appendix A, p. 61.

[7] Language rights presently are found in the *British North America Act*, s. 133, rather than in the *Canadian Bill of Rights*.

[8] Canada, Royal Commission on the Status of Women, *Report*, Ottawa, 1970, p. xi.

[9] *The King v. Alice Stubbs and others* (1788), 2 T.R. 395.

[10] *The Queen v. Crosthwaite* (1867), 17 Ir. Com. L.R. 463. *Chorlton v. Lings* (1868), L.R. 4 C.P. 374. *The Queen v. Harrald* (1872), L.R. 7 Q.B. 361. *Nairn v. University of St. Andrews*, [1909] A.C. 147.

[11] *Beresford-Hope v. Lady Sandhurst* (1889), 23 Q.B.D. 79. *De Souza v. Cobden* [1891] 1 Q.B. 687. *Viscountess Rhondda's Claim*, [1922] 2 A.C. 339.

[12] *Bebb v. The Law Society*, [1914] 1 Ch. D. 286. *Hall v. Incorp. Society of Law Agents* (1901), 38 Scot. L.R. 776. *Cave v. Benchers of Gray's Inn* (1903) The Times, Dec. 3.

[13] *Chorlton v. Lings*, op. cit., 338.

[14] *Jex-Blake v. Senatus of University of Edinburgh* (1873), 11 M. 784.

[15] *In Re Mabel P. French* (1905), 37 N.B.R. 359. *Re Mabel Fench* (1912), 1 D.L.R. 80. *Dame Langstaff v. The Bar of Quebec* (1915), 47 C.S. 131.

[16] *R. v. Cyr* (1917), 2 W.W.R. 1185, appealed [1917] 38 D.L.R. 601.

[17] *Ibid.*, 611.

[18] *In the Matter of a Reference as to the Meaning of the Word "Persons" in Section 24 of the British North America Act, 1867*. [1928] S.C.R. 276.

[19] *Edwards and others v. Attorney-General for Canada*, [1930] A.C. 124.

[20] M.E. Ritchie, "Alice Through the Statutes" (1975), 21 *McGill L.J.* 685, 701-2. See also G. Brent, "The Development of the Law Relating to the Participation of Canadian Women in Public Life" (1975), 25 *University of Toronto Law Journal* 358, 368-370.

[21]*Union Colliery Company of B.C. Ltd.* v. *Bryden*, [1899] A.C. 580.
[22]*Cunningham and A-G for B.C.* v. *Tomey Homma and A.G. for Canada*, [1903] A.C. 151.
[23]*Ibid.*, 155-6.
[24]*Quong-Wing* v. *The King*, [1914] 49 S.C.R. 440.
[25]*Christie* v. *The York Corporation*, [1940] S.C.R. 139.
[26]*Noble and Wolf* v. *Alley*, [1951] S.C.R. 64.
[27]*Bhadauria* v. *Seneca C.A.A.T.* (1980), 27 O.R. (2d) 142.
[28]Section 10 of the Quebec Charter provides: Every person has a right to full and equal recognition and exercise of his human rights and freedoms, without distinction, exclusion or preference based on race, colour, sex, etc. There has been no jurisprudence as to whether s. 10 applies to legislation or only to private activity.
[29]*Re Ontario Human Rights Commission et al. and Ontario Rural Softball Association* (1980), 26 O.R. (2d) 134. See also *Re Cummings and Ontario Minor Hockey Association* (1980), 26 O.R. (2d) 7, decided at the same time but on the technicality that the O.M.H.A. was not an incorporated entity and therefore could not be sued as a "person" under the Ontario Human Rights Code, section 2.
[30]*Bloedel* v. *University of Calgary*, unreported, Board of Inquiry, Jan. 30, 1980.
[31]The *Athabasca Tribal Council* v. *Amoco Canada Petroleum Company Ltd. et al.*[1980] 5 W.W.R. 165.
[32]*Ibid.*
[33]The *Individual's Rights Protection Act*, S.A. 1972, c. 2.
[34]*The Newfoundland Human Rights Code*, R.S.N. 1970, c. 262, as amended.
[35]*Supra*, n. 3.
[36]*An Act to Amend The Individual's Rights Protection Act*, Bill 201, 2nd session, 19th Legislature, 29 Eliz. II, s. 2.
[37]*Human Rights Code of British Columbia*, S.B.C. 1973, C. 119, as amended, s. 11(5).
[38]*The Saskatchewan Human Rights Code*, S.S. 1979, c. S-24.1, s. 47(3).
[39]*Human Rights Code*, R.S.N.B. 1973, c. H-11, as amended, s. 13(3).
[40]*Human Rights Act*, S.P.E.I. 1975, c. 72, as amended, s. 19.
[41]*Human Rights Act*, S.N.S., c. H-24, as amended, s. 19.
[42]*Canadian Human Rights Act*, 25-26 Eliz. II, c. 33, s. 15(1).
[43]*The Ontario Human Rights Code*, R.S.O. 1970, c. 318, as amended.
[44]Saskatchewan, Manitoba and Canada.
[45]*Supra*, n. 27.
[46]Hereafter called the equality clause.
[47]See M. Eberts, *Women and Constitutional Renewal*, *supra*. p. 10.
[48]M. Eberts, "The Rights of Women" in MacDonald and Humphrey, *The Practice of Freedom*, 1979, Butterworths, 237.
[49]*Attorney-General of Canada* v. *Lavell, Isaac* v. *Bedard* (1973), 38 D.L.R. (3d) 481. (The Supreme Court of Canada issued one decision that included both of these cases, so I shall treat them as one decision.)
[50]*Bliss* v. *Attorney-General of Canada* (1978), 23 N.R. 527.
[51]*R.* v. *Drybones* (1970), 9 D.L.R. (3d) 473.
[52]*Attorney-General of Canada* v. *Canard et al.* (1975), 52 D.L.R. (3d) 548.
[53]*R.* v. *Smythe* (1971), 19 D.L.R. (3d) 480.
[54]*Curr* v. *The Queen* (1972), 26 D.L.R. (3d) 603.
[55]*R.* v. *Burnshine* (1974), 44 D.L.R. (3d) 584.
[56]*Prata* v. *Ministry of Manpower and Immigration* (1975), 52 D.L.R. (3d) 383.
[57]*Morgentaler* v. *The Queen* (1975), 53 D.L.R. (3d) 161.
[58]*R.* v. *Hatchwell*, [1976] 1 S.C.R. 39.

[59] *Supra*, n. 51.
[60] *Supra*, n. 8, p. 342.
[61] *Constitutional Amendment Bill*, 1978, s. 104.
[62] P. Weiler, *In The Last Resort*, (Toronto: Carswell/Methuen, 1974) p. 22.
[63] J.D. Johnston, Jr., and C.L. Knapp, "Sex Discrimination by Law: A Study in Judicial Perspective" (1971), 46 *N.Y.U.L.R.* 675.
[64] *Ibid.*, 676.
[65] *Ibid.*
[66] *Ibid.*
[67] A. Sachs, and J.H. Wilson, *Sexism and the Law*, (New York: The Free Press, 1978) p.8.
[68] *Ibid.*, 9.
[69] *Ibid.*, 11.
[70] *Re Lavell and A-G. Canada* (1972), 22 D.L.R. (3d) 182.
[71] *Re Lavell and A-G. Canada* (1972), 22 D.L.R. (3d) 188.
[72] *Ibid.*, 193.
[73] *Bedard v. Isaac et al.* (1972), 22 D.L.R. (3d) 188.
[74] *Supra*, n. 49.
[75] *Ibid.*, 495.
[76] *Ibid.*
[77] Discussed in text accompanying n. 94.
[78] *Unemployment Insurance Act*, 1971, S.C. 1970-71-72, c. 48, s. 17, 25 and 30.
[79] *Bliss v. A.G. Canada* (1977), 16 N.R. 254, 257.
[80] *Ibid.*, 258.
[81] *Ibid.*
[82] *Ibid.*, 259.
[83] *Ibid.*, 260.
[84] *Ibid.*, 261.
[85] *Constitutional Amendment Bill*, 1978, s. 6.
[86] O. Lang, *Constitutional Reform: Canadian Charter of Rights and Freedoms*, Canada, 1978, p. 8.
[87] Also known as the "reasonable relationship" or "reasonableness" or "rational basis" principle.
[88] This section became section 15(1) in the Constitution Bill, 1980 which was put before Parliament. Section 15(1) reads: "Everyone has the right to equality before the law and to the equal protection of the law without discrimination because of race, national or ethnic origin, colour, religion, age or sex." There is no reference to the "reasonable/relevant" principle in s. 15(1); however the same effect is achieved by providing in s. 1 that: "The *Canadian Charter of Rights and Freedoms* guarantees the rights and freedoms set out in it subject only to such reasonable limits as are generally accepted in a free and democratic society with a parliamentary system of government."
[89] *Supra*, n. 49, 494. He said that the "equality before the law" clause did not evoke the American principle. This left open the question whether adoption of the American "equal protection of the law" terminology would cause the Supreme Court of Canada to adopt the American jurisprudence. Mr. Justice Laskin's rejection of the "reasonable classification" principle (see text, n. 90) was more categorical.
[90] *Ibid.*, 510.
[91] *Supra*, n. 50, p. 534.
[92] *Ibid.*, 535.
[93] *Ibid.*, 536.
[94] *Supra*, n. 51. This principle was also applied in *Lavell* by the Federal Court of Appeal and resulted in s. 12(1)(b) being declared inoperative, a finding which the Supreme Court of Canada later reversed using the rule of law principle. See text accompanying n. 72.

[95] *Supra*, n. 55.
[96] *Ibid*.
[97] As reported by Mr. Justice Martland in *Prata* v. *Min. of Manpower and Immigration* (1975), 3 N.R. 484, 490, citing *Burnshine*.
[98] *Supra*, n. 50, p. 537.
[99] Included in the proposed *Constitution Bill, 1980* as s. 15(2) which reads: "This section does not preclude any law, program or activity that has as its object the amelioration of conditions of disadvantaged persons or groups."
[100] Ontario. Royal Commission Inquiry into Civil Rights, *Report*, Vol. 4, No. 2, c. 102, p. 1493.
[101] W. Tarnopolsky, "A New Bill of Rights in the Light of the Interpretation of the Present One by the Supreme Court of Canada," Law Society of Upper Canada, Special Lectures on *The Constitution,* 1978, p. 161, 193.
[102] Bora Laskin, "The Role and Functions of Final Appellate Courts: The Supreme Court of Canada," [1975] 53 *C.B.R.* 469, 479. According to Mr. Justice Laskin "On constitutional issues, issues concerning the division or distribution of legislative power, the courts, and ultimately the Supreme Court of Canada, have the final word (subject to constitutional amendment)."
[103] *Supra*, no. 101, p. 165.

Statement by Native Women's Association of Canada on Native Women's Rights

The impact of the Canadian Constitution on all Canadians is immense, yet the federal and provincial governments are prepared to negotiate without the involvement or participation of many Canadians, and certainly without the participation and involvement of Canada's Native women. The 500,000 Native women living here have never been assured by governments or by Native leaders that they can speak from their communities to the decision-makers. *There must be the true involvement of Native women in determining any constitutional arrangement.*

Native women are concerned that their rights and freedoms have not flowed from the present constitution but rather from an administrative statute. Native women have yet to take their rightful place in Canadian history, recognized as women and as the descendants of the original people. *There must be the recognition of Native Rights, the entrenchment of the rights of Native women and of Native people and the endorsement of the principle that Native people must define what those rights are.*

Native people have been beaten and jailed for following their traditional religions, speaking their languages and carrying out their traditional customs. Too many Native people have lost their way in life because they could not grow up feeling proud, knowing and understanding their culture. They fight to survive in a world alienated from the land and from the harmony among human beings, animals, the land and sky. Women are the bearers of Native cultures, ensuring a life for Native children so they can be proud to be the descendants of the original people. *There must be the recognition of Native culture and heritage that Native women are helping to protect in all matters that affect Native people.*

Whatever the final constitutional outcome of the endeavours of Native leaders and governments may be, the result of actions by the governments and Native leaders will control future generations for many years. They cannot stand aside while their natural and human resources are drained away without their involvement or consent.

These first principles are required to provide an arrangement that gives Native women and their children a destiny that they can participate in fully and direct themselves.

Because Native women want to ensure their rightful place in the Canadian Constitution as descendants of the original people and as women, they feel they must speak out on the need to participate in the upcoming constitutional discussions. The concerns held by Native women on the *Bill of Rights* and social services will be presented to highlight the inadequacies of the present constitution and to point to a direction for change.

I

Native people are the descendants of the original people of this land. Before the Europeans arrived, Native people called themselves by their own names using their own languages. Native people are not the descendants of one nation but rather of hundreds of sovereign nations that lived on this land before the Europeans. When treaties were signed, they were signed by one nation entering into agreements with another nation. But as history has shown, treaties were not honoured in this way. Instead, the federal government developed an attitude of paternalism and assimilation towards Native people, legislating a process of defining who is an Indian and who is not, and confining Native people to specific sections of land.

Native people today are recognized and divided by the government of Canada under many titles. Status Indians are those Native people who the federal government has registered as Indians and to whom the government delivers the provisions of its responsibility under the *British North America Act*. Recently, the Inuit people have been recognized as "Indian" for these purposes. The non-status Indians and the Metis people are descendants of the original people but, for many reasons, are not registered as "Indian" by the government of Canada. Most non-status and Metis people do not have their land base recognized by the federal government.

Native women recognize the urgent need for unity among Native peoples by embracing all women of aboriginal descent as Native women. The divisions among Native people are rooted in the *British North America Act*, for the federal government felt the need to define the membership of the Indian people in order to exercise its constitutional responsibility.

II

Under the present constitutional arrangement, the *British North*

America Act, the federal government has exclusive legislative authority over "Indians and land reserved for the Indians." This is stated under Section 91(24) which is the only reference to Indians, and is wedged in the list of federal powers between "Copyrights" and "Naturalization and Aliens." There is no recognition in the *British North America Act* of the fact that Native nations pre-dated the establishment of the two "founding" nations. Rather than dealing with Native people as sovereign nations, as one would deal with foreign powers, the Canadian Government chose to use legislation to determine the scope of its responsibility toward Native people.

After Confederation, the *Indian Act* was made law virtually unchanged from previous acts passed in Lower and Upper Canada. What is important is not so much the specific provisions of the *Act* but the underlying and often rather overt philosophy of promoting assimilation of Native people based on the hope that the "Indian Problem" would soon die away. The argument has been made that the *Indian Act* cannot affect a person's status or aboriginal rights under the *British North America Act* since these derive from a person's status as a Native person and not from the *Indian Act*. However, judicial interpretations of the supremacy of the *Indian Act,* and the power of the *Indian Act* to determine how one is able to live one's life, has meant that the *Indian Act*, not the *British North America Act* has come to be seen as the embodiment of the rights and privileges of those peoples designated as Indian.

Under the present constitution, Native women face a double bind. Not only is there no recognition of their rights as Native people, there is also no guarantee of their rights as women. Despite the advances made by women toward constitutional equality, Native women today still do not enjoy the full range of rights, privileges and constitutional protection afforded non-Native women.

The federal government enacted the *Indian Act* as a means to carry out its constitutional responsibility and as part of that *Act* instituted a process that determines Indian membership. Earlier acts had a statutory definition of Indians as all persons of Indian blood, their spouses and descendants. The definition was to be applied when determining rights to possess or occupy lands; however, in 1869, the government passed an act aimed at the gradual enfranchisement of Indians. It was in this 1869 *Act* that women who married non-Indians ceased to be Indians in the eyes of the government. There are also provisions stating that, upon the death of an Indian man, his estate passed to his children, not his wife, and that if an Indian was enfranchised, his wife and minor children were automatically enfranchised. It must be noted that the predominant thinking then was that enfranchisement as full Canadian citizens was the most desirable goal for Indians to attain. To put it another way, an Indian person, once he or she had achieved a certain economic or educational status, could be admitted into the fold of Canadian citizenship.

Kathleen Jamieson, in her book *Indian Women and the Law in Canada: Citizens Minus,* outlines the principles embodied in the *Act* of 1869. First, Indians and their lands were to be assimilated, and the number of Indians reduced. Second, the government had to make the rational decisions for the welfare of Indians, who were seen as incapable of such decision-making. Finally, Indian women would be subject to their husbands as other non-Native women are.

Indian people, and certainly Indian women, were never involved in the deliberations of the *Indian Act* of 1869 nor any subsequent act. There was no consideration given to traditional tribal customs and many Indian nations found their matrilinial culture being legislated out of legal existence. But the most significant and overriding fact in any discussion of the *Indian Act* is that Native peoples belong to the only nations of people whose membership are not defined by themselves.

Native women believe in the fundamental, and perhaps rather obvious, principle that Native people *must have the freedom and power to determine their own membership, and in defining that membership there can be no discrimination based on sex.* The federal government's responsibility to Indian people is an addition to, not a substitute for, the rights of all people under the *British North America Act* and the *Canadian Bill of Rights.* Unfortunately, the Supreme Court has not shared that view.

The Supreme Court of Canada ruled in 1973 that the Section 12(1) (b) of the *Indian Act,* pertaining to the loss of status by Indian women when they married non-Indian men, did not violate the *Canadian Bill of Rights.*

Previously, in the *Regina* v *Drybones* case, the Supreme Court of Canada ruled that a section of the *Indian Act* regarding intoxication in public places could not be applied because the treatment of Indians was harsher than the treatment of non-Indians. The section contravened the right to equality before the law as stated in the *Bill of Rights.* It was believed that a precedent had been set that no law of Canada could operate contrary to the *Bill of Rights.*

Armed with this precedent, Jeannette Lavell went to the courts to have the decision to strike her off the Band list because she married a non-Indian overturned. When she was successful in the lower courts, the federal government appealed to the Supreme Court of Canada.

The Supreme Court based its decision to overturn earlier decisions on some fairly complicated reasoning. Rather than ruling only on Section 12(1) (b), the court looked at the entire *Indian Act* and found that, if the *Bill of Rights* was applied on the basis of discrimination, the *Indian Act* itself would be inoperable because it treats Indians differently from non-Indians. The court felt it could not bring down the entire act. As well, the court felt that there were no constitutional roots for the *Bill of Rights* but there were for the *Indian Act*, therefore the *Bill of Rights* would not override the *Indian Act*.

When arguments based on sexual discrimination failed, Lavell called upon the "Equality Before the Law" Section of the *Bill of Rights*. However, the court interpreted equality before the law as the administration and application of the law. Since the *Indian Act* was applied equally to men and women, although with different results, this right according to the court, had not been denied. The ruling was a departure from the precedent set in the *Drybones* case.

The court's arguments are difficult to follow if one accepts the view that discrimination whether based on race or sex is still discrimination. Under Section 2 of the *Bill of Rights* the rights and freedoms of individuals such as equality before the law, must be seen in light of Section 1 which states that these rights exist without discrimination by reason of race, national origin, colour, religion or sex. Nevertheless, the Supreme Court ruling has prevailed. The *Canadian Bill of Rights* holds no promise to Native women in their struggle to halt discrimination.

When the *Canadian Human Rights Act* was enacted the *Lavell* case was before the courts. The Minister of Justice agreed to exclude the *Indian Act* from the body of federal legislation subject to the provisions of the *Human Rights Act*. Native women have found no protection of their rights either under the *Canadian Bill of Rights* or the *Canadian Human Rights Act*.

III

History has proven that the *Bill of Rights* in its present statutory form cannot always be relied upon to protect and uphold the fundamental rights and freedom of not only Native women, but all Canadians. Its status as merely another piece of federal legislation has meant that discrimination and injustices have been allowed to continue.

It has been a hard lesson to learn that, while its originators saw the *Bill of Rights* as an adjunct to the constitution, this was not the court's ruling in the *Lavell* case. One has to wonder, as Walter

Tarnopolsky does in his book, *Canadian Bill of Rights,* how Canada can encourage legislation against discrimination in employment and housing, participate at United Nations meetings on the universal declaration of human rights and the international convention on the elimination of all forms of racial discrimination, and not have an enshrined Bill of Rights. The entrenchment of the *Canadian Bill of Rights* will ensure its supremacy, place it beyond the whims of governments and demonstrate to the courts its true impact and meaning.

But entrenchment of the *Bill of Rights* is only a first step toward ensuring the rights of Native women. Such a move would certainly assist in fighting discrimination. But, as long as the rights of Native people are not entrenched in the constitution, there can be no assurances that the paternalistic attitude of the government of Canada towards Native people, as evidenced through the *Indian Act,* will end. The federal government does have constitutional responsibility toward Native people, as defined by Native people, but this relationship must be based on cooperation and equal partners in a venture to secure the destiny of Native people.

When Native rights are guaranteed in the constitution, with the involvement of Native women at the community level, the Indian Act should be done away with or become the administrative statute it was meant to be. For without such assurances, the demise of the *Indian Act* may be interpreted as the demise of federal responsibility toward Native people. Native women will no longer tolerate legislation they have not designed themselves or been consulted on in a co-operative way.

The Native Women's Association of Canada *supports the moratorium on women being enfranchised when they marry non-Indians* as recently announced by the Minister of Indian Affairs resulting from pressure by most women parliamentarians.

The Native Women's Association of Canada hopes that all Band Councils will pass the required resolutions of support and give Native women time to work on developing a humane and just definition of "Indian." The moratorium will not correct past injustices done to women and all Native people. Native people have been enfranchised for achieving a university education, fighting for their country, wanting to sell the fruits of their labour without official permission, becoming economically self-sufficient, being omitted in the initial registration, or being the children of non-Indian mothers and grandmothers. The moratorium is only the first step toward fighting for the end of other injustices.

The federal government has not chosen a process of constitutional reform that is truly accessible to all people. There is a need for debate at the community level regarding both the constitution and the *Indian Act*. To a certain extent, the federal government has recognized the requirements of Native organizations to consult their constituents and undertake research and has provided funding for these purposes. It has not, however, recognized the concerns of Native women or made an effort to ensure their full participation in constitutional discussions.

IV

With the entrenchment of the rights of Native people in a new constitution, and the guarantee that Native people can define their own membership, the first steps will have been taken towards ensuring a future for Native people that they can control and direct themselves. With such constitutional guarantees and continued federal responsibility for all Native people, many of the concerns about the control and delivery of services to Native people will have been relieved.

Services for Native people are now delivered by both the federal and provincial governments. The federal government provides services for status Indians living on reserves, either by delivering those services itself or by reimbursing the provinces. Status Indians living off reserves and all non-status and Metis people must rely on services provided by the provincial governments which often do not meet Native people's needs.

Governments have never recognized traditional customs and ways when deciding which and how many services to give Native people. Governments have imposed non-Native systems as solutions to the problems faced by Native people. By defining membership of Native people so narrowly, the federal government refuses to recognize the needs of all people of aboriginal descent. The result is inadequate services and wide fluctuations in the level of services offered from province to province.

Native women believe that *all services for Native people need to recognize the uniqueness and vitality of Native culture.* Native people are constantly struggling to live their own cultures with their own customs and traditions, while at the same time, trying to deal with and survive in a modern technological society. The history of Native people in Canada has been one of forced dependency upon the federal government through paternalistic legislation and has meant loss of control over one's own life and destiny. By developing services tailored to fit the needs of Native people, this pattern can be reversed.

Unfortunately, it seems that non-Native society believes that no living culture existed prior to the coming of the Europeans. Governments felt the need to "educate" and assimilate Native people by providing them with educational, judicial and economic systems that were alien to Native people. Children are removed from their families and their communities by agencies who apply non-Native concepts of proper child care, and the children are placed in non-Native homes where they grow up without knowledge or appreciation of their own heritage. Native people in conflict with the law — a law based on values and conventions fundamentally different from those held by Native people — are more likely to be sentenced for crimes against property or for the non-payment of fines. Native women are incarcerated for federal offences in institutions thousands of miles from their communities where they can receive little support from their families. Native children learn a history in schools that consistently degrades their ancestors and reinforces cultural stereotypes. The skills learned in school often leave Native children unable to survive either in their home communities or in urban society, because the educational curriculum is not designed to meet their needs.

Native women must speak out on behalf of their families and especially their children, to ensure they will no longer be subject to the often well-intended but ill-fated attempts by governments to provide services. Native women believe that only when Native people control and deliver the services themselves will they have true control over their own destinies.

Native control over some services has begun. Some Native people living in cities have organized to provide services that governments cannot give, and to ensure that the services the governments do provide are delivered with the active participation of and consultation with Native people. One example encouraging to Native women is that on many reserves Band councils are starting to take control of and manage services, especially child welfare services.

The British Columbia Native Women's Society says that Native women "have an interest in every Native Indian child in the community, for it is understood that what our Native Indian children become will be reflected in what the community is going to be. And what we do to our Native Indian children we are doing to the community and to ourselves. And that if we look after them and make opportunities available to them, and give them the opportunity to take advantages of those opportunities, those Native Indian children will profit by what we can give them and in the long run we will be the gainer by what we have accorded to our children."

Good child care is not measured by material standards but by the care, attention and guidance the child receives from the communities. However, provincial child welfare agencies apply non-Native standards of good child care and take custody of many Native children. Over 3.5 per cent of Native children are in the care of child welfare agencies, compared to 1.35 per cent of all Canadian children (Philip Hepworth, *Foster Care and Adoption in Canada*, CCSD. 1980). Over 76 per cent of status Indian children adopted between 1969 and 1978 were adopted by non-Native families (Department of Indian Affairs). The likelihood of these children ever returning to their home communities or knowing their heritage is minimal.

One Band in British Columbia, the Spallumcheen Indian Band, recently moved to stop the unwarranted apprehension of its children. Between 1951 and 1961 the province removed 70 children from the reserve, often during fruit picking season when the elders took care of the children. Almost an entire generation was removed and many of these children are now alcoholics, incarcerated, have committed suicide or are unable to keep their own families together.

The Band Council has passed a by-law that gives the Band exclusive jurisdiction over any child custody proceeding involving Native children. Children are removed only when there is a family request, in cases of abuse or neglect, abandonment, or when the child is deprived of necessary care due to death, imprisonment or disability of the parents. The Chief and Council are guided in their decisions by Indian customs, and by the wishes of the child, if he or she is old enough. The Chief and Council place children preferably with relatives living on the reserve, another reserve, or off the reserve, with the long-term objective of rebuilding the family. Failing that, the children are placed with Native people on the reserve or off the reserve or, as a last resort, with non-Native people. The decision can be reviewed at any time by the parent or an extended family member, and appeals made at a meeting with the entire band. The family can have the child returned or placed in another home at any time and they are informed of major changes and events in the child's life. The Spallumcheen Indian Band views "parents" as the biological, lawfully-adopted or tribal-law or custom-adopted parents, and "family" as the unit with which the child is a permanent member and usually resides.

The Spallumcheen Band's actions are an example of measures Native women know need to take place across the country. With constitutional guarantees, Native people can begin the process of delivering all services to all Native people. While that process is underway, the federal and provincial governments must sit down with Native people and jointly develop the mechanisms that will ensure that Native people, no matter where they live in this country, can control their own destinies. For, as an unknown author said:

> I need to make my own
> choices . . .
> I need to live with
> dignity . . .
> I need to remember my
> heritage . . .
> I need to be heard and
> understood . . .
> I need to live in harmony
> with my creator. . .
> I need to be accepted
> for what I am . . .
> An Indian.

V

"There is no present or future — only the past, happening over and over again — now." Native women realize that unless they speak out now to protect their children, their land and their rights, the opportunity may never occur again. Whether the future of Native people is as nations under a Canadian Constitution or as nations with their own constitutions, Native women at the community level need to be truly involved in the debates to protect and entrench both their rights as women and as Native people. Flowing from the entrenchment of these two rights is the freedom to control one's own destiny in a manner that protects the integrity of Native cultures and employs traditional Native customs and values.

III. Family Law

From Bad to Worse in One Easy Step: Proposed Transfer of Divorce Jurisdiction: An Assessment

Myrna Bowman

The purpose of this paper is to discuss the proposed constitutional amendment to transfer jurisdiction over divorce from the federal to the provincial sphere. It is not possible to foresee or to describe all of the possible ramifications of such a transfer in this presentation, but the major concerns and arguments are here presented.

The proposal under discussion is that put forward by the Honourable Jean Chrétien on July 8, 1980.[1] This is the most recent version of proposed reform in this area. There have been a number of changes in the original proposal put forward by the federal government in the 1978-79 constitutional discussions. It may change again. The essence of the proposal as it now stands is as follows:

1. Jurisdiction to grant divorces and corollary relief (i.e. custody, maintenance, etc.) will be transferred to those provinces that wish to have such jurisdiction. Other provinces that do not wish to have it will continue to remain under the federal *Divorce Act*.

2. The federal government will have power to set jurisdictional rules which determine when a province acquires jurisdiction to grant a divorce in a particular case; i.e. the federal government will establish a minimum residency requirement which a party will have to meet before they can apply for a divorce in that province. While it has not been specified, it is widely assumed that should this proposal go forward, the present requirement under the *Divorce Act* of one year's residency in the province would be maintained.

3. Either the federal government would retain jurisdiction over the extra-provincial enforcement of decrees of divorce granted under provincial legislation, or, in the alternative, a constitutional provision would require each province to recognize and enforce orders made in another province.

At the time of writing, only two provinces, Manitoba and Prince Edward Island, have steadfastly opposed this transfer proposal. Other provinces, including Ontario and Quebec, have definitely and publicly agreed to the transfer. Still other provinces have continued to waffle, saying one thing to the press and to their people and another in the constitutional talks.

Rationale for the Proposal

A proposal for the tranfer of divorce jurisdiction to the provinces was originally put forward in a Joint Parliamentary Committee report on the Constitution, the Molgat-MacGuigan report of 1972. The justifications advanced for the transfers of jurisdiction at that time were as follows:

- that divorce is a matter of strictly local and private concern and, therefore, one most properly dealt with by the provincial legislatures rather than the federal Parliament;
- that the transfer of jurisdiction to the provinces would enable each of them to make laws to conform more closely to the local and ethical values of Canadians living in that province and be a more genuine and more particular expression of their social philosophy; and
- that a transfer of jurisdiction to the provinces would permit a more integrated approach to family law within the provincial jurisdiction (i.e. facilitate the establishment of unified family courts).

The justifications offered for the present proposal are substantially the same as those set out above. A closer examination of each of these reasons will reveal that they are, to put it kindly, faulty.

First of all, there is the assumption that divorce is a purely local and private matter. One has only to look at the volume of divorces which are granted in our courts today, the number of children involved in those families and the number of those families where one spouse and/or the children become public charges by reason of non-payment of maintenance, to recognize that divorce cannot be treated simply as a matter of purely local and private concern. Every taxpayer in this country must be concerned about the social cost of marriage breakdown, both from the point of view of welfare payments that have to be made to support (usually) the wife and children, and also the social cost in terms of ancillary services and emotional and behavioural problems which may have their root, in part, in the breakdown of the family. While divorce may be a private matter in that it directly affects the relationship between two people, the husband and wife, it clearly has much greater social ramifications.

One could as logically assign criminal law to the provincial jurisdiction on the ground that it is a matter of local and private concern between two people, the criminal and the victim. It is obvious to the meanest intelligence that Canadian society as a whole has a vital interest in criminal law and no one has ever seriously suggested that the jurisdiction should be anything other than federal. It should be equally obvious that Canadian society as a whole also has a vital interest in family law and, specifically, in divorce, and its corollary relief. It is not only a social interest. It is a financial interest to the Canadian taxpayer. It has been widely reported that some 70 per cent of all maintenance orders fall into arrears during the first five years after they are made. A substantial number of those persons entitled to receive maintenance do, in fact, become a charge upon the taxpayer. Not merely the taxpayer in the province, but the taxpayer in the federal sense, since Canada Assistance payments are the major source of funding in all provinces for the payment of welfare. The vast majority of people on welfare consist of women living alone with young children.

The second assumption is that Canadians have social and ethical values and a social philosophy which are delineated by provincial boundaries; that the ethical and social values and social philosophy of people differ not according to their religion, to their ethnic origin, to their individual precepts, but according to the province of their residence. There is no justification offered for this astonishing proposition and it is not one that is widely accepted among family law authorities. Professor Julian Payne of the University of Ottawa, one of the most widely known authors on the subject of family law in Canada, commented that the conclusions of the Molgat-MacGuigan Committee were not substantiated by the submissions made to it.[2] He points out that the differing philosophies, expressed by the persons and organizations submitting opinions to the Committee, failed to reveal any substantial, regional or provincial differences in the area of moral, social, religious, or ethical values. He further comments on the degree of unanimity in the views expressed by the established churches, all advocating the marriage breakdown concept as the sole criterion for divorce.

Common sense would lead one to the same conclusion and supporting evidence is not hard to find. In recent years, public opinion surveys have been taken in various areas related to social, ethical and moral values. If there is indeed a provincial code of ethical and moral values, one would expect that code would be most apparent in such areas as divorce and abortion law; and one would think that if ever a province could be expected to have such a distinctive view on these two topics, that province might be Quebec, which is widely reputed to have a cultural and social philosophy significantly different from those in other provinces. In point of fact, the published divorce statistics indicate that Quebecers, both Catholic and non-Catholic, are divorcing in approximately the same numbers as the rest of us. When views were polled on the subject of abortion law reform, again the views of Quebecers differed little from those of the rest of Canada. In each case the majority favoured law reform in that area.

While it is probably true that pressure groups or institutions in a province may adopt a particular social or moral philosophy which bears upon some issues in family law, there is *no* underlying evidence to suggest that such views necessarily or even probably reflect such a unified view by a majority of the people in that province. The proposed transfer would, however, enable such organizations and groups to impose more effectively their views on the government of their province, perhaps to the detriment of the general populace. Divorce laws should not cater only to narrow interests, however sincere they may be. They should look to the views and needs of the population in general, bearing in mind the diversity of our population which is evident in each and every one of our provinces.

The third justification offered for the transfer of jurisdiction is that it would facilitate the establishment of unified family courts and unified family laws. The argument is made that the resolution of all matrimonial problems in one court rather than two would be preferred, from the point of view of the litigants. This is, undoubtedly, a desirable situation, but there are a number of ways of achieving this result:

- A court would be established to deal solely with these matters having complete jurisdiction in all family law cases. Such a court is usually envisaged as having judges appointed by the provinces, although this need not be so; or,
- A complete jurisdiction in family law could be given to an existing superior court which also would continue to deal with other types of matters.

Certainly the transfer of jurisdiction would enable each province to establish a unified family court at the provincial judges' level. This, however, is only one way of establishing unified family courts. They need not necessarily be established at that level in order to be effective and efficient. Indeed, many people active in the field of family law are not in favour of the specialized court at this level for a variety of reasons. The federal government has established projects in a number of areas of the country, experimenting with different methods of establishing unified family courts. These pilot projects have had mixed success and it would appear that the enthusiasm for this concept is diminishing as experience indicates to practitioners and litigants, that the anticipated advantages are not, in fact, materializing.

At least two provinces have been able to attain the desired end by other means. Prince Edward Island maintains a division of its Supreme Court as a Family Division and that division is clothed with all jurisdiction over family law, both federal and provincial. In Manitoba, the same purpose has been achieved by giving concurrent jurisdiction under provincial separation and property laws to the Court of Queen's Bench which also, of course, has divorce jurisdiction. Although Manitoba has an extensive family court system, and has had one for years, most knowledgeable and experienced lawyers prefer to conduct their cases in the Court of Queen's Bench for a number of reasons. It is their perception, and my own, that the specialized family court at the provincial level does not provide the hoped-for advantages which included inexpensive and speedy resolution of cases and some special expertise on the part of judges of the court. In fact, their experience, as mine, has been that the very opposite of this is true — that proceedings in these courts are generally more time consuming and thus more expensive for the litigants and we have seen no evidence that any special mantle of wisdom or expertise descends upon the person appointed to this bench. British Columbia family law lawyers base part of their opposition to the transfer of divorce jurisdiction on the very fear that, in fact, such a unified Family Court would be imposed upon them by the provincial government.

In looking at the current proposal for transfer of jurisdiction, however, one must wonder whether the one alleged advantage of the proposed transfer, that is, to give the provinces the right to appoint judges who would hear divorce cases and property matters, possibly justifies the immense difficulties that are envisaged by the transfer. Is it really that important that unified family courts be operated by judges appointed by the provinces? That is really the issue. There is no obstacle whatever under the present constitutional arrangements to develop a unified family court as long as the jurisdiction to deal with the cases is given to a Superior Court judge. However, by virtue of Section 96 of the *British North America Act,* Superior Court judges must be appointed by the federal government. This is apparently what irks provincial governments and certainly a large part of their enthusiasm for the transfer of divorce jurisdiction is their desire to have the power to appoint additional judges.

If the power to establish unified family courts at the provincial level and to appoint the judges who will deal with the legislation is of primary importance to some provinces, then surely there is no reason to attain that end by such a draconian means as transferring all divorce jurisdiction to the provinces. That simple objective would readily be accomplished by an amendment to Section 96 of the *British North America Act* which would permit the provinces to appoint judges with powers to deal with matters of divorce and property settlement, while still leaving the power to make laws respecting divorce and corollary relief with the federal government.

Problems Foreseen Should Jurisdiction be Transferred

The original proposal put forward in 1978-79 by the federal government was for the transfer of jurisdiction to the provinces to pass laws respecting divorce, with the federal government to retain the control over the jurisdictional basis upon which the divorce could be granted (i.e. the residency requirements) and the recognition of divorces. This last phrase is an attempt to ensure that a divorce granted in one province would be valid in all other provinces. The final portion of the present proposal relating to enforcement of corollary relief was added recently in an attempt to pacify the opposition of women's groups and family law lawyers across the country who have strongly opposed the transfer. Opponents of the proposal anticipate serious problems in three areas.

1. *Jurisdiction shopping* — It is, in the view of most people involved in the field, highly undesirable that there should be different criteria for obtaining a divorce in different provinces. With the mobility of the Canadian population, there is a basic injustice in permitting people to obtain a divorce in one province while having it denied to them in another. The accident of provincial residence should not govern the granting of such basic and important human relief. Although uniform residency requirements would prevent a quickie "Reno-style" divorce haven from developing in Canada, it would not prevent, but would rather encourage, persons to shop for the most favourable provincial residence to get the very best deal on custody, maintenance and property division as well as on grounds.

For example, a wife might find it worth her while to move to Saskatchewan from Newfoundland for a year to take advantage of a divorce law which would give equal division of property and no-fault maintenance on a divorce granted to her after three months of separation. As a newcomer to the province, of course, she would have to wait out her year before commencing the petition. Still that might be preferable to staying in Newfoundland, her home province, where, for example, the law might possibly provide a five-year waiting period for divorce with maintenance based on fault only and no division of assets at all. Conversely, a wealthy Saskatchewan husband might find it advantageous (and easy) to consider a move to Newfoundland in a similar case, thus avoiding what might be financially painful results of a Saskatchewan divorce.

One can certainly foresee some races to the courthouse in each province to ensure that one's own petition is filed first. There is no indication in the proposal as to how the legislation would deal with a situation, which arises not infrequently, where both parties petition immediately upon the expiry of three years in two different provinces. At the present time, the choice as to which jurisdiction will deal with the divorce is not usually of great significance, but a matter of relative convenience, since the *Divorce Act* is uniform across Canada. Neither party can expect a better or worse deal by reason of the divorce being heard in one place or the other. However, if the provisions for maintenance, custody and property are substantially different between the two provinces, the question of jurisdiction becomes a matter of major concern. It is, I believe, obvious to most Canadians, and certainly to most women, that it is not merely important but imperative that in a matter so central to the life of the individual and to his family, as well as to his relationship with the community and the state, there should be one law which determines when and whether a Canadian is married or divorced. This is so particularly in view of the mobility of Canadians across the country.

It is peculiar to say the least, to find this proposal coming forward in Canada when other jurisdictions are proceeding in precisely the opposite direction. In Australia, where the states have had the jurisdiction over divorce, the problems became so difficult that the states have recently surrendered that power to the federal government. In the United States, they have had the very system which is now being proposed in Canada for a great many years and it has caused them nothing but grief and aggravation. They have been searching for these many years for a uniform divorce code but without success. The anomalies and injustices brought about by 50 different divorce jurisdictions in the United States have made them most envious of the Canadian situation.

2. *Status* — A second area in which major difficulties could result from adoption of the proposal is in those situations where the individual's rights are specifically dependent upon marital status. The marital status of a person is and always has been an important and vital factor in many aspects of life and one which the law has treated as having special significance. If that status is to be terminated, or retained, it should be done on a uniform basis for all Canadians wherever they live. Let me give you three related

examples of the kind of injustices which will necessarily result from the transfer of jurisdiction.

- Canada Pension Plan — Whether a widow's pension and death benefits can be claimed by a separated wife under the Canada Pension Plan depends entirely upon whether or not she is still legally married at the date of the husband's death. If there has been a divorce, no pension could be payable, whether or not the husband has remarried, and whether or not the woman was his dependent at the time of his death. Should such rights depend on whether one or both of the parties lived in province A where a five-year waiting period is required for divorce, or province B where a six-month waiting period is required? It should be borne in mind that many women and, more especially, older women in a vulnerable position of economic dependency, are separated and divorced against their wishes. If the husband is able to obtain a divorce quickly in a province with relatively liberal divorce laws, he will, by so doing, deprive his former wife of the right to this type of dependent's pension while her sisters in another province, under precisely the same circumstances, cannot lose such rights for a significantly longer period.

- Veteran's Pensions — The right to receive a pension as the widow of a veteran depends entirely upon the marriage continuing to subsist in the legal sense until the veteran's death. Once again, if different divorce laws apply in each province, some women will lose these rights because they live in one province while others will retain them purely because they live in another.

- Private Pensions — In almost all private company or union pension plans, the widow's pension will only be paid where there is a legal marriage subsisting at the time of the employee's death. In most provinces (British Columbia and Manitoba are exceptions) such pensions are not divided under the marital property legislation and women who are separated or divorced late in life are left unprotected in their old age.

3. *Enforcement* — It is in the area of enforcement of custody and maintenance orders, that the most obvious difficulties can be anticipated, should the transfer of jurisdiction take place. Anyone who has the slightest familiarity with the area of family law is aware that the enforcement of maintenance orders, particularly where the parties live in different provinces, is one of the most difficult and perplexing problems. As previously indicated, it is estimated that some 70 per cent of maintenance orders fall into arrears soon after they are made. Enforcement of the order when the paying spouse, usually the husband, resides in the same province with the creditor spouse, is difficult and somewhat frustrating. However, when the

parties live in different provinces, the problems are enormous. The high and increasing rate of mobility of the Canadian population means that this problem grows greater rather than less each year. Analytical studies prepared at the request of and published by Statistics Canada[3] amply support the above comment. These studies indicate not only that the mobility rate of Canadians is higher even than that of our neighbours in the United States, but also that, "among the ages where the most geographic mobility takes place, persons who were once married but are no longer living with their spouses at the time of the 1972 census, had consistently higher than average mobility rates."[4] Again, "changes in marital status often entail or are otherwise associated with geographical mobility."[5]

Presently, provincial maintenance orders are enforced in other provinces under a system known as REMO (reciprocal enforcement of maintenance orders) which is a series of provincial statutes for the reciprocal enforcement in each province of maintenance orders made elsewhere. The attorney-general in each province theoretically assumes the responsibility for bringing before the courts of his province for enforcement orders made in another province if so requested by the originating province. Where the original order is made in the absence of the husband, that is, after he has left the province, the original order is a provisional one only and no enforcement can take place until the husband has had the opportunity to put forward his side of the case. After hearing him, the judge will either make a final order which may be less, but is never more, than that made in the original court or may return the matter together with the evidence which has been taken from the husband to the original province for the re-hearing of further evidence from the wife and the re-submission of that evidence to the enforcing province. Ultimately, if the parties live that long, an order may be made. If the original order was made when the husband was in the same province with the wife, then the enforcing province theoretically deals only with the enforcement and not with any variation.

However, where a maintenance order is part of a divorce decree made under the *Divorce Act* of Canada, the order is enforceable without a variation and without question in any province in Canada. The creditor spouse, usually the wife, has the option of having the order enforced by the attorney-general's offices as described above, that is, by transmitting it from her own province through the two governments, or by engaging a lawyer in the husband's province of residence to take the ordinary collection procedures of garnishment of wages, seizure of assets, etc.

The foregoing sounds neat, efficient, and inexpensive. It is none of these. The very best that can be said for the reciprocal enforcement procedures which we have now is that they are better than nothing, but only just! The problems that are encountered are overwhelming to the individual litigant and frustrating to lawyers and judges alike. One of the major difficulties that is encountered is the delay. Many months, even years, can pass before the wife will ever receive a penny through these proceedings. The procedure is almost designed to encourage and facilitate the defaulting husband. Differences in provincial legislation which appear minor to the layperson offer numerous loopholes through which the defaulting husband may make his escape. In addition to this, the promptness with which enforcement proceedings will be launched and pursued in the other province is entirely dependent upon the priority assigned to it by the attorney-general's office in that province. In almost all provinces, this priority is very low if it exists at all. The administration of justice, which includes the provincial family courts, has traditionally been one of the lowest priorities in provincial budgets, and these courts are consistently understaffed, overworked and have a heavy backlog. The second reason for difficulties is the inherent problem with provisional orders in that evidence must be taken in one province, transcribed by the court reporter, transmitted to both government offices and then to the second court. The husband must then be served with a notice of a hearing. The matter is then put onto a court docket and considered again when the husband's evidence is heard. The court may then make a decision or send the case back to the originating province for more evidence, again going through two government offices. The result is that the husband is given every opportunity to minimize the amount of money that he can pay and the wife has little or no opportunity to test the accuracy and completeness of the financial information he provides.

The third area of difficulty is the irresistible urge that most courts in a province seem to have to tamper with an order made in another province. They find it most difficult to resist this impulse to re-hear and re-adjudicate the case. They are only too anxious to consider anything which may be said in their jurisdiction and to find some excuse to vary the order if it is legally possible, or to decline to enforce it, or to enforce it only partially if that is not possible. This tendency is especially evident where a maintenance order is granted on criteria that differ significantly from those criteria in the enforcing province. The courts in a province which have retained the fault standard for the granting of maintenance, for example, will be most reluctant to enforce a maintenance order from a no-fault province and will look for and find any kind of loophole to avoid that enforcement. If property division orders are included, as they would be in the event of the transfer of jurisdiction, then the temptation and the opportunity to look behind the order and attempt to re-adjudicate the case in the absence of the wife will be even greater.

Reciprocal enforcement of maintenance orders by provincial governments has been totally ineffective. This type of legislation has existed in one form or another for more than 25 years now, and it is still so defective as to be almost useless. There is absolutely no reason to think that the provinces would be any better at enforcing orders should they acquire the additional divorce jurisdiction than they have been during the past 25 years. The addition of property division orders would simply magnify the difficulties.

The foregoing description sounds like "lawyer's problems", but behind these technical and procedural complaints, there are "people problems." There are children who don't have warm winter coats. There are families who don't have nutritious diets. There are mothers who cannot make their rental or mortage payments, all because the court-ordered maintenance is not being paid because the husband has left town.

Custody Orders

The inter-provincial enforcement of custody orders has many of the same problems as enforcement of maintenance orders and some unique ones. The problem of "child-napping" in Canada is already a difficult one. It is probably the most heart-wrenching legal problem with which a lawyer has to deal. The anguish that is caused to the parent whose child has disappeared is almost impossible to imagine. If a child is taken across a provincial boundary in Canada, the parent who is entitled to custody of the child faces enormous difficulties in retrieving him or her. He or she is almost in the same position as though the child had been taken to a foreign country.

A provincial custody order made in Manitoba is virtually unenforceable in Ontario and Quebec, and has very little weight in any of the other provinces. Eight of the 10 provinces have now passed legislation which is intended to ensure the return of a child who is kidnapped by one parent from the custodial parent. In most provinces, that legislation looks good but is ineffective. Ontario and Quebec have no such legislation. Ontario plans it. Quebec does not. The reason that it is not effective where it exists is that the provincial governments will not give assistance to the custodial parent in regaining the child.

If my child is taken from Manitoba to British Columbia by my husband while I have a Manitoba custody order, I must locate that child in British Columbia, probably through the services of a private investigator. The police will not help me even after I have located the child. I must hire a lawyer in British Columbia and probably one in Manitoba as well and I must have the case brought on in British Columbia courts at my own expense. Moreover, I will probably have to travel there for the hearing. The provincial authorities in British Columbia will not lift one finger to assist me. The cost to me will be in the thousands of dollars. The same situation will apply in all of the other provinces in Canada with the exception of Manitoba.

If a British Columbia mother has her child brought into Manitoba by her former husband in the same circumstances, the Manitoba Attorney General's Department will use the police facilities to locate the child and will provide legal counsel to the mother at no cost to bring the matter to court in order to have her child returned to her. The Department gives urgent priority to any such cases without any expense to the custodial parent. If my child was taken not to British Columbia, but to Quebec, I might just as well write him off altogether, since there is no legislation present or contemplated which will assist me to regain my rightful custody.

If, however, I have a custody order made under the *Divorce Act*, I can register that order in any Superior Court in Canada and it will be recognized by police anywhere in Canada as a valid order. The police will frequently assist me to locate and regain the child. The Quebec court, like any other superior court in Canada will recognize my divorce decree as a valid order and will enforce it as an order of the Quebec Court.

Any lawyer who practices family law will tell you that only an order made under the federal jurisdiction of the *Divorce Act* is recognized and respected by police and civil authorities throughout Canada and will be acted upon by them. Provincial court orders have little effect outside provincial boundaries.

Do I exaggerate the difficulties which may be anticipated in enforcement of orders? Professor Julian Payne, a previously cited authority on this subject, recently discussed this proposal for transfer and divorce jurisdiction and concluded "The difficulties likely to be encountered under provincial regime with respect to the extra-provincial enforcement of maintenance and custody orders cannot be exaggerated."[6] Professor Payne went on to comment that such problems would only be aggravated by the implementation of the proposed transfer of jurisdiction.

In summary, the enforcement of custody and maintenance orders extra-provincially is already a disaster area. The proposed transfer of jurisdiction can only make it worse and not better. It is common ground to all who wrestle with this problem that improvement in enforcement will only come through more federal involvement and federal enforcement rather than less. A transfer of jurisdiction will simply make divorce decrees as unenforceable as provincial orders now are. A number of suggestions have been under discussion in the legal community over the past year for the improvement of extra-provincial enforcement of divorce orders. These proposals involve the use of federal institutions and accessibility of federal information in limited ways and depend for their viability upon the maintenance of one national divorce law.

In answer to the foregoing complaints and problems, the new proposals would offer the possibility for federal jurisdiction for enforcement of provincial decrees involving maintenance and custody. How could this be accomplished and would it solve the problem? Some proponents of the concept, including Attorney-General, Roy McMurtry of Ontario, say that the solution is to require in the constitution, a "full faith and credit" clause which would require each province to recognize as valid and enforceable in that province a divorce decree including maintenance or custody provisions made in any other province. This is proposed as the ultimate solution to all problems caused by the transfer of jurisdiction. Again, it sounds attractive, but beware of the fine print which will read something like this: "Provided that a Court may refuse to enforce such an order by reason of public policy or by reason of a change in circumstances of the parties."

Such qualifications (and no such clause without qualification, would be acceptable to the provinces) do not, of course, meet the objections of jurisdiction-shopping and status and diversity of grounds which have been previously described. Nevertheless, it is offered as a real solution to our concerns about the enforcement of custody and maintenance orders.

Be not deceived, my friends. This brand of snake oil offers no cure! The qualifications, the fine print, leave two gaping holes in enforceability through which a busload of welfare mothers could be driven. Let me give you a few examples which spring easily to mind.

1. Where a divorce is granted in Manitoba, and the maintenance is sought to be enforced in Alberta, the husband, whether or not he was in Manitoba at the time of the divorce, can delay proceedings, avoid payment for months if not years, and

possibly have the maintenance reduced simply by claiming a change in circumstances, real or imagined. The wife in Manitoba cannot afford to come to Alberta for the hearing or to hire a lawyer there and has no way of checking the accuracy and completeness of the financial disclosure which the husband would allege in support of his new impoverishment. Even if no real change in circumstances is shown, a delay of six months to a year and a half can be experienced in addition to the normal delay involved in obtaining the original divorce.

2. Where maintenance is granted in one province and sought to be enforced in another with very different criteria, the door is left invitingly open for the court asked to enforce the order to refuse to do so since provincial legislation clearly establishes public policy in that province. For example, Manitoba has no-fault maintenance laws. Newfoundland might give maintenance on proof of cruelty or desertion only and deny it altogether if the wife had ever committed adultery. If a Manitoba maintenance order were sent to Newfoundland for enforcement under the new proposal, the Court there could say, and very likely would, on the husband's application, that as no cruelty or desertion was proved or the wife had committed adultery after the separation, that it was against public policy in Newfoundland, to enforce such an order for her benefit. The difficulties faced by the dependent wife in Manitoba in answering the charges made by her husband in Newfoundland are obvious. Again, the same delay factor would operate.

3. In custody matters, the same two qualifications in the fine print would be used to defeat, not to enhance enforcement. For example, a mother may be given custody of a child in a Saskatchewan divorce action. The father, who moves to British Columbia, has the child by agreement for a month's holiday in the summer. He refuses to return the child and the mother tries to enforce her Saskatchewan divorce order for custody. The husband, with very little difficulty, can

- delay the application until the child is back at school in British Columbia and makes new friends, etc. there;
- allege that there is a change in circumstances in that the child now wants to stay with him (children will often say what the parent in charge wants them to say, particularly if offered a new puppy as an inducement);
- argue that it is against public policy in British Columbia to give custody to a mother who is living in a common-law

relationship as opposed to a father, like himself, who is living virtuously alone; and
- claim that by reason of the passage of time, the child is now firmly rooted in British Columbia and it would be traumatic for him to be uprooted from his new home and that this constitutes a further change in circumstances.

4. There are numerous differences in the provincial age limitation for payment of child support. Each province at this time is free under provincial legislation to say that the maintenance for a child terminates at 14, 15, 16, and up to 19 years. The *Divorce Act*, on the other hand, says that upon a divorce, the court can give maintenance to the child up to the age of 16 and beyond that age, without limit, if the child is dependent by reason of illness or disability, or where the child is attending school and living at home with the custodial parent. If the jurisdiction were provincial, then each province would again establish its own age limit and upon the transmission of an order from one province to another for enforcement that enforcement might be refused on the grounds that public policy in the enforcing province established 16 as the age limit for maintenance, whereas the child in question was 17, well within the limit of the originating province. This type of litigation happens now in Canada, where a custody order is made under provincial legislation. The transfer of jurisdiction and the proposed full faith and credit clause would *encourage* the proliferation of such cases.

Whether it be custody or maintenance, it would be a very dull and unimaginative lawyer indeed who could not conjure up some argument on behalf of the defaulting husband on the grounds of a change of circumstances or public policy. It is a well-known fact that delay is the best friend of a person who is seeking to resist the enforcement of a maintenance or custody order. The longer the maintenance order is unpaid, the more the husband saves. The courts are loath to enforce arrears in these cases, thinking themselves lucky if they can extract maintenance on a current basis, much less collect the arrears. The longer he hangs on to the child, the stronger his case for retaining him.

The transfer proposal, even with its latest embellishment, offers obvious advantages to two groups of people only: provincial politicians whose nature it is to aggrandize power, and lawyers who will face more complex and lengthy legal disputes in matrimonial cases and will, quite rightly, charge accordingly. The first group does not deserve any such benefit and the second group does not want it. To the ordinary men and women of Canada, the proposal offers no advantages and massive disadvantages to men and women alike.

The United States experience with their "full faith and credit" clause has been abysmal, even though their clause does not contain the exceptions or fine print above discussed. With this apparently unqualified clause, the validity of divorce decrees, as well as the corollary relief are regularly attached by indirect means relating to the constitutionality and adequacy of the procedures and the validity of the evidence as to jurisdiction which had been heard in the originating court. It is this type of problem, unsolved for 200 years in the American experience, that we will import into Canada and encourage to flourish and multiply.

I have addressed this subject as a lawyer experienced in the field of family law. Are the opinions expressed here shared by others in the field? Indeed they are. The British Columbia Bar Association and particularly its Family Law Section, are vigorously opposed to the transfer. The Manitoba Bar Association is unanimously opposed to it. Family law sections in all but one of the other provinces are also opposed to the transfer, and the Canadian Bar Association in August of 1979 passed a resolution opposing the transfer. An experienced Supreme Court Judge (Family Division) Mr. Justice Charles McQuaid, of Prince Edward Island, said in a recent newspaper interview on the subject of the transfer, "It would be a real horror show."

Other distinguished legal writers and teachers on the subject share the view that the transfer is a highly undesirable change in the law. Professor Julian Payne, whose views have been previously cited, pointed out in a recent article that: "The experiences in the United States indicates the havoc that may ensue from the absence of a national divorce regime."[7] In the same article, Professor Payne concluded that the proposal does not solve the difficulties in respect of enforcement and variation of corollary relief, nor the problems of competing jurisdiction over divorce in many cases.

Another authority, J.G. Castel, Professor of Law, Osgoode Hall Law School, York University, Toronto, writing on the same topic, noted that in the United States the divided jurisdiction has made interstate divorce the most persistent and perplexing of the full faith and credit problems in that country. After examining the potential difficulties, he concludes: "In the absence of compelling reasons for transferring competence over divorce from the federal parliament to the provincial legislature, it might be preferable to leave things as they stand."[8] He goes on to comment that the proposed change would give rise to added litigation, inconsistent judgments regarding marital status and general confusion.

The full scope of the problems which will result from a transfer of jurisdiction as proposed, cannot now be foreseen. In the last two years, the proposal has been modified on several occasions, each time the assurance being given that the new improved proposal will solve the perceived problems, That is *not true* and I hope that the women of Canada at least will not be so gullible as to accept these assurances. The more bandaids, slings and crutches that have been applied to this proposal, the more clearly it can be seen as the cripple it is. In the text of the new proposal of July 8th Mr. Chrétien says:

> While the solution to the problem of enforcement does not lie wholly or even mainly in constitutional change, we must be certain that we will *improve* and not *worsen* the present situation. It is not enough that we do not make things worse. We must make them better than they are now.[9]

If that is truly the objective of constitutional reform in this area, then the best and only thing to do with this proposal is to forget it as quickly as possible.

Notes

[1] Jean Chrétien, "Statement to the Continuing Committee of Ministers on the Constitution", July 8, 1980.

[2] Julian Payne, "Divorce and the Canadian Constitution", *Conciliation Courts Review*, Vol. 18, no. 1 (June 1980), p. 58.

[3] Statistics Canada. "The Frequency of Geographic Mobility in the Population of Canada", Ottawa, 1978, p. 31.

[4] *Ibid.*, p. 33.

[5] *Ibid.*

[6] Julian Payne, "Divorce and the Canadian Constitution", p. 60.

[7] *Ibid.*

[8] J.G. Castel, "Recognition of Provincial Divorces in Canada", *McGill Law Journal*, Vol. 24, No. 4, p. 651.

[9] Jean Chrétien, "Statement", p. 2.

Property Division on Marriage Breakdown in the Common Law Provinces

Carol Mahood Huddart

The Problem

Our most fundamental partnerships, which are formed to meet our most basic needs for companionship and support in every aspect of our lives, and to raise our children — with or without the ceremony of marriage — are encompassed in a fragile and confused legislative framework. Individual Canadians forced to deal with issues arising within the area of family law are faced with confusion, complication and all the resultant financial and emotional expense; while business partnerships are able to learn the rules, live by them in a relatively orderly way, and frequently lobby successfully for change.

The purpose of this paper is to discuss the problems created for Canadians by the provincial governments when they enacted legislation providing for property division on marriage breakdown that is not uniform across Canada. To provide background, the fundamentals of the provincial schemes will be described in very general terms. While the Appendices provide a more detailed overview of these basic features, the cost of attempting to deal with nine complex enactments in a few paragraphs is oversimplification to the point of danger. Each reader should refer to the enactments as amended for any specific provisions.

In 1867, in a far less mobile society with a much smaller population, for which ecclesiastical authority was emphasized, the Fathers of Confederation had considered "Marriage and Divorce" suitable for federal control. One hundred and one years later the Parliament of Canada finally acted to the everlasting credit of the Senate of Canada and its Committee on Divorce. In 1968, the *Divorce Act* of Canada brought the beginnings of a stronger and more uniform treatment of families, when divorce and the ancillary relief relating to maintenance and custody were made uniform across Canada. There was a good argument for including property division in the ancillary relief, but the Government of Canada chose not to upset the provinces by including property in the *Divorce Act, 1968*.

Pressure for more liberalization of our divorce laws continued. The federal government's response came in 1972 when the Minister of Justice agreed that the grounds and procedure for divorce should be reconsidered with a view to making them more compatible with current social reality, but deferred such reconsideration until all the provinces would have enacted more equitable property-sharing provisions under their power over "property and civil rights." Again the Government of Canada chose this route in preference to attempting to legislate property division between spouses on marriage breakdown as an incident of their "marriage and divorce" power so as not to risk confrontation with the provinces, always anxious for more power.

By August, 1980, all the common law provinces had responded to this federal proposal, to the injustice done Mrs. Murdoch and to the articulate voices of women demanding a fair share of the marital property at the end of the dream. The government of Quebec had introduced matrimonial property reform in 1979, changing the legal regime from a community of property to a community of acquests.

Provincial Matrimonial Property Legislation

Property division legislation is in place in all common law provinces, although it is yet to be proclaimed in New Brunswick. Each piece of legislation is unbelievably intricate, open to many different interpretations,[1] and raises dozens of questions. Ontario's *Family Law Reform Act*, the first, has been in effect only since April 1, 1978. Thus, the courts have not yet had an opportunity to settle on a consistent approach to the legislation. Few scholars have commented on the legislation.

Although the general scheme of the legislation in all ten provinces is now similar to Quebec's 1979 legislation, each provincial scheme is a distinct system in its details. We have 10 different systems of dealing with matrimonial property on marriage breakdown; we have 10 different ways of dealing with matrimonial property during marriage; and, we have 10 varieties of result on death.

Generally speaking, all the acts are based on the stated principle that "marriage is an equal partnership" unless something different is "put in writing." All assume that unmarried living together means you "keep what you have" unless you agree in writing otherwise or make a contribution that might qualify you for a "constructive trust." All agree on a version of a "deferred community of acquests" — a 50/50 sharing of some or all property acquired during marriage on its termination.

- **Private Ordering**

All provinces permit some form of private ordering,[2] which allows a couple to arrange their affairs as they prefer within the boundaries established by the legislatures in the interest of public policy, and recognize that the needs and circumstances of each "partnership" are different.

If we think of a "domestic contract" (to use one word to include all private ordering within a family relationship, whether legally married or not) as the constitution of the family, in the same way a company's Memorandum and Articles of Association or Letters Patent and By-Laws are a company's constitution, we can consider the problems created by the lack of any uniform or consistent framework for the "constitution."

If a couple enter a "cohabitation contract" in Ontario with proper legal advice will it be legally effective if they move to Prince Edward Island two weeks later to take up their permanent residence? What if they marry two years later on that Island and then 35 years later retire to British Columbia, all without amending their agreement or making a new one on marriage? Lawyers who read the various acts and consult their texts on conflicts of law are not able to answer all the questions that situation poses. British Columbia recognizes only those "marriage agreements" which take effect on marriage. There is no provision for cohabitation contracts in Manitoba, Saskatchewan, Alberta or British Columbia, where such contracts might well be considered unenforceable as being against public policy, while Ontario and the Atlantic Provinces make them acceptable by their statutes.

All provinces agree on the need for domestic contracts to be in writing, signed by both parties and witnessed, but Saskatchewan and Alberta go further and require acknowledgment of independent legal advice. Manitoba has added the concept of a "spousal agreement" to their existing "matrimonial settlement", the latter with special requirements for registration to be enforceable.

As Appendix A shows, the limitations to private ordering vary from province to province, with custody and access being exempted most frequently in marriage or cohabitation agreements and rights regarding the matrimonial home in those and some others. Only British Columbia has an express provision for variation of a domestic contract generally. Couples who attempt to order their affairs to suit themselves and thereby avoid the statutory property division are affected, since their rights are different from province to province under the statutory division, and since conflicts rules, to be discussed below, are at best complicated and at worst incomprehensible.

- **Division in the Case of No Private Ordering**[3]

Essentially there are two basic systems: The first system includes a 50/50 sharing presumption which applies to "family assets" as defined by a use test. This system has been adopted in the provinces of Ontario, British Columbia, Newfoundland, Nova Scotia and Prince Edward Island. The test applies regardless of the origin or source of the property except that Prince Edward Island excludes the value of property acquired before marriage. Judicial discretion may be used to vary the equal division within guidelines that are different in every province. There is no such presumption for "non-family assets" although the court may provide for some sharing of such property on criteria set out in each act, again all different. The definition of "family assets" (under whatever name) varies significantly from province to province with, for example, British Columbia specifically including "a right . . . under an annuity or a pension, home ownership or retirement savings plan" [s.45(3)(d), *Family Relations Act*], regardless of their "use" and assets to which a spouse has contributed.

The second system includes a 50/50 sharing presumption which applies to all assets acquired during marriage in the provinces of Alberta, Saskatchewan, and Manitoba. Each of these provinces has its own exceptions, exemptions and other considerations.

New Brunswick combines the two systems. Some other fundamental differences are important, as a glance at Appendix B will show. In Newfoundland, Nova Scotia, New Brunswick and Saskatchewan, a surviving spouse may claim a division on the death of the other spouse, whereas in the remaining provinces the surviving spouse must claim a division before death or be satisfied with what he or she has already and receives by will, statutory succession rights or under dependants' relief legislation. In Saskatchewan, either spouse may apply for a division during marriage. Everywhere else the division can take place only on marriage breakdown (a term I am using to include a decree nisi or a decree absolute, a decree of nullity, a judicial separation or any order declaring the marriage irretrievably broken down), except that Manitoba allows division if one spouse is dissipating the family's assets, New Brunswick directs division of the proceeds of sale of any matrimonial home (as defined in the *Marital Property Act*), and Ontario and the Atlantic Provinces allow an application at any time for compensation for contribution to some or all assets, restating Mr. Justice Dickson's decision in *Rathwell* v. *Rathwell*[4] that still applies in all common law provinces.

All provinces except British Columbia require an application to be made to a court for the division to take place. In British Columbia the division is automatic on the occurrence of a separation agreement, decree absolute of divorce, decree of nullity or a declaration of marriage breakdown, which division can be varied by an application to vary under section 51 of the *Family Relations Act*. Thus, a matrimonial home owned before marriage by a spouse in British Columbia would be divided equally on marriage breakdown, while in Alberta the value of the equity at marriage would belong to the owner. Only the increase in value would be shared. In British Columbia the equal division can be varied but in Alberta only the increase in value can be varied.

A British Columbia man's boat, in which his wife never set foot, but which he used to take the children fishing, would be a family asset. The same boat, not being used by *both* spouses, would be a non-family asset in Ontario and not presumptively divided. A full-time homemaker in British Columbia will get a 50 per cent interest in her husband's pension as a property right, while a New Brunswick homemaker will have to rely on a maintenance claim that will probably end on her cohabiting with another man or remarrying or becoming self-supporting. The wife who helps her husband in his business is more likely to get an equal share in British Columbia than in Nova Scotia where she will be "compensated for her contribution" to "business assets" and the onus will be on the British Columbia husband to prove that the business is *not* a family asset while the Nova Scotia wife will have to prove her contribution.

While all 10 provinces agree in principle on the division that should take place on marriage breakdown, the provincial systems of property division do not treat all Canadian citizens equally. The rights of spouses will depend upon the province that has jurisdiction at the time of marriage breakdown.

Conflicts[5]

Which province will have jurisdiction over the division of property on marriage breakdown is not always clear. In the absence of an express agreement to the contrary, the common law suggests that the law of the husband's domicile at the time of marriage will control the couple's property regime (*Loustalan* v. *Loustalan*)[6] on the theory of an "implied contract." If this law includes provision for division of property on marriage breakdown it should prevail.

However, will a New Brunswick court accept such a theory if the parties married in British Columbia where the husband was domiciled, moved to New Brunswick two years later and separated there 20 years later? Will it allow the implied contract to prevail over the provisions of the *Marital Property Act* which has its own conflicts rule which restates the traditional common law rule as to which law should apply to division of property on divorce? In this *Act*, division of moveables will be governed by the law of the place where the spouses had their "last habitual residence" and division of immoveables by the law of the place where they are located. Will the decision be the same if the parties lived in British Columbia for 30 years and moved to New Brunswick one year later before the separation? What will a New Brunswick court do if faced with an application by a husband to divide assets if the wife has returned to British Columbia to her family and petitioned for divorce and a property division there where she could seek half his federal government pension?

If an Ontario domiciled man married a British Columbia domiciled woman in Ontario and they shortly settled in British Columbia, will a British Columbia court five years later apply Ontario law to the moveables? British Columbia has not affirmed the common law rule in its *Family Relations Act*, but a British Columbia court might well decide that only a marriage agreement complying with section 48 of the *Family Relations Act* could prevail over the provisions of the *Act*. If the parties had made a cohabitation agreement in Ontario (which would become a marrige agreement upon marriage by Ontario law but not by British Columbia law) will that contract prevail over the British Columbia statutory division?

There is no case law respecting the move of parties from one "separate property" regime to another. Prior to the enactment of these new provincial marital property laws all "separate property" regimes were sufficiently similar that the questions were never raised. With the differences in the "deferred community" systems in our reformed provincial laws a Canadian couple must now face the issue.

In the United States similar conflicts have arisen and the so-called "doctrine of mutability" has been developed to deal with them. Property acquired in one state is governed by the law of that state to the extent rights have vested, that is, become the absolute property of one or both parties. When the parties change their domicile, the property acquired in the new domicile is governed by the law of that state. By this doctrine a Saskatchewan woman could apply for a division before the couple move to Prince Edward Island. Her property rights would vest. She would then take her property with her to Prince Edward Island. If the parties separate there, will their property be subject to a new division on the basis of the "use test" and the conflict rules contained in Prince Edward Island's legislation or will the wife be allowed to keep what she has "acquired" by court order regardless of the use she has made of it?

99

As an alternative the Saskatchwan and British Columbia courts might apply the "doctrine of immutability" that prevails in Europe. In this case, rules respecting property are set at marriage and never changed thereafter. Thus, the husband's domicile at marriage would govern for the duration of the marriage including division on marriage breakdown and would not take into account the fact that seven other provinces have chosen to impose the alternate common law rule.

Will Canadian courts follow *Devos* v. *Devos*[7] and enforce a marriage agreement between the parties validly entered at the place of marriage? Will such a contract be subject to the variation provisions in section 24 of Saskatchewan's *Matrimonial Property Act* or section 51 of British Columbia's *Family Relations Act*?

There are some theoretical answers to these questions but to date there have been no decisions. The only certainty is that more Canadians will find themselves embroiled in cases involving conflicts than in the past, when there was only a rare case involving Quebec or, more likely, foreign countries. In every marriage breakdown where the parties have lived in more than one province, time and cost will be involved as their lawyers deal with competing claims as to jurisdiction and conflicting laws. Given the general philosophic agreement underlying not only the common law legislation but also the Quebec legislation the differences in detail are unfortunate and probably unnecessary. Yet in matrimonial law we are now a balkanized country. For money matters in our marriages each of us is a citizen of our province, not our country.

Tax Considerations[8]

Conflicts problems may be interesting for the academic and a guaranteed income for the lawyer, but their ramifications in a country with a uniform tax system are considerable. To begin, two essential points about income tax law need to be made. In the first instance, property division has tax implications that make the after-tax division different from the before-tax division. Second, laws that vary from province to province make equality in the tax system difficult to achieve. The underlying problem is that provincial marital property laws consider marriage a partnership while the *Income Tax Act* assesses individuals. It is a problem Quebec has faced since the government of Canada first imposed an income tax.

The impact on an individual Canadian whose marriage has broken down will vary depending on when an agreement is reached, whether it takes account of the tax ramifications of various alternative settlement possibilities, whether or when a court order is made, and what law is applied in dividing the property. We live with uncertainty and the possibility that tax will have to be paid (by one or both parties) to accomplish a division of assets and may leave less for both just when they need more to maintain the separated family.

The province of Quebec, with more experience in this area, has moved to deal with these issues under its *Taxation Act,* 1979. If Canadian couples are to be treated equally Parliament will have to make the changes in the *Income Tax Act* necessary to take account of the variety of marital property regimes across Canada. Whether this can be achieved before the conflicts questions discussed above are settled and the property reform acts receive more definitive interpretation is doubtful. No one envies Revenue Canada its task.

Implications on Death

British Columbia, Ontario and Prince Edward Island do not permit applications for property division to be made on the death of a spouse. They do allow an action commenced prior to death to be continued after death against the estate of the deceased as do all the provinces. Thus, in these three provinces the spouse with less "divisible" property might choose to separate if and when death is imminent! British Columbia probably permits the surviving spouse to make an application against the estate of the deceased where marriage breakdown occurred prior to death to enforce the automatic division that occurred on the happening of the triggering event.

In Alberta, British Columbia, Manitoba, Ontario, and Prince Edward Island, the matrimonial property laws do not provide for division on death. In these provinces the surviving spouse can claim, on intestacy, his or her rights against the deceased's estate under succession legislation, or be satisfied with the provision made in the deceased's will or seek relief under the dependent's relief legislation.

Manitoba, Ontario and Prince Edward Island have introduced changes to this legislation to make the division on death comparable to division on marriage breakdown. In the case of British Columbia,[9] a surviving spouse must look to the provisions of the dependents' relief legislation and make a claim based on the deceased's failure to make "just and adequate provision" for a dependent, taking into account all competing claims. After divorce or annulment there is, with minor exceptions, no recourse.

The proposition that a spouse in any part of Canada should have more rights to share in marital property on the termination of a marriage by marriage breakdown than he or she has on its termination by death is unacceptable. However, it is the situation that prevails in British Columbia today. The surviving spouse is dependent on the deceased spouse's will as varied by judicial discretion or in the absence of a will on the provisions of the *Estate Administration Act* which denies the surviving spouse a claim if separated for more than one year and not eligible for maintenance.

In some provinces, these statutory or testamentary rights on death are additional to the matrimonial property rights (e.g. Saskatchewan) while in others the surviving spouse must elect (e.g. Manitoba). Again conflicts questions arise. If a man in British Columbia who possesses a home in Newfoundland dies, his widow may be able to pursue successfully a claim to a half interest in the Newfoundland property in a Newfoundland court regardless of the beneficiary of it in her husband's will. A Newfoundlander with a winter home in Victoria would not have the same opportunity under Newfoundland's conflict rules. Thus, Canadians who move from province to province, or have property in different provinces, are faced with uncertainty. Canadians' rights will depend on where they happen to be resident at the termination of marriage.

Guardianship, Custody, Access, Protection of Children and Adoption

The problems of a balkanized Canada have been with us for a long time with regard to our rights and obligations regarding children. This will be the case more often in the future as fathers less and less automatically hand over the entire care and control of children to mothers. While this area is beyond the scope of this paper I want to draw attention to one point:

Conflicts between custody orders made under the *Divorce Act* and adoption or protection of children orders made under provincial legislation are increasing. Are we now to have conflicting orders in guardianship, custody, and adoption if the over-riding federal legislation is removed? Are children to have two or perhaps three domiciles? Are children to have several "parents" depending on the varying definitions in our 10 provincial statutes? Reflect on the problems of children moving from country to country and consider them in relations to our 10 provinces and the numbers of people who move between them.

Enforcement

Property orders made in the superior courts of our provinces and domestic contracts made pursuant to provincial laws are useful only to the extent they are enforceable. Otherwise, they are only expensive pieces of paper. All lawyers practising family law are conscious of some basic facts — most clients cannot afford the expense of resolving their legal problems, financially or emotionally, on marriage breakdown. A large percentage of our clients will move from one province to another during their lives and thus into foreign jurisdictions. Enforcing court orders or separation agreements in foreign jurisdictions is expensive, time-consuming and frequently futile. Pursuing original claims in foreign jurisdictions is even worse and usually useless. The existing system only works for those with substantial property, enabling them to hire the best in legal, investigatory, and financial advice. For some of those the process is futile as foreign countries refuse to order their residents or nationals to comply with orders of a Canadian court or with agreements made here.

Given the present situation, most do not bother trying. They simply do what they can to get along — all too frequently dependent on family or government resources, especially where children are involved. "I'll just quit my job and move out of the province" is one of the best threats a person can make to force an agreement he wants because it is so effective.

This situation exists largely because governments are jealous of their own powers and zealous in protecting their own residents from "foreign" laws on the assumption that they know best. To illustrate the difficulties, consider the alternatives available to a woman who has negotiated a separation agreement or obtained a court order in Ontario for a cash payment against a husband who has moved to British Columbia. That women can sue her husband in British Columbia on her original cause of action (i.e. begin again) or on the judgment of the Ontario court or she can apply to register her judgment pursuant to the *Court Order Enforcement Act.* Her application under this reciprocal enforcement of judgment legislation will be refused if a British Columbia court considers that the Ontario court acted (a) without jurisdiction under British Columbia conflict of law rules, or (b) without authority under Ontario jurisdiction rules concerning either the cause of action or the subject matter, or (c) if neither party was resident or carrying on business in Ontario and the husband did not attorn to the Ontario jurisdiction, or (d) the husband did not appear and was not duly served, or (e) the judgment was obtained by fraud, or (f) if an appeal is pending or the time for appeal has not expired, or (g) if the judgment is "against public policy" in British Columbia, or (h) if the husband would have a good defence if an action were brought on the judgment. The opportunities for delay (and time to leave British Columbia) are obvious. There is no right to use summary judgment procedures.

This reciprocal enforcement of judgment legislation does not distinguish between orders made in other Canadian provinces and those made in other jurisdictions. An Alberta order is to be treated the same as an order of an Alabama Court or an Argentinian Court. (Contrast this with the treatment of a Federal Court judgment which can be automatically registered and enforced throughout Canada.) Yet even this inadequate procedure is not available between Quebec and British Columbia.

The use of the second alternative to sue on the "foreign" judgment may be faster because of the right to use summary judgment procedures. In this instance additional defences are available if the process was contrary to natural justice or if there was a manifest error in fact or law.

In sum, the underlying problem is that a system was set up for commercial contracts of substantial size. It does not take account of the needs of average people of limited means. There is a fundamental lack of trust between the competing jurisdictions. Thus, we have so many protections for the "local" person that the "foreign" person frequently loses out. This may have been appropriate for English courts dealing with the laws of European countries in the nineteenth century. It certainly is not appropriate for Canadians within our own country.

Summary

On the basis of this discussion, the problems for a Canadian who moves from province to province or who owns property in more than one province may be summarized as follows:

- What provincial law or laws will govern the matrimonial property regime?
- What effect, if any, will be given a marriage agreement made in accordance with the law of the place where the parties were married?
- How will the *Income Tax Act* affect his or her particular situation? Is the result certain?
- Is it better to separate, divorce or die in one province rather than another?
- What effect will a judgment or a separation agreement have in provinces other than the one where it was obtained?

For Canadians as a group, two issues are paramount:

- Is it fair that the share a spouse receives on marriage breakdown should depend upon the happenstance of residence and the peculiarities of the conflicts rules when that share can vary so much from province to province?

- Will the treatment of all Canadians be equal under our tax laws if provinces continue to have substantially different matrimonial property regimes?

Underlying the discussion, general and specific, is the fundamental principle: each Canadian is a citizen able to move freely for whatever reason of the heart or head within Canada. Should something so fundamental as our family rights and obligations, our marital status, or the status of a child be different depending on our choice of residence? Are we one country or 10?

The Solution

The ideal solution for Canadian families is a uniform family law for Canada following the Australian example, where the states, with much broader powers under their constitution than have our provinces, have ceded jurisdiction in all family law to the federal government. The Government of Australia has established a Family Court *to deal with all family matters*. This Court is informal, has judges specially trained to deal with family problems and has attached to it a conciliation service to assist in resolving disputes involving children. It works. Given our history and the special situation of Quebec with its civil law system, this may be perceived as a politically unrealistic solution.

With the introduction of the popular *société d'acquêts* in Quebec, a "deferred" community of acquests in the Prairie Provinces and a sharing of family assets defined by use in the other common law provinces, the two matrimonial property systems are now similar in principle. It should not be beyond the capacity of Parliament and the federal Department of Justice to devise a matrimonial property regime and complementary tax law that would meet the essential objectives of each of the provinces as they are set out in the legislation we have been discussing. The discretion available to judges under the legislation could allow the "social and cultural" environment and the "unique history" of each province to be taken into account. However, if this solution is not possible, there are other alternatives.

1. The common law provinces can cede jurisdiction over family law to the government of Canada leaving Quebec with its own system, but with an agreement from Quebec:
    (i) to give full faith and credit to orders under the federal law,
    (ii) to establish the rules under which Quebec can take jurisdiction, and
    (iii) to determine the conflicts rules that will apply.

This "special status" would recognize the historical and cultural features unique to the civil law.
2. The present system can continue with a system of federal enforcement procedures, perhaps registration of any order under specified legislation (family law legislation) in the Federal Court with enforcement under its rules by provincially appointed sheriffs and some adjustments to help those people who cannot establish residency for the purpose of divorce in any province.
3. "Marriage and divorce" jurisdiction can be transferred to the provinces with concurrent federal and provincial legislation reserving to the government of Canada:
   (i) rules as to jurisdiction,
   (ii) rules as to conflicts of laws,
   (iii) a federal registry system utilizing the proposed (provincial) Unified Family Courts for enforcement,
   (iv) guaranteed full faith and credit for orders of courts of provinces with the court or original jurisdiction retaining the sole power to set aside or vary (unless the action has been transferred pursuant to rules — see (v) below),
   (v) a procedure for transfer of the action to another province for all purposes under defined circumstances by consent or court order in the same way venue is changed within a province,
   (vi) provision for the Federal Court to have jurisdiction in those situations where the parties cannot fall within the jurisdiction of any one province or where two provinces claim jurisdiction under the rules.

Before the situation is made worse by transferring jurisdiction over marriage and divorce to the provinces these provisions should be in effect in every province.

4. Introduction of the Australian model with legislation for provincially-appointed Unified Family Courts to administer the law. This fourth alternative would mean that efforts would be needed at the provincial level to ensure quality of service to all who come before them at least comparable to the quality of service now offered in the superior courts of our provinces. That challenge should be met before section 96 is amended to permit provincially appointed judges to hear all matters relating to the family.

In my view, preference should be given to the first or the last alternative. With the exception of Ontario, British Columbia and Quebec, the provinces do not want the entire jurisdiction over

marriage and divorce to themselves. Therefore, I see a compromise between these two as the only politically available alternative. Such a solution must have the following essential ingredients if it is to serve the Canadian family:
- The substantive law should be the same throughout Canada regarding the family's "constitution" including provisions for private ordering of an alternative regime and the limitations to that ordering.
- One court should be able to deal with all matters relating to each individual family and it should have access to conciliation and mediation services or have them attached to the court to assist in disputed custody and access cases.
- Rules respecting the transfer of an action from one court to another (a) where all family members move to a new part of the province or country or by agreement and (b) where the family divides and lives in different parts of the province or country.

If everyone involved in the family law system works together, with only the best interest of the family in mind, all except (b) above will be easy to achieve. Providing for a workable system for variation and enforcement where mother and some or all of the children live in one place and father and perhaps some children live in another will be the tough problem. Here I suggest that the provincial and federal governments seeks the advice of the Family Law Subsection of the Canadian Bar Association and of the provincial officials responsible for administering the Reciprocal Enforcement of Maintenance Orders legislation. Those with experience of delays, frustration and futility in this area are the best persons to devise a practical solution. Once the policy decision has been made, a functional solution will be possible.

The parochial attitude presently illustrated by our family property legislation will undoubtedly be repeated in areas of ancillary relief now included in the *Divorce Act* of Canada (maintenance, custody and access) if the legislative authority over divorce is transferred to the provinces. There will be no fundamental differences but sufficient difference in detail to cause problems for individual Canadian families. The underlying philosophical and social values will be the same but the provinces and the courts, jealous of their jurisdiction, will continue to permit individuals to delay and frustrate enforcement of *ex juris* orders. Surely we Canadians have a right to expect more of our governments than that.

Appendix A
PRIVATE ORDERING

Province	Newfoundland	Nova Scotia	Prince Edward Island	New Brunswick
Title	Matrimonial Property Act	Matrimonial Property Act	Family Law Reform Act	Marital Property Act
Effective Date	July 1/80	October 1/80	December 31/78	Not proclaimed as of September 30/80
Types of Agreements	Marriage Contract (s. 31) Cohabitation Agreement (s.32) Separation Agreement (s.34)	Marriage Contract (s. 23) Separation Agreement	Domestic Contract (Part IV) (marriage cohabitation, separation) (ss.51-53)	Domestic Contract (Part III) " (ss.34-36)
Formal Requirements	writing signed, witnessed (s.35)	" (s.24)	" (s.54)	" (s.37)
Scope	all except custody & access unless separation agreement (ss.33-4)	no limitations	as Nfld but cannot limit Part III rights to matrimonial home	all except children unless separation agreement or cohabitation agreement
Effect	binding except as to children (s.38) [s.16(b)(v) s.2(3) & 8(b)] & dum casta clauses (s.39)	" (s.26)	binding except as to maintenance [s.19(4)] & children (s.55)	prevails (s.40) except as to children (s.38) or where no indept legal advice [s.41(6)]
Variation	No provision	probably by s. 13 and by s.29	as to maintenance [s.19(4)] & children (s.55)	No provision except as to children

108

Ontario	Manitoba	Saskatchewan	Alberta	British Columbia
Family Law Reform Act	Marital Property Act	Matrimonial Property Act	Matrimonial Property Act	Family Relations Act
April 1/78	October 15/78	January 1/80	January 1/79	April 1/79
Domestic Contract (Part IV)	Spousal Agreement [s.1(f)]	Interspousal Contract (s.38)	Agreement between spouses (s.37)	Marriage Agreement (s.48)
"	(marriage settlement, marriage contract or separation agreement, or "writing")			"ante-nuptial or post-nuptial settlement", "separation agreement"
(ss.50-52)				
" (s.54)	Marriage Settlement Act, s.3 writing, signed with affidavit of witness & registered	writing, signed, witnessed with independent legal advice (s.38)	(s.38) plus acknowledgement	writing, signed & witnessed (s.48)
"rights & obligations" (s.51) except custody & access	"assets" [s.1(f)]	"property" [s.38(4)]	status, ownership & division of property (s.37)	management, ownership & division of property [s.48(2)] and perhaps maintenance (ss.57 & 75)
binding except custody & access, matrimonial home, & maintance where default unconscionable [s.18(4)] or destitute	binding (s.5) unless separation agreement	binding (s.24) unless "grossly unfair or unconscionable" after marriage	makes property division (Part I) inapplicable but not possession of matrimonial home (Part 2)	binding after marriage
as to children (s.55) & maintenance [s.18(4)]	no provision	s.24	no provision	s.51 if "unfair"

Appendix B
PROPERTY DIVISION

Province	Newfoundland	Nova Scotia	Prince Edward Island	New Brunswick
Who?	spouses [s.2(1)(e)]	spouses [s.2(9)] including widow(er)	spouses [s.2(f)]	spouses [ss.1&3(3)] including widow(er)
When?	separation, annulment, divorce or death (s. 19)	'' (s. 12)	divorce, annulment, separation (s.5)	divorce, annulment, separation, (s.3) or sale of matrimonial home (s.20)
What?	"matrimonial assets" [s.16(b)] 50/50 compensation for contribution to "business assets"	"matrimonial assets" 50/50 (s.4) & may order division of non-matrimonial assets	"family assets" 50/50 [s.4(a)] less ante-nuptial value [s.5(4)] can order division of non-family assets	"family assets" & "marital property" 50/50 (ss. 3&4) and can order a division of other assets (s.8)
How?	application [s.19(1)] except matrimonial home jointly held (s.6)	application (s.12, 18)	application [s.4(1)]	application (ss.3&4)
Where?	Unified Family Court Supreme Court District Court	Supreme Court	Family Division Supreme Court	Court of Queen's Bench
Variation	Yes, s.20	Yes, s.13 as to matrimonial assets	Yes, s.5(5)	Yes, ss.6 & 7
Non-economic misconduct a factor?	No	No	No	No

110

	Ontario	Manitoba	Saskatchewan	Alberta	British Columbia
	spouses [s.1(f)]	spouses (s.2) not separated before May 6, 1979	spouses [s.2(k)] including widow(er)	spouses [s.1(e)] including widow(er) (s.11)	spouses (s.1)
	separation divorce or annulment (s.4)	" & dissipation (s.12)	on application (s.30)	no more than 2 years after decree nisi, annulment or separation (s.5)	no more than 2 years after decree absolute annulment or separation (s.43)
	"family assets" [s.3(b)] 50/50 & can order division of non-family assets [s.4(6)] & compensation for contribution (s.8)	assets acquired during marriage 50/50 with exceptions (s.30)	"matrimonial property" [s.2(h)] except that acquired before marriage and other exceptions (s.30) 50/50	property acquired during marriage with exceptions [s.7(2)] 50/50	"family assets" (s.43) 50/50
	application [s.4(1)]	accounting (s.14)	application (s.21)	application (s.3)	automatic or occurrence of triggering event (s.43)
	UFC SCO County or District Ct	CQB or County Ct	CQB or District Ct	SCA or District Ct	SCBC
	Yes, s.4(4)	"family assets" [s.13(1)] "commercial assets" [s.13(2)]	Yes, s.21 including variation of an earlier order (s.8) with leave if no longer spouses [s.26(2)]	Yes, but not as to exempt property (s.8)	Yes, s.51
	No	possible as to family assets [s.13(1)]	No	possibly 58m	No

Notes

[1] My interpretation is drawn from my own reading of the nine "property reform acts", some advice from Professor A.J. McClean given to the members of the Family Law Subsection of the Canadian Bar Association in Montreal on August 26, 1980, and a paper presented by Professor T.J. Wuester, to the 31st Tax Conference of the Canadian Tax Foundation and subsequently published in the Report of the Thirty-First Tax Conference, Canadian Tax Foundation, 1979 (CTF Conference Report) under the title *Through Western Matrimonial Property on Horseback*.

[2] For a discussion of this concept see Mnookin, R.H. *Bargaining in the shadow of the Law: The Case of Divorce* AFCC Mid-Winter Conference, Family Law Colloquium, "Family Law in the 1980's" Los Angeles, 1979 and Eisenberg, R.A. *Private Ordering Through Negotiation: Dispute — Settlement and Rulemaking,* 89 Harvard Law Review 637 (1976).

[3] While Ontario and the Atlantic Provinces ensure that cohabiting couples can order their own affairs by agreement, others have no such security. None of the provinces provide for property division on separation. So all cohabiting couples are dependent on the law of trusts. *Becker* v. *Pettkus* (1979) 20 Or (2d) 105 (C.A.) is now before the Supreme Court of Canada. In that case the Supreme Court will have the opportunity to affirm the Ontario Court of Appeal's decision and to set out what rights a "common law" spouse has to property acquired by the joint efforts of the couple but registered in the name of the other. It is hoped the Court will make a far reaching and comprehensive decision in principle as some of the justices did in the *Rathwell* case.

[4] (1978) 2 *WWR* 101 (SCC).

[5] For further reference see Castel, J.G., *Conflict of Laws: Cases, Notes & Materials*, Fourth Edition, Toronto, Butterworths, (1978); Wuester, T.J., "Marriage, Property and Some Conflicts of Laws Problems," Continuing Legal Education Society of British Columbia Programme on Marriage Agreements, April, 1980 (CLE papers).

[6] (1900) p. 211.

[7] (1970) 10 *DLR* (3rd) 603 (Ont. CA).

[8] For more detailed discussion see Ellis, James, *Income Tax Considerations and Marriage Agreements,* CLE papers; McNair, D. Keith, *The Income Tax Implications of Matrimonial Property Law Reform — The Common Law Provinces,* CTF Conference Report.

[9] Fraser, Paul & Horn, John, *The Conduct of Civil Litigation in B.C.,* (Butterworths, 1979), c. 52.

Family Law and The Constitution

Nicole Bénard

Even though family law and the constitution are concerns of a legal nature, they arouse emotional reactions. It is not necessary to recall in detail the nationalist tradition of Quebecers, who are distinguished, by both culture and history, from other Canadians and who more readily identify with the provincial institutions they control.

The general problems of the status of women are not linked to nationalism, but the feminist movement cannot be removed from the cultural milieu which gave it birth. The evolution of women depends on social, political and legal developments. This is what prompts us to claim full and complete jurisdiction over family matters for Quebec. A review of the historical, cultural and legal factors that justify this demand would be useful.

A single body of criminal law is used in all provinces of Canada. With respect to civil law, however, the Quebec Code is derived from French law while English Canada has chosen common law, which is not a codified system. Common law is an unwritten tradition; it has been developed and changed by judicial rulings, and tradition, usage, custom and precedent play an important role. It is derived from Britain and often baffles the "Latin mind", which is accustomed to precise and strict classification systems and places greater emphasis on the letter of the "code."

Since the *Quebec Act* of 1774, all governments have recognized the Quebec Code, on which the civil law system is based. The jurists of 1867 yielded to the demands of the representatives from Lower Canada and left it up to the provincial parliaments to codify and amend the civil law and procedures in force in their areas of jurisdiction. Each province was deemed better able to decide upon the most contentious issues since its government was closer to the concerns of its citizens. Influenced by religious authorities, who were bitterly opposed to divorce, the Quebec representatives asked the federal government to assume legislative responsibility for this area. The consciences of Quebecers were relieved by the fact that divorces had to be obtained from Ottawa.

For the last two centuries, Canada's two main language groups have reviewed the law and interpreted it in different ways. Of course, the Quebec Civil Code has undergone major changes and will continue to do so as a result of the persistent efforts of women, but it is still closely adapted to the values and customs of the Quebec people. Quebecers will not renounce their civil law system and, for their part, Quebec women fully realize that a nation's thinking cannot be radically changed.

Civil laws govern the status and "being" of the individual, the family structure, and property, which is viewed as a fundamental right of the individual. Provincial governments look after the immediate interests and needs of their citizens, and Quebec women feel that their government is performing this task well, even though they may retain a few grievances against it. The province is the only government over which Quebecers exert any real influence, since they are a minority in a federation which is not necessarily concerned with their particular interests. As a result, it is logical to want broader powers for the provincial government and, in fact, to have it assume power in all areas. Quebec women will support the action of women at the national level. However, in order to improve the status of women, it is first necessary to bring about a radical change in thinking and this has a greater chance of being accomplished through the decisions and actions of provincial governments.

As groups and as individuals, Quebec women have worked tirelessly in unions, political parties and government departments. Their efforts have led to the creation of a Council on the Status of Women and, most importantly, to a review of family law recently initiated as a result of feminist demands. Quebec women are no longer afraid of divorce on religious or other grounds and they accept the consequences as readily as their marriage obligations.

This brings me specifically to the legal matrimonial regime in Quebec.

Marriage

Section 92.13 of the *British North America Act* gave the provinces jurisdiction over matters of civil law, and thus the responsibility for determining the legal matrimonial systems in their area of jurisdiction. Until 1970, people who were married in Quebec without a marriage contract were automatically included under the community property regime. If the union was dissolved, each spouse received half of the community property. In other provinces, separation of property was the legal system that ensured each spouse had exclusive ownership of any property to which he or she held personal title.

Unless they were married under a system other than the community property regime, Quebec women, for over a hundred years, were entitled to half of the property accumulated by the family. Certain provinces have only recently granted women the right to share the family home and possessions — a right that half of Quebec women have enjoyed for a century. This perhaps explains why the Quebec legislator was slow in granting women rights to the assets acquired by couples married under the separation of property system, and in introducing a reform proposal such as Bill 89.

Since 1970, people who were married in Quebec without a marriage contract have come under the "deferred sharing" regime. The property and possessions acquired after marriage by each spouse is shared by them. Each looks after and disposes of them as he or she pleases and if the marriage is dissolved, each is entitled to half of the other's assets. This makes it different from the separation of property system used in the other provinces and in which possessions acquired before marriage remain the personal property of each spouse.

The deferred sharing regime gives women a certain degree of protection: if the marriage breaks down, any woman who was married under this system is entitled to part of the property accumulated by the family, even when it is in the husband's name. The major drawback is that the spouse who owns the assets, administers and disposes of them as he or she pleases during the marriage. There is nothing that prevents that spouse from squandering them without the other spouse knowing.

Divorce and Family Law

As for divorce, some would like the federal government to retain jurisdiction over it under the pretext that Quebec's law reform proposal does not cover no-fault divorce. It is unfortunate that the "fault" of one or the other spouse must still be used as grounds for divorce, but we have no guarantee that the situation will change if the federal government retains jurisdiction in this field. The federal government must consider the wishes of all the provinces, and some of them have rather conservative views on the matter.

Bill 89, entitled *An Act to Establish a New Civil Code and to Reform Family Law*, deals with divorce, its causes and effects. It would have been more comprehensive if a bill creating a family court had been tabled at the same time. According to the Civil Code Revision Board, this court could be given exclusive jurisdiction over all aspects of family law, including those related to children. The court would be governed by rules of procedure adapted to the specific nature of family disputes, presided over by judges who specialize in the field, and assisted by qualified staff.[1]

The family court would exercise exclusive jurisdiction in all civil matters, including marriage, legal separation, divorce, adoption, support payments for children and parental authority. It would also have jurisdiction over certain criminal matters associated with youth protection; over cases of failing to provide maintenance and over those sections of the *Criminal Code* dealing with incest, assault, and rape of a spouse.

The report of the Civil Code Revision Board states that this court should be autonomous, that is, it should operate independently of existing judicial structures. It could also be integrated into the provincial court system. The authors examine the constitutional problems raised by an independent court but do not put forward any solutions.

The present constitution would seem to grant Quebec the authority to create a family court with the judges being appointed by the federal government. The disadvantage is that the federal government would not be obliged to respect the appointment criteria established by the province. The aforementioned report concludes that major changes are needed in sections 96 to 100 of the *British North America Act*. Given the complex problems raised by overlapping jurisdictions, it would be simpler to grant Quebec exclusive jurisdiction over divorce. The province could then introduce comprehensive legislation incorporating all matters related to the family.

Alimony

The Quebec government has already adopted an *Act to Promote the Collection of Alimony*. Bill 183 does not respond to all the aspirations of women, but it does represent an improvement over the situation that had existed. Section 169.1 stipulates that the courts have authority to order that payments be tied the annual index established in section 119 of the *Act Respecting the Quebec Pension Plan* (Chapter R-9). However, particular circumstances of the individual may justify the selection of another index. I would be sorry to see the Supreme Court declare article 169.1 of the *Civil Code ultra vires*, or rule that it does not apply to cases involving alimony payments following a divorce, under the pretext that the Canadian constitution grants legislative authority in the field of divorce to the federal government and not the provinces. A lot of my colleagues are anxiously awaiting the opportunity to contest the application of this Act but it is impossible to predict what the courts' decision will be. If it is necessary to wait for a case to reach the Supreme Court before acting in other cases, women, once again, will suffer a waste of time, money and energy.

It is also argued that if the provinces exercised full jurisdiction in the area of divorce, problems would arise in executing judgments as they relate to custody and alimony. However, even though the federal government has exclusive jurisdiction over divorce, such problems already exist. Unfortunately, the solution depends on how far one must go to assert one's rights, rather than on the distribution of powers.

With the exception of Nova Scotia, Saskatchewan, the Northwest Territories and the Yukon, all the provinces have signed agreements on the execution of alimony judgments. According to these agreements, a creditor need only file a certified copy of the judgment rendered in another province with the registrar of the Superior Court in the debtor's district of residence. As soon as this document is filed, the judgment acquires the same force and effect as if it had been delivered in the province of origin.

It is up to the debtor to request a review of the judgment if he feels that the payments claimed are too high in relation to his income and needs. But this system is not as effective as one would wish: the geographic distance separating creditors from debtors at times prevents them from obtaining information that is essential to the execution of the judgment. Distance also means high travel expenses, which can prevent one of the parties from appearing in court when the judge sets the amount of payments, and the other party from attending when the court reviews the payments or custody conditions. As a result, if Quebec were to obtain exclusive jurisdiction over divorce, the situation would not necessarily be worse than it is at the present time.

An Interesting Proposal

After lengthy discussions, in February 1979, provincial government officials and their federal counterparts appeared to have succeeded in reaching agreement on four major points.

The provinces would have exclusive jurisdiction over marriage. The federal and provincial governments would share jurisdiction over divorce, with the provinces having predominant authority: one province might decide to exercise full jurisdiction, while another might allow the federal government to legislate in this area. The provinces would have exclusive authority over property matters, while the federal government would see to it that all regions of the country recognized divorce judgments issued in Canada or abroad.

Finally, a special constitutional provision would enable the provinces to appoint judges to a "unified" family court.

In my opinion, this formula seems satisfactory for Quebecers. Women who fear that their governments will use this power ill-advisedly could appeal to them so that they would leave some jurisdiction over divorce to the federal government. Quebecers believe that their provincial government is no less qualified than the one in Ottawa to represent them in areas that affect their private lives. This is why they fail to understand the reservations of other Canadians.

This occurs, also, in relation to the problem raised by the appointment of judges. The women of other provinces have no confidence in their governments in this area, whereas in Quebec the method of appointing judges is neither better nor worse than that of the federal government. When the proposed agreement is finalized, it will be easier for Quebec to include in the act creating the family court, selection criteria for the judges who will be responsible for administering justice in this area.

. . . and One Other Objection

On the other hand, what the Honourable Jean Chrétien proposed in July 1980 is unacceptable. Here again, to believe that the provinces are interested in becoming "divorce havens" is to have no faith in provincial governments. To judge by the fears aroused in Canadian women by the conservatism of their leaders, Mr. Chrétien's apprehensions are unfounded. The situation will in no way be altered if the federal government is granted exclusive jurisdiction over the execution of judgments rendered in the various provinces. We should improve the existing interprovincial agreements and conclude new agreements. In any case, Quebec will not surrender part of its jurisdiction in this area to the federal government.

It is important to consider the consequences of yielding partial jurisdiction over the execution of divorce judgments to the federal government. It would also have to be given partial jurisdiction over other areas, in particular marriage and succession. Quebec women will never agree to this.

Women in the various regions of Canada do not speak with one voice where family law is concerned. It must be kept in mind, however, that the object of our struggles is the equality for women and the elimination of injustices against them. We want to be guaranteed that this objective will be achieved, but the best guarantee is still a change in attitudes. Together, we must constantly strive to reach this goal.

Note

[1] Civil Code Revision Board, *Rapport sur le tribunal de la famille*, Montreal, 1975.

Statement by the Fédération des femmes du Québec on Jurisdiction in Family Law

From both legislative and judicial standpoints, the sharing of jurisdiction over family law has an impact on the lives of individuals and communities and, in particular, the settlement of family disputes. A unified body of family law would be an appropriate solution. However, the consolidation of family law requires that a single government hold both legislative jurisdiction and judicial responsibility. The judicial structure of Quebec, which differs from the other provinces, and the sharing of jurisdiction in the field of civil law make the administration of justice more complex.

Because provincial governments are more closely linked to the concerns of their citizens and, as such, interpret their aspirations better, it is up to the provinces to legislate in this area. Since they already bear the major part of the responsibilities with regard to family law, it would be natural and simpler to give them the responsibility for unifying family law.

Some will protest perhaps that Canadians would not receive equal treatment before the law if the provincial governments were to exercise exclusive jurisdiction over divorce, as was proposed during the constitutional talks. The mere fact that the same *Divorce Act* is administered in the same way in Canada offers no guarantee of equality before the law for all.

It has been suggested that the federal Parliament should legislate in the area of matrimonial property to ensure identical treatment for all. This suggestion may seem logical to our "compatriots" in the anglophone provinces, but it is unacceptable to Quebec. The Quebec matrimonial regimes which form an integral part of the *Civil Code*, already provide for the sharing of a couple's property, and Quebecers will not give them up. Quebec must have a comprehensive body of family law. The more one chips away at the civil law, the more the identity of Quebecers will be endangered. Quebecers are the only Canadians who are faced with two philosophies, one stemming from the common law and the other from the French civil law. This situation does not promote unity. To a certain degree, the judicial process will be more humane if a single government is granted jurisdiction over the entire field of family law. It is commonly acknowledged that many aspects of family disputes are interdependent and inseparable. The family courts called for by the Fédération des femmes du Québec would adequately meet the needs of all citizens. The Civil Code Revision Board has presented recommendations on the operation of such courts that are both relevant and in line with the needs of the Quebec population.

The Fédération des femmes du Québec approves of the so-called "best effort draft" proposal, which would enable the provinces to appoint judges to preside over the administration of family law. The appointment criteria for judges established by the Quebec government are similar to those of the federal government, and a feared reduction in legal services seems unfounded to us.

IV. Overlapping Jurisdictions and Women's Issues

Overlapping Jurisdictions and Women's Issues

Audrey Doerr

The debate on constitutional reform in Canada in the last decade or more has yielded an abundance of proposals for change. While there has been no lack of proposals for reform, there has been a notable lack of consensus on the nature of reform respecting particular issues and the means whereby final agreement is to be reached. From the viewpoint of women, the relative lack of discussion on the effect of constitutional reform as it pertains to women's issues has been equally noteworthy. As citizens concerned with achieving equality of status under the laws in this country, women have a fundamental interest in the constitutional debate.

The purpose of this paper is to address the question of overlapping jurisdictions of federal and provincial governmental activities and their implications for the types of women's policies and programs that have been developed. The first section of the paper treats the particular dilemma of overlapping jurisdictions respecting the current division of powers and the resulting implications for reform in this area. The second section considers three particular areas of governmental action respecting women's interests to demonstrate how the characterization of women's needs is affected by problems arising from the division of powers and overlapping jurisdictions. Finally, the concluding section offers observations and options in the approach to women's issues relevant to constitutional reform.

The current agenda for constitutional renewal has included, *inter alia*, matters respecting entrenchment of a charter of rights, division of powers, resource sharing, patriation, powers affecting the economy and institutional reform.[1] Moreover, each level of government has had its own set of priorities on matters respecting reform. From the federal government's perspective, the entrenchment of a charter of rights including language rights is a priority issue. The federal government has argued for the inclusion of a charter of rights on the grounds that not only would safeguards against government interference with these rights be afforded to individuals, but the ambiguities of federal and provincial jurisdiction respecting human rights would be removed.[2] For their part, the provinces have concentrated their concerns on the clarification and adjustment of the division of powers between federal and provincial governments and on ways and means whereby provincial influence in central institutions such as the Supreme Court and the Senate would be increased. Power-sharing is a popular term among representatives of both levels of government. In particular, the division of responsibility on economic matters is a major issue. Which level of government controls the key economic levers will be crucial to the future shape and form of economic and social development in Canada.

It is a self-evident truth to state that women are not among the key actors in this process. As a matter of interest, there are only two women in the 33-member federal Cabinet and 14 women in the 282-member federal House of Commons. Of the 193 Cabinet posts in the 10 provinces, 10 women occupy ministerial portfolios. There are only 30 elected women members in the 10 provincial legislatures out of a total of 1,192 elected members. The low participation rates of women will be a recurring theme throughout this discussion.[3]

With the possible exception of human rights and family law, women's issues had not prior to 1980 surfaced in the discussions. One may surmise that these issues either lack priority or are assumed in the context of more general problems respecting the economy and the society. Let us begin by looking at some of the general problems.

Division of Powers and Overlapping Jurisdictions

The essence of a federal system of government is the division of powers between the two levels of government. The co-ordinate yet independent status of each level is central to the federal principle.[4] The *British North America Act* of 1867, however, provided for a quasi-federal union dominated by the central authority. The federal government held the residual power exercised primarily through the emergency and declaratory powers (the preamble to section 91 and section 92.10.c., respectively) on legislative matters and the executive powers of disallowance and reservation (sections 56 and 57 respectively). Furthermore, the appointment of lieutenant governors, superior court justices in the provinces and Senators from the provinces was the executive prerogative of the federal government in addition to the authority to make appointments to federal executive, ambassadorial and judicial positions.[5]

Judicial interpretations of the division of powers in sections 91 and 92 and sections 93 to 95, nevertheless, reinforced the autonomy of the provinces within their fields of jurisdiction.⁶ Until 1945, it could be said that the courts maintained the balance of power in arbitrating disputes which arose between the two levels of government. However, the political and administrative process replaced judicial rulings as a primary means of resolving conflict from that time. A main reason for this shift was the changing economic and financial circumstances of governments.

The division of taxing responsibility under the constitution gave the federal government an unlimited power to tax (section 91.3). The provincial governments had restricted taxation powers (sections 92.2 and 92.9). In addition, interprovincial tariffs were forbidden by section 121. Finally, federal and provincial crown lands were exempt from taxation (section 125). During the depression, provincial financial structures all but collapsed. Demands for social services and the lack of provincial revenue to meet them required federal intervention but, in many areas, federal interference was prohibited on constitutional grounds.⁷

In 1940, unemployment insurance was made the responsibility of the federal government (section 91.2A) pursuant to an amendment to the *British North America Act*. From 1941, as a result of inter-governmental agreement, the levying of personal and corporation income taxes by provincial and municipal governments was suspended and assumed wholly by the federal government. Tax rental payments in lieu of tax revenues were then made by the federal government to the provinces. In 1945, a program of family allowances was introduced ostensibly to increase consumer spending while, at the same time, serving broader social goals. The White Paper on Employment and Income in 1945 charted a major role for the federal government in postwar reconstruction.

Although the federal government came to control the principal revenue sources during the 1940s and continued to refine these fiscal arrangements in consultation with the provinces during the 1950s and 1960s, the responsibilities of the provinces continued to expand and fiscal imbalance increased. That is, demand for the provision of services which fell under provincial jurisdiction continued to expand without commensurate increases in the provincial revenue base. For its part, the federal government used its spending power to assist provinces in developing and delivering services, especially social services, and to help offset the fiscal imbalance at the provincial level. By the 1960s shared cost programs and joint undertakings abounded. The Canada Assistance Plan, the Canadian Pension Plan,⁸ Medicare, and the Post-Secondary Education and Technical and Vocational Training Programs were primary examples.

At this juncture, it is useful to review briefly the exercise of the federal spending power and the problems that it has created with respect to the division of powers. The spending power of governments is usually considered to pertain to the spending activities of those governments on programs operating under the authority of legislation passed by their respective legislatures. In constitutional terms, however, the spending power has meant the power of the federal Parliament to make payments to people or institutions or governments for purposes on which the federal Parliament does not necessarily have the power to legislate. The federal government has claimed the right to exercise the spending power for several purposes, including: the equalization of opportunity for individual Canadians; the equalization of provincial public services; the equalization of opportunity for individual Canadians through regional economic development; and, special projects of national importance.[9] The constitutional basis for this spending power is found in section 91.3 of the *British North America Act,* which gives the Parliament of Canada the power to raise money by any mode of taxation, and section 91.1A, which gives Parliament the right to make laws respecting public debt and property. The latter includes every kind of federal asset, including the Consolidated Revenue Fund.

The exercise of the federal spending power on any matter falling within sections 91 or 95 is unquestioned. If it is used for matters that come under sections 92 or 93, the legislation authorizing the expenditure cannot amount to a regulatory scheme falling within provincial powers.[10] To claim authority to exercise its spending power, the federal government must normally characterize the nature of its use under one of the several purposes mentioned above. In certain respects, however, it may be said that a national interest can be found in any activity of government. For example, the federal Technical and Vocational Training Program of 1966 was justified as an area of federal concern because training was necessary to support national economic priorities. It was not "education in the constitutional sense."[11]

Over the years, federal-provincial fiscal relations have become increasingly sophisticated and complex. The continued need for increased revenue at the provincial level has resulted in elaborate intergovernmental financial arrangements. The current legislation pertaining to the period 1977 to 1982 provides, among other things, for: fiscal equalization payments based on 29 tax revenue sources, fiscal stabilization payments to provinces, tax collection agreements, provincial personal income tax revenue guarantee payments, and established programs financing.[12] The main shared cost programs covered by the *Act* are Post-Secondary Education, Hospital Insurance, Medical Care and Extended Health Services. Block-funding or lump-sum payments in health services was introduced in 1977 to give provinces greater flexibility in the administration of federal funds received. Alternative payments for standing programs also provides for a system of tax abatements for particular programs.

The need to maintain national minimum standards in major social programs and to provide for redistribution of wealth to overcome regional disparities remains the primary *raison-d'être* for extensive federal involvement in provincial fiscal relations and areas of provincial jurisdiction. The point has often been made, nevertheless, that provincial criticisms of the federal spending power have been directed to *how* it has been used, not the exercise of the power *per se*. For some provinces, federal funds are absolutely essential to maintain the delivery of a minimum level of services. Withdrawal of federal support could, in many provinces, result in a substantial decline in services.

In general terms, the problem of overlapping jurisdictions is inherent in any division of powers between the federal and provincial governments. No constitutional division of responsibilities can be made so precisely as to eliminate all ambiguities. Second, to the extent that regional economic disparities continue, there will always be occasions on which the central government will have to play a role in ensuring that minimum national standards are provided. Finally, in recent years, overlap has been generated by actions of provincial as well as federal governments. Provincial "intrusions" in areas such as foreign affairs and communications and claims for involvement in federal decision-making processes, particularly those respecting the economy, have also occurred.

Efforts to deal with the problem of overlapping jurisdictions in the constitutional renewal process have included re-examinations of existing governmental activities, on the one hand, and attempts to redefine categories into which responsibilities might be grouped on the other. The first approach has sometimes been referred to as the "intrusions exercise." In 1977, a continuing committee of ministers and officials on the Constitution conducted a round of discussions on the major irritants in the intrusions of *chevauchements* of one level or another in an endeavour to overcome problems of overlap. Second, efforts to identify responsibilities and place them in categories that determine which government has jurisdiction have been extensive. The *British North America Act* set out three categories of legislative authority: powers that were exclusively federal, powers that were exclusively provincial, and concurrent powers. As noted, the federal government held the residual power. Current formulae extend these categories. For example, the Task Force on Canadian Unity recommended a seven-fold categorization system.[13] In addition to two categories for exclusive federal and provincial powers, they suggested two categories of concurrent powers: central paramountcy would operate for one; provincial paramountcy would operate for the other. Furthermore, they recommended a limited list of those areas where central laws would be administered by the provinces, a limited list of those powers requiring joint action by Parliament and by the provincial legislatures, and a category of special overriding central powers with limitations specified.

You may well ask where all this puts us with respect to dealing with problems of overlapping jurisdictions. To begin, a division of powers must flow from some statement of principles of the respective role of each level of government. Nevertheless, experience has already demonstrated that a national interest may be found in many areas of provincial jurisdiction and, to a certain extent, the converse has also been claimed. In practical terms, the constitutional division of powers has hardly acted as a constraint on government activity at either level.[14] Even during periods of restraint in government spending, such as the one experienced in the last several years, there has been little evidence of efforts to rationalize joint federal-provincial activities in ways that maintain service standards but reduce costs. Government activism has promoted inter-dependence and it would not be far-fetched to suggest that the division of legislative powers has become horizontal rather than vertical in nature. The entrenchment of a charter of rights and the clarification of key powers may reduce ambiguity in some areas but there are undoubtedly many other areas of governmental responsibility in which joint action and joint responsibility will remain.

Women should have a particular interest in the problems of overlapping jurisdictions since the areas in which their main concerns lie — human rights, employment, education, training, welfare, etc. — are fields in which both levels of government have been active despite the fact that most of these fields are ones of provincial jurisdiction. With these considerations in mind let us turn to a discussion of legislative activity respecting women's issues in several key areas.

Women's Issues

The constitution does not provide for any matters or jurisdiction over "women's issues." As we know, women's rights as persons under the Constitution were not established until 1930 with the *Edwards* case, although progress had been made by that time with respect to women's suffrage! Concern with women's status emerged as part of human rights activities internationally particularly after World War II but did not gain force nationally until the 1960s. The treatment of women as a clientele group by government did not emerge until the 1960s. The age of participatory democracy brought special attention to "disadvantaged minorities" and it was into this category that many government-sponsored women's activities fell. Women, like native peoples, needed special encouragement to develop their potential as citizens. While native peoples are a *bona fide* minority, women constitute half the population and the only perceptible justification for using a minority-group approach can be said to stem from the low participation rates of women in different areas of public life.

The problems of women, nevertheless, cover a broad range of public policy issues. In the first instance, there is the issue of human rights. The most important of these is freedom from discrimination on the basis of sex. This issue affects all women, whatever their circumstances. Second, there is the issue of equal status and opportunity. A broad interpretation of this issue covers areas of government activity from education and training to employment and citizenship. Although women constitute half the population, the issue of equal status raises different concerns for women in different circumstances. Governmental programs in many of these areas are, therefore, directed to serve special needs of particular groups of women. Women themselves express differing degrees of interest in women's issues. For example, a single professional woman with a university education is concerned primarily with obtaining equal status and opportunity in law and in practice in her career pursuits. Married women with children who want to combine a dual role of homemaker and worker will be concerned with a broad range of problems on the job and in the home. For a single female parent with no professional training and little financial support, the issues may be ones respecting income support or job development and training and day care. Native women and the handicapped are doubly disadvantaged groups since they are affected by problems particular to their circumstances as well as those pertaining to women generally. Thus, the range of activities and experiences are important to women's concerns and action must be directed at all groups to move toward a society in which equal status is more than a hollow phrase.

The following discussion will consider three areas. The first is relevant to all women who wish to be part of the labour force. The second pertains to women who, for whatever reason, need special encouragement in their participation in the labour force and society. The third relates to the role of women as mothers as well as members of the labour force. In each case, the problems of overlapping jurisdiction affect the impact of government activity on women's issues.

1. Employment Legislation

Labour and employment is an area of governmental jurisdiction in which the levels of government act separately but have related interests. In the first instance, both levels of government have their own labour forces in respect to workers in their public services. Provinces exercise control over private sector labour forces in their jurisdiction except in matters pertaining to interprovincial agreements and federal workers.[15] To the extent that employment and the creation of jobs is a national economic concern, the federal government can also exercise influence in the private sector through tax provisions or subsidizations.

Creating a climate of equal opportunity in the labour force is a primary goal for women in Canada. Equal economic status and equity in treatment have been pursued along several avenues, most notably equal rights and equal pay legislation. One of the effects of a federal system such as Canada has is the scope of reciprocal influence that can occur between and among the several governments. For example, a legislative initiative in one jurisdiction can act as a catalyst or bring pressure to bear on the other jurisdiction to act. The area of human rights legislation is an interesting example of this type of federal-provincial interplay. The *Canadian Bill of Rights*, which prohibits discrimination on the grounds of sex, was passed by the federal Parliament in 1960. Some provinces also included an anti-discrimination clause in human rights legislation.[16] In 1977, the federal government passed the *Human Rights Act* and established a Human Rights Commission for appeals of violation under the *Act*, which covers areas of federal jurisdiction. Human rights commissions have also been established in many provinces.

It should be noted that section 92(13) of the *British North America Act* gives provinces jurisdiction over "property and civil rights in the provinces." With respect to "civil rights," judicial interpretations have inferred that such laws would not affect federal powers of legislation or matters of a general nature. Conversely, the federal government may pass laws in this area to establish uniformity across the nation but any federal act that provides for such uniformity shall not have effect in any provinces unless and until it is adopted and enacted by the respective legislature.[17] Thus, the entrenchment of a charter of rights in the constitution requires federal and provincial concurrence to have national effect.

Equal pay provisions have been included in federal and provincial legislation. New Brunswick's *Employees' Fair Remuneration Act* was passed as early as 1961. Other provinces acted, for the most part, in the late 1960s and early 1970s. At the federal level, the *Canada Labour Code* has, since July 1, 1971, prohibited differences in wages between male and female employees "employed in the same establishment performing the same or similar work under the same or similar working conditions on jobs requiring the same or similar skill, effort and responsibility." The federal *Human Rights Act* contains a similar equal pay provision.[18]

Gail Cook and Mary Eberts have examined critically the implications of the types of phrases used in equal pay legislation.[19] They point out that equal wages are upheld in the legislation only if women perform the "same" or "identical" work as men in the same working establishment. The problem which this type of legislation addresses, therefore, is that of lower wages for women than men in similar jobs. Furthermore, with few exceptions, equal pay provisions have pertained to wages rather than total compensation, that is pension and other benefits.

Federal and provincial governments have lagged behind equal pay standards recommended at the international level. The Equal Remuneration Convention, #100 passed by the International Labour Organization in 1959 and ratified by Canada in 1972, promotes the application of the principle of equal remuneration regardless of sex for work of equal value. In order to devise the means for assessing the value of work, it was proposed that measures be taken to promote the approval of jobs on the basis of work to be performed. This approach broadens the concept of equal pay for it does not require that male and female employees work at the same or similar jobs in the same establishment.

Varying provisions in equal pay legislation might be construed as barriers to interprovincial mobility of workers. If less protection is offered under legislation in one province than another not only is the condition of work for women unequal across Canada, it may also lead to concentration and, hence, higher participation rates of women in one province or indeed in one sector of the labour force than others. Although job opportunities and regional rates of pay are issues which affect both men and women, women may have to deal with the added disadvantage of discriminatory wage practices in some areas. A current federal proposal as one aspect of support for economic union in Canada is the entrenchment in the Constitution of "the mobility rights of citizens, as well as their right to gain a livelihood and acquire property in any province, regardless of their province or residence or previous residence, subject to laws of general application."[20] It would be interesting to know if the intention of that proposal would also include the elements of the principles of non-discrimination and equal pay for work of equal value for women!

Equal opportunity legislation has been used as an alternative as well as a complement to equal pay legislation. By and large, this has been pursued by broadening the provision of existing human rights legislation so that sex and, in some cases, marital status have become prohibited grounds of discrimination along with race, religion, national origin, etc. in hiring practices. Equal opportunity provisions available to women in Canada vary from jurisdiction to jurisdiction and anti-discrimination measures often contain significant exceptions.[21] Equal opportunity legislation is important, nevertheless, because, short of affirmative action, it addresses the problem of recruitment and selection to jobs rather than equal pay once an individual is in a job. The problem of classification, the core of the issue in determining equal work, equal qualifications and experience, however, is still a major problem.

The federal government has pursued equal opportunity practices over the last decade and could perhaps be considered one of the better employers so far as women are concerned. The Public Service Commission which administers the *Public Service Employment Act* has followed a three-stage strategy in providing equal opportunity. As outlined in its 1979 report,[22] the first stage was one of consciousness raising. This led to a second stage of initiating action to eliminate the more obvious forms of discrimination. Steps were taken to ensure that women were considered as candidates for positions at all levels, were more frequently chosen as selection board members and were offered opportunities for training in the Career Assignment Program and the Senior Management Development Program. In the late seventies, annual departmental action plans and labour market surveys were requested from departments. In early 1979 an exclusion order was passed allowing female correctional officers to be recruited to work in male institutions on an experimental basis. Recognition has also been given to volunteer work and salary bands rather than individual salary levels in the selection process.

Despite these and other efforts, the statistics are discouraging. The current distribution of women in occupational categories in the federal public service has changed only marginally in some occupational categories. The 1979 statistics compiled by the Public Service Commission provide the following breakdown.

Table 1
Percentage of Women by Occupational Category in the Federal Public Service[23]

Category	Percentage
Senior Executive	3.7
Scientific and Professional	21.8
Administrative and Foreign Service	24.4
Technical	10.0
Administrative Support	79.7
Operational	18.7
Total (all categories)	34.6

In her study of "Sex and the Public Service," Kathleen Archibald reported in 1967 that 65.5 per cent of positions in the then "Office" category were occupied by women.[24] Assuming some approximation of this group (pre-collective bargaining classification) with the Administrative Support category, one could observe that the percentage of women in these types of occupations has increased. However, in other categories such as the professional groups female participation has risen. Archibald reported the 1967 figure at 7.8 per cent compared to the 21.8 per cent above. Finally, the total percentage of women in all categories in 1967 was 26.5 per cent compared to 34.6 per cent above.

A main finding from the 1979 statistics was the continued high rates of turnover of women in public service jobs.[25] While it was known that women generally resigned more often than men, it was found that the disparity increased at senior managerial levels (below senior executive) where the proportion of women resigning was twice as great as the participation rates in those groups.[26] Despite the deficiencies of the data, it was reported that family-related issues were considered to be the major factor underlying the resignations of women.

On a broader plane, the participation rate of women in the labour force as a whole is low, relatively speaking. Figures obtained from a May 1980 Statistics Canada report show the following:

Table 2
The Labour Force — 1980[27]

	Men	(000's) Women	Total
Population (15 years or more)	8,808	9,159	17,967
Active in Labour Force	6,924	4,592	11,516
Not Active in Labour Force	1,884	4,567	6,451
Participation Rate	78.6%	50.1%	
Unemployment Rate	7.3%	8.7%	

The key figure in the first instance is the participation rate for women. The national average is 50.1 per cent. Only four provinces are above the national average: Ontario (54.4 per cent), Manitoba (51 per cent), Alberta (57.4 per cent) and British Columbia (50.4 per cent). While there are undoubtedly many factors to explain the low participation rates, such as the exercise of choice on the part of women who do not want to work, the lack of perceived opportunities for entering the labour force or obtaining appropriate training and credentials to do so, lack of day care facilities, etc., the statistics are troublesome. In view of the legislative guarantees for non-discrimination, equal pay and equal opportunity, one might have expected higher participation rates.

The relationship between participation rates and employment patterns and division of powers and overlapping jurisdictions may seem remote at first glance but several considerations arise. For those who would like to see an entrenched charter of rights in the Constitution, pressure for equal rights on job-related matters like equal pay should be considered. Protection of this kind, however, is safeguarded in individual cases by an expensive judicial process. Legislative action at both levels of government would continue to be required particularly on matters respecting equal opportunity. There would be a continued need for improved and extended provisions for job recuitment, job classification and job promotion. The participation rates also tell us that the problems extend beyond legislative guarantees. They lie in developing women as a resource pool for a larger number of jobs in the labour market. It is here that the problem of overlapping jurisdictions wields its full force on women's issues. Let us examine some of the complexities of joint governmental action in the fields of education, training and voluntary activities.

2. Joint Programs in Education, Training and Volunteer Work

Many government programs which directly affect women's interest such as health, welfare, education, training, etc., fall within provincial jurisdiction. It is these precise areas in which overlapping jurisdictions have been created mainly through the use of the federal spending power and which have been enshrined, for the most part, in federal-provincial financial arrangements legislation. By and large, federal and provincial spending programs have treated women as part of general programs, as in the case of training, or as special groups, as in the case of funding voluntary associations. The key consideration, therefore, is the extent to which women have been the recipients of or participants in these programs.

Education and training are means whereby women can prepare themselves for participation in the labour force. The provincial governments exercise exclusive jurisdiction over education pursuant to section 93 of the *British North America Act*. It is an area of jurisdiction which has been guarded jealously as a primary basis for provincial autonomy and cultural development, especially in the case of the province of Quebec. However, the federal government has economic interests in this field in that the education and training of individuals develops a critical national resource. Problems of employment and unemployment, for example, are related to the programs which may or may not exist in educational and training institutions.

Provincial governments exercise sole authority at the primary and secondary school level. With the exception of federal funds which are made available to provincial governments for the development of special language programs in the schools, there is little joint activity. School curricula are developed at the provincial level. Local school boards are the creatures of provincial governments. At the post-secondary level, however, the federal government has claimed a substantial role. Following a recommendation of the Royal Commission on National Development in the Arts, Letters and Sciences (Massey Commission) in 1952, annual federal grants to universities were made available. As the Royal Commission had stated in its report: "The universities are provincial institutions; but they are much more than that . . . . They also serve the national cause in so many ways, direct and indirect, that theirs must be regarded as the finest contribution to national strength and unity."[28] When the Canada Council was established in 1957 a section of the *Act* provided for grants to universities.[29]

Such heady nationalism did not pass without criticism. For example, the Royal Commission of Inquiry on Constitutional Problems in the Province of Quebec (Tremblay Commission) in 1956 rejected any federal intervention. Education was the cornerstone of provincial autonomy and cultural development. For its part, the province had refused to accept the annual federal university grants until 1961 when a tax abatement arrangement in lieu of the grant was provided to the province.

The activities of federal granting councils such as the National Research Council, the Canada Council and more recently the Social Sciences and Humanities Research Council and others provide federal support for scholarly scientific and artistic undertakings in universities. Since 1964, the federal government has through the Canada Student Loans program operated by the Department of the Secretary of State extended federal support to individuals wishing to attend university. Many provinces operate their own programs as well.

An area of federal intervention into the provincial educational field which generated considerable jurisdictional conflict at the time of its inception was the training of adults. In 1960, the *Technical and Vocational Training Assistance Act* was passed by the federal Parliament.[30] Under this *Act*, federal aid was directed to post-secondary institutions to provide assistance in training the unemployed. Provisions were also included respecting the retraining of individuals who were employed in jobs which were likely to become obsolete. Moneys made available under this *Act* were used by the provinces to expand their post-secondary educational systems.[31]

In 1966, the federal government took a major initiative in this field. A Department of Manpower and Immigration (renamed Employment and Immigration in 1977) was established and the post-secondary and training policy was revised. Mr. Pearson, the then Prime Minister, expressed the federal government's position in these terms: "The federal government believes that it has a constitutional and necessary role in the training and development of our adult labour force for economic growth and full employment."[32]

Therein lies a brief background to the current basis for federal-provincial arrangements respecting the training and retraining of adults. Provincial institutions are used for the delivery of training programs funded jointly or wholly by the federal government. Furthermore, in the last decade, federal manpower programs have been expanded and complemented by direct job creation programs such as Canada Works, Young Canada Works, Local Employment Assistance, and Summer Youth Employment Programs, as well as a number of subsidy programs such as employment tax credit programs.[33]

What impact have these federal initiatives had on women? At the university level the world seems to be unfolding as it should, at least to a limited extent. In the first instance, female university enrolments for 1980 are, as a whole, comparable to male enrolments. Female enrolments at the elementary and secondary school levels are approximately 48.6 per cent of total enrolments.[34] Female undergraduate enrolment at universities is approximately 45 per cent of total enrolments.[35] However, women tend to be concentrated in programs in faculties of arts, education, nursing and pharmacy. There is a considerably lower participation rate of women in faculties such as science, commerce, engineering, dentistry, medicine and law. What is even more disturbing, although demographic trends may change the pattern over time, is the participation rate of female university graduates in the labour force. Women with university degrees constitute approximately 33 per cent of the total group of persons with university degrees who are active in the labour force. Secondly, the participation rate of women who have university degrees is 73.5 per cent as compared to 91.4 per cent of men with a university education. The unemployment figure for these people is 5.6 per cent for women and 3.3 per cent for men.

Training and retraining programs have had limited positive impact for women. The assessments of these programs, and there have been several, including one currently underway by the Economic Council of Canada, reveal a number of general shortcomings. The C.D. Howe Institute Study, *New Directions for Manpower Policy*, revealed three main weaknesses.[36] First, the programs have a heavy orientation toward classroom training with too little emphasis on on-the-job training or industrial training and an apprenticeship where people can acquire real work experience. Second, graduates are often unable to make use of training received due to poor matching of the type and number of training positions with job opportunities. Finally, the jurisdictional distinction between training and education has often resulted in poor co-ordination and conflict between federal and provincial activities. The key issue, nevertheless, has been identified as poor matching of job training and employment opportunities.

In addition to these general problems, female participants are confronted with several other difficulties. In a recent study of the impact of federal employment strategies on women, it was found that for 1978-79 women represented 33 per cent of full-time institutional trainees and 29 per cent of all industrial trainees in adult occupational training programs.[37] However, female participation was 48 per cent in programs over which the federal government had maximum control (these included institutional occupational skill training, language training, basic training for skill development, basic job readiness training, work adjustment training programs but not the apprenticeship programs). Second, the dependent care allowances for women with children enrolled in these programs are minimal. A recent increase in the allowance in 1979, for example, was accompanied by a reduction in training allowances for those living with a parent or a working spouse. No wonder the characteristics of trainees have tended to be young, single, relatively uneducated and without dependents. Finally, and perhaps more important, is the degree to which these programs have continued sex-stereotyping in jobs. Eight occupational groups accounted for 85 per cent of all female skill trainees started in 1978-79 and these occupational groups consisted primarily of traditional female jobs.[38] Over 50 per cent of the women were trained in stenographic and typing occupations. A look at some statistics of full time enrolments and spring graduates in post-secondary career programs in community colleges (institutions which, by an large, handle the training programs on a province-by-province basis) is revealing. To demonstrate the point, I have selected a representative sample of provinces and the enrolment figures in two categories.

Table 3
Training Enrolments by Province and Sex 1978-79[39]

Province	Secretarial		Electrical & Electronic Engineering	
	Men	Women	Men	Women
Newfoundland	0	72	127	1
Nova Scotia	0	46	80	1
Quebec	8	3,577	2,773	36
Ontario	69	2,715	1,937	76
Alberta	0	739	507	7
British Columbia	5	93	303	5

I need not comment on the salary differentials between these two occupational categories.

Female participation in direct job creation programs has been about 31 per cent or less in Young Canada, Summer Youth Job Corps and Local Initiatives Programs.[40] These and other direct job creation programs have resulted primarily in poorly-paid sex-typed and short duration jobs with little training opportunities for women.[41] Greater federal government control might improve the participation of women but would that be enough to overcome difficulties of transition from short-term to permanent employment? The jurisdictional problem with these programs is that support is given to community-based projects in which provincial governments may or may not have an interest.

The question of women's interests in respect of overlapping jurisdictions focuses on the need for better co-ordination of training and employment programs between federal and provincial governments and joint efforts to break traditional work patterns. If the training programs emphasized an internship component, for example, one could envisage some improvement in operations. Job-matching could occur at the point of entry to the program. However, if it was a federal program, public service internships might be restricted to federal jobs. Co-operation would be necessary to ensure the success of such a reorientation. Universities are now placing an emphasis, albeit on a limited basis, on co-operative education programs which include internships as part of degree requirements. Although these efforts have had a limited impact to date, internships in governmental and private sector jobs are sought out. A shift in emphasis of this kind could also be accompanied by efforts to break sex-stereotyping in occupational categories. Equal opportunity practices in internship programs could encourage the training and development of female electrical engineers, plumbers, chefs and so forth.

A main obstacle to reform of these programs lies not only in the federal design but also with the fact that the institutions and instructors are under provincial jurisdiction. Government officials whom I talked to in the course of preparing this paper indicated all sorts of problems ranging from the difficulties of diverting funds from one program to another to resistance from tenured community college instructors to changing course curricula.

Direct job creation programs suffer from broader economic influences as well. Unemployment and inflation are facts of life. Effecting structural shifts in a depressed labour market whether through government sponsorship or private initiative is a slow and painful process. Creating new jobs to replace obsolescent jobs would seem to warrant a high priority in these programs but, to date, only limited evidence of this can be demonstrated. Entrepreneurship is sorely needed and women would do well to exploit their own potential in this regard.

A final example here of overlap and potential jurisdictional conflict relates to the funding of voluntary association activities. Citizenship is, by and large, a federal matter, falling under section 91.25, naturalization and aliens. The Citizenship Branch of the federal Department of State provides a number of programs including grant programs to support volunteer activity. Of the nine grant programs offered, two are directed to women: Women's Programs and Native Women. The objectives of these programs are, in the first instance, to provide support for women's groups that are promoting a greater understanding of the status of women in Canada and developing the knowledge and skills necessary for effective participation by women and, in the second instance, to enable native women's groups to undertake an active role in the overall development of native people and to participate in matters of concern to themselves.[42] The grants' criteria are generally broad but preference is given to community-based projects.

These types of programs both by the amount of funds provided and the focus of their activity could, for the most part, by styled as consciousness-raising activities. While volunteer work is important to many women and the communities in which they live and may now be recognized as work experience in particular employment jurisdictions, it does not tackle labour force problems in a major way. The programs are designed to promote community relations and to enhance the efficacy of female participation in these areas. The community orientation of these activities may be said to reflect the social values behind the programs and to help maintain an easy balance with provincial interests.

In summary, the case of employment legislation is one in which the standardization of federal and provincial standards may be a desirable objective related to the process of constitutional renewal. In the second area of joint programs, several types of action might be considered. Education is a provincial and community matter and control at that level is important. Nevertheless, federal support to university education has helped to provide national standards of excellence which might not have developed otherwise. Federal and provincial programs with respect to training and direct job creation require re-examination. Reorientation and consolidation are possibilities to be considered. Women get caught in the jurisdictional tussle between the educational goals of the provinces and the employment objectives of the federal government. At the local level, it is often difficult to appreciate the extent to which a community-based project may be supportive of provincial or federal interests. Nevertheless, the intergovernmental sensitivity is there. If joint programs are to continue in this area, better co-ordination is needed. From women's standpoint, efforts to increase their participation, break traditional job patterns and provide opportunities for obtaining on-the-job experience as well as training are essential. Strong political commitment at both levels of government in support of women's concerns is required.

A major barrier to female participation, whether it pertains to training, education or advancement in employment, seems to be the creation of the necessary conditions to allow for participation. More than 35 per cent of women who work are also mothers, and the annual rate of increase of these women in the labour force in recent years has been between eight and nine per cent.[43] The dilemma of dual roles and the assistance needed to provide opportunities, let alone equal opportunities, takes us into a third area in which problems of overlapping jurisdictions may arise.

3. Day Care — The Dilemma of Characterization

The first part of this section examined the problem of overlapping jurisdictions in an area in which each level of government acts separately. The second part examined areas of jurisdiction in which provincial and federal governments act jointly. The following discussion considers an activity for which neither level of government is doing much acting at all.

Day care is probably one of the most sensitive and controversial issues facing women. Although the question of federal and provincial jurisdiction has been used as a means of avoiding governmental action on this question, the real issue is much deeper than a jurisdictional conflict. It is, above all, a question of philosophy and values. Rather than presenting statistics on existing facilities and creating cause for pessimism, the basic assumption in examining this issue will be that the existing facilities are inadequate. I doubt there would be much disagreement with this assumption.

As noted, the principal criterion for the division of powers between federal and provincial governments is that matters of a general or national character should be the responsibility of the central government and that matters of a purely local nature should be the responsibility of regional governments. To date, day care has been characterized as a matter of a local nature, a provincial responsibility primarily identified as an extension of the education system or, on a limited basis, as welfare in the case of needy families. For example, the Canada Assistance Plan which, as noted, is a shared-cost program involving federal funds, provides for day care services for needy individuals. For the most part, day care facilities are established by institutions or in communities on an ad hoc basis. Government intervention has been limited, presumably reflecting prevailing social values.

Thus, there are several issues here. First: What, if any, role should government have in child care especially for pre-school children? Second, what are the dominant values with respect to child care and the responsibilities of child rearing? Third, in what respects could day care be considered a national and local matter? In the first instance, it is interesting to consider the recommendations of a 1945 report called *Post War Problems of Women*. During World War II, the participation rate of women in the labour force rose to 30 per cent. In recognition of their service during the war, the Advisory Committee on Reconstruction stated: "women have played their full part as responsible citizens and expect to be treated consistently as such in the coming years. Their hope is to be full members of the community."[44] The report identified four main groups of women: married women raising families; single women earning their own living; married women who for economic reasons or by choice were engaged in full or part-time work; and women on farms. An emphasis was placed on the right of women to choose their lifestyle but the presumption that happier homes made a happier democracy was explicit.[45] Not surprisingly the recommendations of the sub-committee which examined women's problems directed its attention to women in the home. The proposals included the coverage of housework (for domestics, not wives) under the *Minimum Wages Act*, training for household work, the introduction of children's allowances, health insurance, etc. Furthermore, it was recommended that nursery schools should be extended and included in the educational system, that is, under provincial jurisdiction.[46]

Not only was there little follow-up on the day care proposals, but social attitudes also served to push the issue into the background in the ensuing years. Social values and attitudes in the decades following the war supported child care as a responsibility of parents, particularly the mother.[47] It would not be far-fetched to say that this was a period in which it was disgraceful for a married women to work unless it was absolutely necessary financially.

When the Royal Commission on the Status of Women examined the question of day care facilities in the 1960s, they looked to international examples to demonstrate the lack of development in this area in Canada.[48] The commissioners rejected the idea that private initiative could cope with the problem and stated uncategorically that governments had to assume the major responsibility, no doubt because of the anticipated costs as well as control over service standards. Given the precedents of federal assistance in the fields of health, education and welfare, the Commission believed that the federal government should assume a continuing responsibility. They, therefore, recommended that the *National Housing Act* be amended to provide for loans for building day care centres and for day care facilities in housing developments including universities.[49] Furthermore, they recommended the passage of a *National Day*

Care Act that would establish a federal-provincial shared cost program to develop facilities. They also recommended the establishment of Child Care Boards in each of the provinces to ensure standards were being maintained. In other words, the approach was to propose a joint or overlapping jurisdictional responsibility in this area.

Nevertheless, a minority report by one of the commissioners emphasized the relative adequacy of existing provisions under the Canada Assistance Plan for welfare purposes and contended that:

> In any event, whether conceived as extensions of the school system or not, the provision and operation of day care centres obviously comes under provincial jurisdiction and that is where I think they should remain.[50]

Although the recommendation respecting the amendment of the *National Housing Act* was partially implemented, no action has been taken with respect to the passage of a *National Day Care Act*.[51] The Advisory Council itself reports that day care, like other social services, is under provincial jurisdiction. Thus, a government role has been recognized but it has been the provincial governments which have defined the nature and extent of day care services. Pressures for the formation of a national association on day care have yet to yield concrete results.

The second issue of social values is difficult to discern. Current studies stress the changing lifestyles of individuals and the break-up of the nuclear family. Single parents and singles are becoming an increasingly large proportion of the adult population but married women who combine dual roles of homemaker and worker are becoming an increasing proportion of the work force.[52] It may be argued that changing lifestyles and social and economic circumstances of individuals combined with the increasing number of women entering or wanting to enter the work force necessitates the reconsideration of and renewed efforts in the provision of day care services. The right to choose is essential; but opportunity to choose must be created.

If we accept the idea that government has a role to play and that prevailing social values would allow some further degree of government intervention, then the question of defining the role and responsibilities of governments arises. If day care is characterized, as it has been, as an extension of educational or welfare services, it remains an integral part of family and community relations at the provincial and local level of government. A limited national interest has been defined respecting the health and well-being of Canadians and through the linkage of day care and welfare services. Further action along the lines recommended by the Royal Commission on the Status of Women could be pursued with the result that responsibility for day care by governments would increasingly overlap. A national day care act establishing a shared cost program to finance day care facilities would probably involve provincial governments in the delivery of services, with the federal government determining minimum levels and standards of services. The unpopularity of shared cost programs at the provincial level of government, however, would likely ensure that little progress would be made if this line of action were followed. It is enough to consider the problems pertaining to joint training programs to search for other alternatives. Furthermore, the current preoccupation with accountability of and in government argues against extending these kinds of joint undertakings.

An alternative approach might include a reconsideration of the purposes of day care services. If these services, especially for pre-school children, were construed as an integral part of employment conditions rather than part of education and welfare, employers, in particular government employers, could act separately allowing initiatives to be taken at either level of government. Standards of services across jurisdictions might vary as in the case of non-discriminatory, equal pay and equal opportunity practices, but the programs would be focused more directly on the problem, that is, creating equal opportunity for women including those who want to combine the roles of homemaker and worker.

A primary obstacle to any approach to extending day care services, however, is the cost. At a time when maternity leave and benefits are still granted begrudgingly in different jurisdictions, if at all, the additional request of day care facilities as part of an employment package might not be well received by employers, male co-workers or the general tax-paying public. Even extending day care services as part of the educational system at the provincial level would run into the problem of limited funds. Restraint in provincial government expenditures on education has been practiced for a number of years now. Day care would also have to be assigned some priority vis-à-vis other measures which are currently provided or are being sought. Paying wages to housewives and including them in calculations of the Gross National Product might be viewed by some as an alternative to extending day care facilities. Tax deductions to individuals for child care payments might be lost if day care services were to be included as part of employment provisions by institutions and governments. Women on welfare who can now opt to stay home and take care of their children might resent having to go to work if day care facilities are provided with employment. Attempts to maintain a little of everything would require trade-offs and compromises with respect to all the measures that directly and indirectly assist working women with children.

We have, therefore, come back to the issue of defining the problem and setting priorities. The status quo will persist unless new perspectives on this issue are developed. In addition, priorities amongst the several kinds of actions possible are also needed. And all this will probably have to occur in an environment of economic uncertainty, high unemployment and inflation and a growing conservative sentiment in popular opinion in western democracies. Federalism complicates the process further for the distribution of power and its exercise must recognize social and cultural diversities.

Conclusions

Generally speaking, overlapping jurisdictions in one form or another have become the norm rather than the exception in fields of governmental activity respecting women's issues. In assessing the impact of the range of programs and policies discussed in this paper, several observations may be made. First, the federal government has assumed an initiating role in many of these areas. It has been concerned with establishing national standards of employment legislation or setting an example as in the case of equal opportunity practices. In education and training areas, it has taken the initiative by defining a role distinct from that of the provincial governments. Federal involvement in education has been justified on the basis of national economic goals; in the case of welfare, on the basis of national well-being of Canadians. Federal participation in these areas has been achieved through the exercise of the federal spending power.

For their part, the provinces have co-operated with the federal government although jurisdictional sensitivities have resulted in open conflict from time to time. Provincial jurisdiction over property and civil rights in the provinces, education and matters of a local nature are guarded jealously. Provinces have not always wanted federal intervention in these areas and some provinces have resisted more than others. Joint programs have generated problems. Lines of responsibility and accountability of governments have often been blurred and initial goals and objectives displaced as the programs have been nurtured and sustained over time.

Women's interests have been served by federal initiatives in that the promotion of equal rights and equal opportunity have improved their status. The federal commitment to equal opportunity within its employment sector has helped to provide a good employer example to others. Variations in political commitment and governmental activity across provincial jurisdictions may be viewed in light of the influence of political and social influences at the regional and local levels. National interests may be declared at the federal level, but the local circumstances will influence and create differences in policy implementation and delivery of services. Diversity as well as unity must be recognized and accommodated within a federal system.

Given the achievements of women in advancing equal status over the past decade, it is difficult to ascertain why participation rates in employment and training sectors continue to be low. The need for day care services to assist married women with children in particular to enter the labour force and to help them advance their careers when in the labour force seems paramount. The characterization of this problem and the strategies necessary to evoke governmental response are related closely to the question of the division of powers in our federal system.

The issue of division of powers and overlapping jurisdictions is of immense importance to women. Which level of government exercises authority and financial resources over particular issues will determine how women will have to address and even define their problems in the future. The federal experience demonstrates that much can be achieved through co-operation even though conflicts are common and serve to reduce effectiveness of government initiatives. Regionalism is and has been a strong force in Canada despite concerted efforts by the central government to promote unity. National goals and priorities must be compatible with regional and local interests. And yet, interdependence requires that governments develop ways and means of sharing power, whatever the distribution formula of legislative responsibilities. Women must consider what their values and priorities are with respect to our federal system, and how their interests would be affected in a renewed constitution. To put a turn on the classic Canadian cliché: Women's issues, are they federal or provincial jurisdiction?

Notes

[1] From "Suggested Agenda for the Meeting of First Ministers on the Constitution" tabled in the House of Commons, June 10, 1980. See Canada, *Debates of the House of Commons,* June 10, 1980, p. 1977.

[2] See D.V. Smiley, *Canada in Question: Federalism in the Seventies,* 2nd ed. (Toronto: McGraw-Hill Ryerson, 1976), pp. 14-18.

[3] As a matter of interest, the participation rates for women in respect of the statistics set out in this paragraph are: federal Cabinet six per cent; House of Commons 4.9 per cent; provincial cabinets five per cent; provincial legislatures 2.5 per cent.

[4] The classic reference here is K.C. Wheare, *Federal Government.* (Toronto: Oxford University Press, 1963), pp. 1-3.

⁵See *British North America Act* sections 9 to 14 and section 96. In fact, the Prime Minister exercises the appointment prerogative through submissions to the Governor-General by Governor-in-Council. The list of appointments made in this way are contained in a Minute of the Privy Council first issued in 1896 and re-issued on four subsequent occasions.

⁶Judicial interpretations, particularly those of the Judicial Committee of the Privy Council have been the subject of much academic discussion and dispute. The case of *Hodge v. the Queen* was one which helped to provide a cornerstone for provincial autonomy in that the Justices declared that the provincial legislatures had "authority as plenary and as ample within the limits prescribed by section 92 as the Imperial Parliament in the plenitude of its power possessed and could bestow. Within these limits of subjects and area the local legislature is supreme and has the same authority as the Imperial Parliament, or the Parliament of the Dominion would have under like circumstances . . ." *Hodge v. the Queen* (1883) 9 A.C. 117.

⁷See *A.G. Canada v. A.G. Ontario (Labour Conventions Case), (1937)* A.C. 327; and, *A.G. Canada v. A.G. Ontario (Unemployment Insurance) (1937)* A.C. 355.

⁸To enact the Plan, an amendment to the *British North America Act* (section 94A) was passed in 1964 enabling the Parliament of Canada to make laws in relation to old age pensions in Canada provided it did not affect existing or future laws on the subject in the provinces.

⁹Canada, *Federal Provincial Grants and the Spending Power of Parliament* (Ottawa: Queen's Printer, 1969), pp. 4-8.

¹⁰*Ibid.*, pp. 10-14.

¹¹Canada. *Proceedings of the Federal-Provincial Conference,* Ottawa, October 24-28, 1966 (Ottawa: Queen's Printer, 1968), p. 15.

¹²Canada. *Statutes, 1977,* 25-26 Eliz. II, Ch. 10, "Federal Provincial Fiscal Arrangements and Established Programs Financing Act, 1977."

¹³Canada. Task Force on Canadian Unity, *A Future Together: Observations and Recommendations* (Ottawa: Supply and Services, 1979), pp. 88-9.

¹⁴See A.C. Cairns, "The Other Crisis in Canadian Federalism," *Canadian Public Administration,* Summer 1979, Vol. 22, no. 2, pp. 175-95.

¹⁵For a discussion of federal views on Sections 121 to 123 of the *British North America Act* respecting interprovincial flows of goods, see Canada, Discussion Paper, "Powers over the Economy: Securing the Canadian Economic Union in the Constitution," document 830-81/036, July 9, 1980, mimeo, pp. 16-19. Mobility of workers is not referred to explicitly in the current Constitution.

¹⁶See Department of Labour, *The Law Relating to Working Women* (Ottawa: Information Canada, 1975), for a summary of legislative provisions in federal and provincial jurisdictions.

¹⁷See A.S. Abel, *Laskin's Canadian Constitutional Law,* 4th ed. (Toronto: Carswell, 1973) pp. 365-70 for discussion. A particular citation on this subject is *Valin v. Langlois,* (1879) 3 S.C.R. 1.

¹⁸Canada. *Statutes of Canada, 1977,* 25-26 Eliz. II. Ch. 33, "Canadian Human Rights Act," section 11.

¹⁹See Gail Cook and Mary Eberts, "Policies Affecting Work," in Gail Cook, ed., *Opportunity for Choice* (Ottawa: Information Canada, 1976), pp. 143-202 and especially pp. 174-178.

²⁰Canada. "Powers over the Economy: Securing the Canadian Economic Union in the Constitution," July 9, 1980, p. 24.

²¹Gail Cook and Mary Eberts, "Policies Affecting Work," in Cook, *Opportunity for Choice,* pp. 178-80.

²²Canada. Public Service Commission, *Annual Report 1979,* Vol. I (Ottawa: Supply and Services, 1980), pp. 17-20.

²³*Ibid.* Vol. II, summary of statistics from Table 14, pp 16-17.

²⁴Kathleen Archibald, *Sex and the Public Service* (Ottawa: Queen's Printer, 1970), Table A-1, pp. 142-43.

[25] Canada, Public Service Commission, *Annual Report 1979*, p. 19.

[26] *Ibid.*

[27] Canada. Statistics Canada, *The Labour Force* (Ottawa: Supply and Services, 1980), statistics drawn from Table 1, p. 15.

[28] Canada, Royal Commission on National Development in the Arts, Letters and Sciences, *Report* (Ottawa: King's Printer, 1952), p. 132.

[29] Canada. *Revised Statutes, 1970*, Ch. C-2, "Canada Council Act, 1957," section 8.

[30] The first federal legislation in this area was the *Technical Education Act* of 1919. For discussion of background to the 1960 Act see J.S. Dupré, et al. *Federalism and Policy Development: the case of adult occupational training in Ontario*, (Toronto: University of Toronto, 1973) chapter one.

[31] *Ibid.*

[32] Canada. *Proceedings of the Federal-Provincial Conference*, Ottawa, October 24-28, 1966 (Ottawa: Queen's Printer, 1968), pp. 14-15.

[33] See Patricia Dale, "Women and Jobs: The Impact of Federal Government Employment Strategies on Women," (Ottawa: Canadian Advisory Council on the Status of Women, 1980) pp. 37-79.

[34] Canada. Statistics Canada, *Elementary and Secondary School Enrolment 1977-78* (Ottawa: Supply and Services, 1979), Table 4.

[35] This and the following statistics are drawn from: Canada. Statistics Canada, *Education in Canada. A Statistical Review for 1977-78* (Ottawa: Supply and Services, 1979), Table 24 and Statistics Canada, *The Labour Force* (Ottawa: Supply and Services, 1980), Table 4.

[36] From Barbara Goldman, *New Directions for Manpower Policy*, (Montreal: C.D. Howe Research Institute, 1976), p. 40 as cited in Patricia Dale, "Women and Jobs," p. 48.

[37] Dale, *ibid.*, p. 51.

[38] *Ibid.*, p. 57.

[39] Canada, Statistics Canada, *Enrolment in Community Colleges, 1978-79* (Ottawa: Supply and Services, 1980), from Table 4.

[40] Dale, "Women and Jobs," p. 72.

[41] *Ibid.*, p. 76.

[42] Canada. Department of State, "Citizenship Activities of the Department of the Secretary of State," August 1978, mimeo, p. 5.

[43] See Julyan Reid, "Changes in Family Lifestyles and their Implications for the Care and Well-Being of the Child," (Ottawa: Department of National Health and Welfare, October 1977), mimeo, Table IV p. viii.

[44] Canada. Advisory Committee on Reconstruction, VI. PostWar Problems of Women. *Final Report of the Sub-Committee*, November 30, 1943 (Ottawa: King's Printer, 1945), p. 7.

[45] *Ibid.*, p. 9.

[46] *Ibid.*, p. 14.

[47] Reid, "Changes in Family Lifestyles," pp. 2-5.

[48] Canada. Royal Commission on the Status of Women, *Report* (Ottawa: Information Canada, 1970), pp. 267-8.

[49] *Ibid.*, p. 220.

[50] *Ibid.*, p. 444.

[51] Canada. Canadian Advisory Council on the Status of Women, *The Royal Commission Report: Ten Years Later*, (Ottawa, October 1979), pp. 44-45.

[52] Reid, "Changes in Family Lifestyles," pp. 8-9.

Statement by the
National Action Committee on the Status of Women

Overlapping Jurisdictions:
A Pitfall in Supplying Services to Women*

The National Action Committee on the Status of Women is a voluntary feminist organization comprised of more than 150 non-governmental groups — national, provincial and local — operating in all regions of the country and in both official languages. We estimate that we speak for more than six million women in Canada. The Committee was formed initially to press for implementation of the recommendations of the Royal Commission on the Status of Women and continues to work for implementation of Commission recommendations but adds new issues as problem areas are identified. Our lobbying activities focus on the federal level but we also serve as a source of information and to assist in co-ordinating the efforts of provincial and local groups.

The purpose of this paper is not to offer a solution to the jurisdictional problems but rather to outline the parameters within which we believe solutions should be sought. The primary considerations include:

- A high priority must be given to meeting women's needs, as *they* define them, with the kind of support services they require. Where old institutions have proven to be inadequate, new ones must be developed, with regular funding and status equal to the old.
- Provision must be made for equalization, so that women in the poorer provinces are not denied much-needed services.
- Solutions must recognize that Canada is comprised of Indian and Inuit peoples, as well as two distinctive founding nations with different languages, histories and cultures. The francophone heritage is central in Quebec, with minorities of varying sizes in the other provinces. English speaking Canadians predominate in the nine other provinces and two territories. For that reason, Quebec cannot be a province exactly like the others, and

---

*The National Action Committee acknowledges the help of many member groups and individuals in providing information for this paper. Jill Porter, NAC Executive Member, acted as co-ordinator for the research and writer of the paper.

Canadians outside Quebec cannot expect Quebeckers to have the same attitudes to, or confidence in, federal institutions which they have.

- Apart from general political and historical factors, there are very particular circumstances which shaped the different jurisdictional preferences as between Quebec and other Canadian women. Quebec, in the last number of years, has moved from lagging behind the other provinces and the federal government in the provision of services, and in recognition of women's rights, to being ahead. Thus, while women of the other provinces express fear of provincial jurisdiction in certain areas, Quebec women do not. Indeed, for some Quebec women, federal jurisdiction menaces as a *regressive* force.

- In areas such as the social services, which have traditionally been under provincial jurisdiction, new procedures and institutions must be devised to ensure adequate services across the country, without resorting to undue centralism. An upper house, comprised of provincial representatives, and ensuring adequate representation of women, might be the means for the ongoing planning and evaluation of social services.

- Decisions as to minimum standards, portability of benefits, and the like can be made by negotiation among the provinces. Too often a federalist solution has been advanced as the quickest and most convenient answer only because of the lack of institutions for working out alternative proposals. *Ad hoc* First Ministers' meetings have been a dismal failure in this respect. Agendas have been too long, and the time too short, so that women's concerns have failed to make it onto the agenda at all, or have subsequently been dropped.

Some important questions with respect to control over the field of social welfare have already been raised in federal-provincial talks. The provinces have argued in favour of a more consultative process and a stronger provincial role. The federal government has expressed concern with the unlimited nature of its commitments to cost-shared programs and responded, in 1977, with revisions to funding arrangements for hospital services, medical insurance and post-secondary education. The two factors mentioned present a major challenge to the realization of standardized social programs in Canada. The field of social services appears, in federal-provincial negotiations, to have great trade-off value in comparison to other areas in which the federal government wishes to retain its power.

The Committee has examined some of the current ramifications for women in areas in which planning and funding services are divided between the two levels of government. The problems caused in the provision of services in areas such as rape crisis centres and transition houses, child care, health care and pension and maternity benefits are considerable. It is as yet unclear to what extent constitutional arrangements can alleviate our problems in these areas, but a new federal-provincial framework is required to aid in the development of an effective network of services. In our view, the formula used must be based on the objective of developing quality services and of allocating funds in an equitable and efficient manner.

Crisis Intervention Services — Rape Crisis Centres and Transition Houses

Obtaining funding for women's services is still an uphill struggle. The major source of funding for social assistance is the Canada Assistance Plan. Each province, with the exception of Quebec, has entered into an agreement with the federal government under the provisions of the Plan. Costs of social programs are shared on a 50/50 basis between provincial and federal governments. Provinces and municipalities make their own funding arrangements to meet provincial commitments. Since the federal contribution is matched with provincial expenditures, the initiative to identify the need for a service and to provide the initial funding before arrangements are made under the plan lies with the provincial government.

Since most services dealing with the specific needs of women come under provincial funding mandates, the federal, as opposed to federal-provincial funding, arrangements are limited. Federal funding is sometimes available for projects of a research or demonstration nature or for projects operating at the national level. Employment and Immigration programs such as Canada Works, Opportunities for Youth, etc., have been utilized by some women's groups but the programs are not designed to support ongoing community services.

Despite growing public awareness of, and concern with the problems of sexual assault and wife battering, governments have apparently not been convinced of the need to provide adequate support systems for victims. Lack of funding, lack of co-ordinated efforts between levels of government and lack of consistent standards have been identified by women across the country as the most common, recurring problem encountered.

Financial restraint hits social services first. Social services are, to a large degree, still considered "economically unproductive" and are minimized during financially troubled times. Cutbacks at all levels of government have affected seriously the development of comprehensive social programs. The CAP arrangement does not seem to provide adequate stimulus for the provinces to initiate activities in this area.

Some provinces, as part of their current austerity programs, have developed a policy of not providing funds to any "new" programs. For example, the Winnipeg Rape Crisis Centre has, for some time, been operating out of the Community Health Centre as part of the Klinic's counselling services. Recently, the United Way agreed to finance one staff position and administrative costs. Until then, all the counsellors had been volunteers and minimal expenditures had been paid out of the agencies' general budget because applications for funding had been repeatedly turned down. United Way funding has greatly facilitated the operation of the program, but centre workers feel that additional funding is badly needed to provide at least two more staff positions. The counsellor and approximately twenty volunteers are currently providing a twenty-four hour crisis intervention service, secondary victim counselling, and public education programs for the entire southern Manitoba region. The provincial government which provides the major portion of the Klinic's funds has, for the past three years, refused to allow additional positions to be created, or the addition of any new programs. Therefore, even though the Rape Crisis Centre is not by any standards a "new" service, it is not considered eligible now because it was denied funding in the past.

Establishing a sustained funding base after start-up assistance has been obtained, constitutes another major problem. For example, Kaushee's Place, the Yukon Women's Transition House, which opened its doors in March, is probably in the most financially secure position of any centre in the country, at the moment. It took about three and a half years of proposal writing and some tragic experiences, but the need for a Transition House was eventually established. The service is operated by a 14-member board composed of representatives of various organizations, including the Indian Women's Association, the Women's Centre, Mental Health, etc. On the basis of the inter-agency element of the project, a three year Health and Welfare grant was awarded. It provides funds for training and evaluation costs, and the salaries of four staff members. The house has been provided by the Department of Public Works. A summer Youth Employment Grant enabled organizers to hire staff to renovate the building. Capital costs are covered by an ARDA grant and a private foundation contributed $15,000 towards the purchase and operation of a van. Local women's organizations have raised and donated approximately $3,200, and the Territorial Council provides a per diem rate of $24.50 per client.

So what's the problem? The Youth Employment grant runs out this month, after three years the Health and Welfare grant money will be depleted, donations are not likely to continue at the current rate and the Territory now believes that the per diem rate is too generous. The subsidy is used to cover operational costs, the co-ordinator's salary, and a child care worker's salary. It is now the only long term funding in sight. Eventually, alternate funding will be needed to pay five or six salaries. Although the community is extremely supportive, it is unlikely that local resources will be able to maintain the current standard of operation. This particular transition house shelters not only battered women, but, in addition, accepts referrals from a number of agencies, including Corrections and Alcohol and Drug Services, and, as a result, requires a versatile staff team, intensive training programs, and effective liaison and education work.

The provision of services to women has often suffered the effects of a lack of coordinated effort between levels of government. Provincial governments have been at best reluctant, frequently resistent, to picking up where the federal government leaves off. Federal programs like Canada Works, demonstration grants, etc., are designed to self-destruct. At the end of a specified contract period, projects are expected to be absorbed into the provincial stream. Unfortunately, this does not follow as a natural consequence. Often such services simply shut down or are maintained by volunteers because of the lack of follow-up support.

The Ottawa Rape Crisis Centre is a notable survivor of the process. Like the Whitehorse Transition House, the Centre received a demonstration grant for three years of operation. At the end of the contract, no provincial monies were forthcoming, the United Way apparently could not accept the Centre's application for assistance, and the regional government was unmoved by its plight. The Centre's successful public education program was put on hold, and the 24-hour crisis service was operated by one co-ordinator working with volunteers. The Region eventually granted $15,000 with a warning that the Centre should not reapply, because it was not, after all, a municipal responsibility to support such services.

In 1980, two and one half years after the original application was submitted, the United Way granted the Centre $10,000. Effective lobbying by the Ontario Coalition of Rape Crisis Centres has resulted in a total grant of $150,000, $10,000 of which goes toward the operation of the Ottawa Centre. These funds will pay two full-time salaries and operational costs, and , it is hoped, begin to pay of the $50,000 debt accumulated by the Centre.

Lack of consistent standards leaves women with very little control over the quality and type of service which can be made available. The Winnipeg Rape Crisis Centre is a prime example of what happens when the government is willing to provide only the barest minimum. An enormous amount of work is left to be done by volunteers, and quality of service is neither assisted or encouraged. Transition House workers throughout the province of Ontario are concerned about the lack of uniform standards for women's shelters. Per diem rates are set by the municipalities and varied, in 1979, from $5 in some regions, to $15 in others. The standard of service, naturally, varies equally drastically. Women in Thunder Bay, Ontario, are particularly anxious to see some minimum standards established. Their "Community Residence" is a shelter owned and operated by the city. The residence provides accommodation to women and children who are in need, and who are residents of Thunder Bay. The residential requirement means that women from outside the city limits must obtain authorization from a social service supervisor before they can be admitted to the residence. If they are eligible for shelter, they get precisely that — shelter. There are no group activities, no child care programs, no opportunity to participate in the operation of the house. Workers are not involved in public education programs, referrals or counselling services. There is apparently considerable variation in opinion as to what constitutes adequate service, and what constitutes need.

Fortunately, there are other services available in Thunder Bay. Beendigen Native Women's Crisis House provides a "safe, home-like atmosphere, babysitting, information and referrals to community agencies, professional counselling . . ." Although it is primarily provided as a service to native women, Beendigen has responded to the needs of non native, non-residents, as well. Crisis Homes, Inc., is a volunteer organization dedicated to identifying and serving the needs of battered women. The group has tried to make a non-traditional counsellor available at Women's Place to assist battered women, but reports that "a tremendous amount of energy is needed for the on-going search for funding to provide the service . . ."

While per diem rates provide a certain amount of income for transition houses, they are paid only if the user qualifies for social assistance, and, as is the case in Thunder Bay, only if she is a resident of the municipality. This constitutes a major problem in Nova Scotia, where there are sixty municipalities, and only one transition house. If a woman from outside Halifax seeks refuge in the house, the workers must contact the municipality where *her husband* lives, to see if *she* qualifies for assistance. If not, the policy of the house is to provide refuge and to assist the woman in establishing herself, without the subsidy. If the municipality does agree to pay, the house must try to recover the money spent in sheltering the woman. The province argues that this level of social assistance is a municipal concern. The municipalities argue that their budgets are not high enough to cover the $26.50 maximum per diem, and are therefore reluctant to agree. The financial situation often results in a high vacancy rate in the Halifax transition house. The vacancies, in turn, are interpreted as proof that such shelter is not really required in the province, and the one resource available to Nova Scotia women is further undermined.

The financial situation of transition houses across the country is much like that of child care centres. The per diem subsidy arrangement implies that only women with rock-bottom incomes are in need. Residential requirements which exist in a number of places further limit women's access to services and result in increased operating costs to the house. The provision of "welfare" subsidies to low-income women is not an adequate funding mechanism to ensure that all women of all economic means and in all geographic locations have access to crisis intervention services.

Furthermore, rape crisis centres which do not fall exactly into the "social assistance" category do not have even the questionable benefit of per diem subsidies. The recent action on the part of the Ontario government is encouraging, but such decisions remain highly discretionary and dependent upon the attitude and priorities of the legislative body — the government in power. Rape crisis centres should also be recognized as a permanent and vital service, requiring secure and dependable funding.

Child Care

The Canadian Commission for the International Year of the Child estimates that there are over 600,000 children under the age of seven who require, but do not have access to, child care, and an additional one million "latch key" children. With regard to services that do exist, shortage of spaces, high child/staff ratios and low standards are common concerns across the country.

Child care programs originated as part of the welfare system and they continue to be funded as such. The federal government plays a minor role in the child care system by providing funds through the Canada Assistance Plan, but the responsibility for the administration of programs rests with the provincial and/or municipal levels of government. In most parts of Canada, the province establishes the policy and standards and the programs are implemented at the local level. The quality, quantity and availability therefore varies widely across Canada.

Provincial governments are in the business of providing assistance to "needy" families, rather than providing direct assistance to the facility. To governments, this funding scheme represents a positive means of "following the child." To child care centres it means a continuing struggle for survival, poorly paid staff, low standards and increased fees. Child care, as it exists now, is thereby available to two income groups: those who qualify for government assistance and those who can afford to pay rates which are normally high to cover the operating costs of the centre. Moderate and middle income families fall between these categories, so a great number of children who require child care come from families which cannot afford the full cost.

In the province of Nova Scotia, for example, a two member family with an income of $4300 is eligible for the full subsidy of $7.75 per day. The income ceiling for subsidization is $11,300. A formula of subsidization is determined for incomes between the exemption and ceiling rate, but once the family income exceeds the ceiling, a daily fee of $8 must be paid. A single parent woman who works 40 hours a week for 50 weeks a year at $4.50 per hour would therefore not be eligible for a full subsidy. For an eight member family, the exemption is $7,900, and the ceiling is $14,900.

Per diem funding has resulted in financial crisis for many centres. If a subsidized child is absent for any reason, the centre does not receive the per diem fee, although operating costs remain the same. In Manitoba, where the user fee is $9.50 per day, most centres are not able to provide hot lunches because the rate is too low to cover the real costs of child care which, for infants, is estimated at around $15.00 per day. Because the rates are too low, and because they are based on attendance, many centres are forced to close, lay off staff, eliminate things like lunches, equipment and supplies or increase fees.

A serious consequence of high user fees is that many parents must send their children to private, unlicensed centres. Manitoba women estimate that this group constitutes 60 per cent of the families in their province. In British Columbia, where fees are up to $160 per month, one woman described sending her two children to an unlicensed centre where the "roof leaked, the floors were rotting . . ." and where she was asked to "attend work parties, take home laundry, work at fundraising events, write letters of appeal and attend organizational meetings." In the Yukon Territory, a mother who works part time sends her children to a private sitter who "has eight or 10 kids in her two bedroom apartment." She would not leave her children there full time, but feels that it is all right for them to be there occasionally. The part time fee in a child care centre in Whitehorse is $120 per month.

Women in several provinces have commented that the present funding structure obscures accountability for the actual expenditure of funds. In British Columbia, the Department of Health, the Ministry of Human Resources, municipal governments and the federal government are all involved in the financing of child care. It is difficult to tell what has actually come from where. Funds are often lumped together and reports are conflicting. The Ontario government, as well, has been known to include federal funds in its expenditure figures. In 1978/79 when Ontario claimed to have spent $37,774,459 for day nurseries, the provincial expenditure was, in fact, more like $14,165,422. In Alberta, the provincial day care budget has been increased, but the result is that municipal contributions have been eliminated and subsidies have been reduced to $175 from $190. Parents who quality for subsidies are now required to pay a minimum $40 per month per child.

In 1970, the Royal Commission on the Status of Women recommended that "the federal government immediately take steps to enter into agreement with the provinces leading into the establishment of a National Day Care Act under which federal funds would be made available on a cost-sharing basis for the building and running of day care centres meeting minimum standards, the federal government to: (a) pay half the operating costs; (b) during an initial seven year period, pay 70 per cent of capital costs; and (c) make similar arrangements with the Yukon and Northwest Territories." The recommendation was supported in 1972 by the National Action Committee, and, again this year, was reiterated by the Canadian Commission for the International Year of the Child. Other than some provisions in the *National Housing Act,* whereby funds may be provided for child care facilities in CMHC-financed projects, we have yet to see any federal initiatives in this area. Some provinces provide capital assistance towards the construction or purchase of facilities, but, for the most part, funds are for specific projects only. In Ontario, capital financing is available to Indian Bands, associations for the retarded and "approved" non-profit societies. The Quebec government provides subsidies of up to $6,000 for centres in "less favoured" neighbourhoods, and non-profit societies in British Columbia are eligible for up to $10,000 on a cost shared basis for "special needs" nurseries or $1,000 for out of school programs.

It appears that as long as child care is regarded as a welfare service provided to "families in need", rather than as an essential service utilized by all socio-economic groups in all parts of the country, there is little hope for improvement. A system for ensuring the ongoing operational support of quality child care is needed. All levels of government, employers and educational institutions should demonstrate an interest in the provision of quality care for the children of this country.

Health Care

Prior to 1977, contributions of the federal government toward hospital and medical services depended upon the amount committed by the provinces for health plans. The provinces expressed dissatisfaction with this arrangement, because it left them with little discretion over spending of the funds. The federal government, at the same time, was becoming increasingly concerned with the degree of its commitment to cost-shared programs.

The solution to these problems was to shift from cost-sharing arrangements to block funding for hospital insurance, medicare and post secondary education. Under the new established programs financing arrangements, 13.5 tax points are transferred to the provinces and an equivalent cash contribution is made. Extended health care payments of $25.00 per capita are intended to assist the provinces in providing nursing home care, home care and ambulatory services, although the provinces are not required to introduce new programs in order to qualify for payments. In fact, although the established programs financing arrangements are intended to encourage the provinces to provide better health care services, the provinces are not legally required to spend the money in the health sector. The federal and provincial governments share the responsibility for providing adequate health care. Under the current arrangements, federal responsibility ends at transferring tax points and funds, and the provinces have the freedom to determine how the money will be spent.

Some provinces have begun to reduce their financial commitments to health care. One way of reducing expenditures has been to curtail increases in physician fees, with the current "opting out" or "extra billing" problem resulting. Extra billing exists in all provinces except British Columbia, Quebec and Newfoundland. British Columbia has the highest fee for service rate in the country undoubtedly to reduce the motivation for doctors to "opt out." Minor extra billing occurs in Nova Scotia and New Brunswick. Extra billing appears to be the critical factor in reducing or limiting reasonable access. Women and children are disproportionately affected by user charges. When women are required to pay extra fees, transportation costs and drug costs, they are likely to delay regular checkups for themselves and their children and may be reluctant or unable to seek needed medical assistance. Clearly, extra billing limits accessibility, and has a much greater effect on the poor, than upon the middle and upper economic groups. The federal government, under the *Medical Care Act,* has the responsibility of protecting the comprehensive and universal nature of the medicare system, yet, under the established programs financing arrangements, seems to have no instrument for doing so.

In the 1970s, several provinces recognized the need for quality community health centres. Ontario, Manitoba, and Nova Scotia produced reports emphasizing programs for promotion of health and home care services and the active participation of the community in decision-making. Community health centres were seen to be a viable means of improving services and containing costs. In some regions, these plans were implemented but for the most part, the medical profession and existing health care structures were not at all receptive and as a result provincial enthusiasm waned. The obvious exception was Quebec, where 144 such centres now exist. In British Columbia, there are now five, as opposed to 29 in the early 1970s. In Ontario there are only two or three community health centres although there are a number of health service organizations. In the Prairies, a few hospitals have been coverted into multi-purpose health centres.

At about the same time, women began to design their own clinics aimed at providing information, assistance in decision making, and medical attention in matters specifically relevant to women. It was documented that costs to the province could be greatly contained by the provision of such services in clinics, rather than in standard medical facilities.

Women in Nova Scotia began sponsoring medical clinics in 1978. Their format ranged from one-day-per-week consultations in church basements to continuing programs in hospitals. Funding for the programs was sporadic. One group received a LIP grant to produce a handbook, others sought Planned Parenthood affiliation, support from public health departments and organizations, held bake sales, etc. A provincial conference on women's health was sponsored by the federal Department of State. The Nova Scotia clinics stressed the value of education for preventive care, fitness, healthy lifestyles, etc. No treatment or prescriptions were administered. The women at first met resistance from the professional sector, but found the Lung Association, Planned Parenthood and other agencies most cooperative. The Nova Scotia Medical Association, which had initially been hostile, later responded with "cautious tolerance."

No provincial funds were initially provided, but now, the ministry agrees to pay sessional fees to doctors. Under the present structure, however, there is no mechanism to reimburse nurses or paraprofessionals for *their* services. The women are reportedly hopeful that provincial funds will be forthcoming, but ironically, the only funding they have received to date in the area of health care, a provincial responsibility, has been from the federal government.

In Manitoba, the Pregnancy Information Service was founded in 1973 to fill the gap which existed in counselling and referral services for women with unplanned pregnancies. PIS is one of two services available in Winnipeg which offers comprehensive, non-judgemental counselling. It is operated by volunteers with the help of Klinic, Inc. The service has, to date, received four short-term federal grants over a period of six years and has received no indication that on-going funding is possible. For over three years, Klinic, Inc. has been refused funding for additional staff or counselling services. Last year, the provincial government refused funding for a Reproductive Health Centre. The concept was supported by the medical community, as well as 13 women's organizations. The Centre would have provided a service which is currently badly needed; for example, women have apparently waited as long as 10 months for a tubal ligation at the Health Sciences Centre. Sixty per cent of Manitoba women seeking abortions are referred to the United States because of lack of service in the province.

The Badgeley Committee Study on the Operation of the Abortion Law pointed out that there are serious geographic and socio-economic inequities in access to safe medical abortion, even when continuation of the pregnancy would, or would be likely to, jeopardize the life or health of the pregnant women. Less than one-fifth of publicly financed Canadian hospitals have even established therapeutic abortion committees, yet no abortion is legally possible without one. Moreover, the mere establishment of a therapeutic abortion committee is no guarantee that the hospital in which it exists will ever approve an application for abortion. Many hospitals which have Therapeutic Abortion Committees have not provided *any* abortions.

Provincial ministers of public health, outside the province of Quebec, have refused to approve free-standing women's clinics where birth control could be dispensed, tubal ligation performed, breast examination provided, and first trimester abortion could be available. Many women are forced to travel hundreds of miles for a medical procedure which we believe should be available to them in the hospitals which ostensibly serve their communities. After tabling of the Badgeley Commitee report, the conclusion of the federal government was that the law is adequate, but that access and facilities, both the responsibility of the provinces, are not. The government of Quebec declined, in the aftermath of the Morgentaler case, to prosecute any qualified physicians operating in adequate facilities.

Dr. Wendall Watters of McMaster University polled all other ministers of public health as to legislative and legal sequelae to the Report on the Operation of the Abortion Law. Four provinces, Prince Edward Island, Newfoundland, Nova Scotia and Alberta reported little or no exchange of information or discussion with the federal government after publication of the report. Two provinces, British Columbia and New Brunswick indicated merely that the provisions of Section 251 of the Criminal Code are being honored in their provinces.

Saskatchewan and Ontario were the only provinces which replied that they had taken special measures following the tabling of the Badgeley Committee report. In Ontario, the report of the Caudwell Committee, established to examine the implications of Badgeley, apparently completed in 1978, has yet to be released. The Ontario Minister of Public Health has declined to approve two applications to establish women's clinics. In Saskatchewan, a full review of operation of the abortion law was carried out. An interministerial committee considered the problem, and all hospitals eligible to establish therapeutic abortion committees were encouraged to do so. Discrepancies in statistical gathering were apparently cleared up and grants for family planning were increased.

Health care is one area of provincial responsibility in which the needs of women are not being met. Opting out, extra billing, lack of adequate services mean, for women, access to only the most basic, mediocre health care at considerable expense. Inequities in the provision of health care exist, in many provinces, due to the discretionary power of individual provinces in the expenditure of "health care" funds. Health care will become affordable, accessible, and responsive to our needs only if some element of control over provincial spending is regained.

The Canada Pension Plan

The Canada Pension Plan is intended to provide basic income support to all Canadians in the event of retirement, disability, or loss of family income caused by death. There is ongoing consultation among federal and provincial welfare authorities to review Canada's Income Security System. Substantial changes to the Plan cannot become effective without the consent of two-thirds of the provinces, having two-thirds of the population.

A prime example of the major problem caused by jurisdictional overlap occurred in 1977. The federal government, at that time, introduced legislation which would, in the event of dissolution of marriage, permit Canada Pension Plan credits. Another provision would allow men or women who leave the labour force for a maximum of seven years to raise children, to eliminate those child-rearing years from the calculation of average lifetime earnings for pension purposes. The first proposal received unanimous support. The second, known as the "drop-out" provision, received the support of nine of the 10 provinces, as well as the National Action Committee, the National Council of Welfare and the Canadian Advisory Council on the Status of Women. Unfortunately, the dissenting province was Ontario, and, as a result of the two-thirds of the population requirement, Ontario was able to virtually veto the drop-out proposal. Premier Davis argued that the CPP should not be a vehicle for "redistribution of income," and child-rearing contributors across Canada lost the right to benefit from the Plan. Should one province hold so much power in the decision-making process?

The Prime Minister has announced that a National Conference on Pensions, involving federal and provincial levels of government, labour, business and pensioner groups, will be held. The Conference will consider federal reform proposals dealing with portability, accessibility, protection against inflation, retirement income for homemakers, and flexibility in retirement age. Employers will be encouraged to allow pension-splitting, and to provide widow(er) benefits. The National Action Committee views the proposed reform as a positive action, but, recalling our experience with the "drop-out" clause, we question the probability that concensus will be reached on *these* issues. Ontario, because of its large population, wields incredible influence, and has strongly vested interest in any discussion of pensions. Perhaps it would be more reasonable if, in future, a vote of two-thirds of the provinces, without regard to population, were to govern future change.

The National Action Commitee on the Status of Women believes that all women should have pensions, in their own names, regardless of their length of time in the work-force. Such pensions must be adequate and portable.

Maternity Leave and Benefits

Women who are fully productive contributors to Canadian society and the economy, also bear Canada's children. Maternity benefits provisions of the *Unemployment Insurance Act,* however, penalize women in the work force for having children. The *Act* provides three areas of "special benefits": retirement, illness, injury or quarantine, and maternity benefits. Both the retirement and illness provisions require a "major attachment" to the labour force of 20 weeks. In the case of maternity benefits, however, 10 of these weeks must be between the fiftieth and thirtieth weeks before the expected date of confinement. There are no circumstances under which male claimants are required to have more than 20 weeks of work to qualify for benefits. In 1978, and 1979, 13,478 women were ruled ineligible for maternity benefits, under the additional 10-week requirement.

The National Action Committee, at every opportunity, raises the need for an equitable and comprehensive maternity benefits/parental leave scheme, with the Minister of Employment and Immigration and other appropriate cabinet ministers. Their standard response is that maternity leave is a matter of provincial jurisdiction. Yet the provinces, with the exception of Quebec, have seen their role as a limited one primarily offering protection against dismissal. They justify the narrow view of their role by pointing out that maternity benefits are provided through the unemployment insurance scheme.

The imperfections and anomalies of the *Unemployment Insurance Act,* have combined with judicial decisions in the Stella Bliss and Maria Santos cases to further reduce the limited benefits available. In the *Santos* case which was argued in the Federal Court before Mr. Justice A. H. Lieff, the Canadian Textile and Chemical Union, represented by Laurell Ritchie, argued that the "magic 10" rule is discriminatory and a violation of the *Canadian Bill of Rights.* Mr. Justice Lieff, in dismissing the appeal, concluded that: "I feel bound to follow the unanimous decision of the Supreme Court of Canada in *Bliss,* and find that this case provides a complete answer to the able arguement made on behalf of the appellant."

The Union has filed a complaint on behalf of Mrs. Santos, with the Federal Human Rights Commission. Three *Unemployment Insurance Act* restrictions, Section 30(1), 30(2) and 46, which were used against women in the *Santos* and *Bliss* cases, have been widely criticized by women's groups and the Canadian Human Rights Commission as discriminatory.

In conclusion, the National Action Committee on the Status of Women is committed to developing practical proposals for constitutional reform in the full range of areas of conern to women. We do not pretend that this will be easy, but we do believe that an effective social service system, which will provide both high standards of service to all Canadians and respect the concerns of our sisters in Quebec is possible. We invite you to join with us in the formation of practical proposals to that end.

Women, Poverty and The Constitution

Louise Dulude

There is no doubt that poverty is a woman's issue and that women have a vital interest in influencing and monitoring government policies in that area. This task has not been made easier by the fact that the division of powers between various levels of government in the field of income security is very unclear. Before considering the tangle of federal and provincial relationships in the area of poverty, however, it is useful to remind ourselves of two basic facts. In the first instance, poverty in Canada is overwhelmingly a female phenomenon. Three out of every five adults whose incomes are below the poverty line in this country are women. Second, poverty is not something that only happens to a few women who probably deserved it anyway. The frightening truth is that the majority of Canadian women are very vulnerable to becoming poor, for poverty is a natural consequence of the role they have been taught to play in our society.

To begin, our original constitutional document, the *British North America Act*, did not have much to say about poverty. The closest it came to it was in a sentence listing hospitals, asylums, charities and charitable institutions among the subjects under provincial jurisdiction. As the Senate Committee on Poverty stated in 1971 in commenting on this matter:

> This was not a deliberate omission. The question simply did not arise. It never occurred to the legislators of the time that massive governmental intervention on behalf of the poor would ever be necessary. Local charities were already in business; local charities were quite enough.[1]

As it turned out, they were not enough for very long. By World War I, the majority of the people in Ontario and Quebec had left the farm and were living in urban centres. The old charity system, based as it was on the extended rural family and the assumption that even the poorest could grow their own food, completely fell apart. The first income security measure to be introduced in Canada was Ontario's Workmen's Compensation, enacted in 1915 to help men who suffered industrial injuries and to prevent them from suing their employers. When similar schemes in British Columbia and Manitoba were challenged as *ultra vires* provincial legislative powers, the courts upheld their validity stating that these laws regulated the contract of employment and, therefore, came under the provincial area of jurisdiction of "property and civil rights in the province."

Meanwhile, women's groups were successful in obtaining provincial assistance for deserving mothers who had been abandoned or widowed with small children. After the first such program was enacted in Manitoba in 1916, many other provinces quickly followed suit. Unlike workers' compensation, no one accused these schemes of being unconstitutional, possibly because it was assumed that they came under the provincial heading of "charity."

Another possible reason that mothers' allowances, as they were called, were never challenged is the wide support they received from both liberal and conservative groups: the former because they were an improvement over private charity, the latter for reasons best expressed by conservative humorist Stephen Leacock. As he commented:

> Social policy should proceed from the fundamental truth that women are and must be dependent. If they cannot be looked after by an individual . . . they must be looked after by the State. To expect a woman, for example, if left by the death of her husband with young children without support, to maintain herself with her own efforts, is the most absurd mockery of freedom ever devised.[2]

The two next important moves belonged to the federal government. In 1927, it passed a law providing for its reimbursement to the provinces of 50 per cent (later 75 per cent) of the cost of the pensions they paid to needy people over the age of 70. In 1935, in the depth of the depression, the federal government enacted the *Employment and Insurance Act*, which was to create a national unemployment insurance system. The pension cost-sharing law was never challenged, although it generated a political storm in Quebec, where it was judged unethical if not illegal because it skewed provincial priorities. Another problem was that the poorest provinces (meaning the Maritimes) could not come up with their share of the costs. In spite of this, all provinces finally took full advantage of the federal offer by 1937.

The *Unemployment Insurance Act* was not as successful. It was challenged and struck down by the courts for two reasons: it attempted to regulate employment, which came under the provincial area of civil rights; and, it dealt with insurance, which in earlier decisions had been deemed to fall under exclusive provincial authority. If the provinces had not all been anxious to get federal money at the time, that might have been the end of the issue. As it was, they all consented to an amendment to the *British North America Act* to give the federal government exclusive jurisdiction over unemployment insurance as of 1940.

Similar reasons also led all the provinces to agree to a 1951 amendment giving the federal government concurrent jurisdiction with the provinces over old age pensions paid directly to the elderly. This was thought to be necessary because the new 1951 federal *Old Age Pension Act* — which extended these benefits to everyone aged 70 and over, whatever their income — involved the levying of a special pension tax which might have put the program in the forbidden "insurance" category.

The only other formal constitutional disagreement over income security involved family allowances, which the federal government introduced in 1945 to stimulate the economy and sweeten the pill for married women who were being forced out of the labour force after the Second World War. When this measure was challenged in the courts, it was found valid because it served a national purpose and did not infringe on provincial authority in the areas of "paternal" (sic) powers and the regulation of school attendance.

In addition to upholding such direct federal payments to individuals, the courts also decided in other cases that the federal government had the power to spend the money it raised through taxes on anything it wanted, as long as the legislation authorizing these expenditures did not amount to a scheme that would regulate subjects falling within provincial authority. This gave the green light to all federal cost-sharing and conditional grants to the provinces.

The most recent use of this federal "spending power" in the welfare field occurred with the advent of the Canada Assistance Plan (CAP) of 1966, which integrated all the former federal-provincial cost-sharing programs — for the aged, the blind, the disabled and the unemployed — into a single plan, and provided federal funds for needy mothers for the first time. Under CAP, federal contributions are set at 50 per cent of all provincial and municipal expenses for social assistance payments and welfare services. The introduction of CAP encouraged many provinces to integrate and expand their own welfare services.

To sum up these constitutional developments, then, the legal situation is the following: Provincial governments can set up programs in any area in the income security field, with the sole exception of unemployment insurance. The federal government, as well as exercising exclusive authority over unemployment insurance and concurrent authority over pensions, has the power to create programs such as family allowances, which serve the national interest and do not infringe on provincial rights, and can make conditional grants and establish cost-sharing plans in any area in which provincial governments will co-operate.

Finally, and in addition to all this, each level of government can use its taxing powers to extend whatever benefits it wants to the population through the tax system. The best known examples of this are tax exemptions for dependent children and the new federal refundable tax credit for low-income mothers. To obtain a clearer picture of the implications of this situation, let us consider existing programs respecting the two largest groups among poor women: the elderly and women with dependent children.

After more than 50 years of legislation by all levels of government, Canadian benefits to low-income elderly people include a comprehensive federal guaranteed income program consisting of two levels of benefits. The first is the universal old age pension and the second is the Guaranteed Income Supplement (GIS) for low-income pensioners only. Secondly, in six provinces, income supplement programs are in place which increase the basic guarantee to the needy elderly by four to 13 per cent. The administration of these provincial supplements is co-ordinated with that of the federal GIS. Finally, there is the Canada/Quebec Pension Plan.

Putting the Canada/Quebec Pension Plan aside for its does not yet help many women, we find that the present income security system for senior citizens aged 65 and over is moderately simple, very humane — only mail-in declarations are required — and would generally be quite satisfactory if the benefits it provides to unmarried elderly people were not so low. In spite of the recent increase in the GIS, these elderly singles, who are mainly widows, are still getting maximum federal pensions that are below the poverty line.

Benefits for low-income mothers are a little more complicated. For single-parent mothers who have no personal income and have not just left a paying job, there are the following programs:

- Federal family allowances.
- Provincial family allowances in Quebec and Prince Edward Island.
- Provincial social assistance (or mothers' allowances), cost-shared by the federal government.
- Saskatchewan's Family Income Plan (FIP), which pays a supplement to low-income parents, as well as a similar program which is due to begin in Manitoba in 1981.

- The once-yearly federal refundable child tax credit for parents with lower-than-average incomes.

In this case, the basic program is provincial social assistance, which is the most humiliating income benefit scheme because it still entails a close verification of the recipients' assets and lifestyle. The other, complementary programs require little or no personal disclosure. When all these benefits are added up nevertheless, the income that results is far below the poverty line in all provinces. This problem is particularly acute in New Brunswick and Quebec, which share the dubious honour of having the worst social assistance rates in Canada.

Comparing our relatively simple and almost adequate programs for the elderly to the patched up, inadequate system of aid to low-income mothers, it is tempting to conclude that the federal government does a better job and that poor women would be better served if all of income security came under that level of government. This would not be a valid comparison, however, because pensions and social assistance are subject to very different practical and political considerations. Moreover, the history of income security shows that the federal government was not at all interested in the problems of poor mothers until very recently.

Similarly, since so many diverse and complex factors determine whether any division of powers over a particular area is good or bad for women, it is very difficult to sort them out. To accomplish this, one would first have to analyze the needs of the various groups of people who receive income security benefits to find out whether one level of government is better equipped to meet them than the other. For example, it has often been argued that it is preferable to entrust provincial governments with programs for single parents and low-income workers, because the federal remote-computer approach to income security is too impersonal and too slow to adequately serve their needs.

Secondly, one must determine whether there exist, beyond the need of recipients, overriding factors that make it advisable to give jurisdiction to one particular level of government in a given area. One example of this is the citizenship rights of all those who helped build our country, which are invoked to support the granting to all senior citizens of an identical basic pension, whatever their province of residence. Another is the importance of unemployment insurance as an instrument of national economic policy.

A third set of factors concern the desirability of concurrent or parallel jurisdiction in any one field. In the past, this type of interaction has had both good and bad effects. On the one hand, it has unquestionably resulted in more uniform programs with higher benefits. On the other, it has generated complex multi-layered programs that are difficult to understand and very resistant to political pressure.

Finally, since we are not in a position to remake the world from scratch tomorrow, it is important to take account of the present constitutional situation. One relevant element of that situation is that the division of powers over income security is not a burning issue between the federal government and the provinces at the present time. This is evidenced by the fact that income security was not even included in the list of topics that were discussed in the current round of constitutional talks.

This omission indicates that important changes have taken place since the constitutional debates of the early 1970s, which eventually foundered because the federal government and the province of Quebec disagreed over who would have jurisdiction in the areas of family allowances, unemployment insurance and supplements for the elderly. Income security has not completely dropped out of sight since then, however, because one of the subjects discussed at the time of the 1978-79 constitutional talks was the question of limiting the spending power of the federal government in areas of provincial jurisdiction.

The seeming inevitability of the curbing of the federal spending power will be detrimental to women, who have often benefitted from the stimulative effect of federal cost sharing and grants in provincial areas such as medicare and social services. The only consolation is that most of the proposals which have been made so far deal only with the exercise of the spending power in relation to "new" or "future" programs, which means that the limits that are adopted are very unlikely to apply to existing cost-sharing programs such as the Canada Assistance Plan.

To conclude, I wish to emphasize that the most important thing for women in the area of income security is not so much who has the power, but rather what is being done with it. Whichever government or combination of governments exercise authority over social assistance, pensions or unemployment insurance, for example, the resulting programs will always be complicated and require close attention. As long as women continue to be so vulnerable to poverty, it is simple self-protection on their part to insist on an income security system that provides humane and adequate benefits.

Notes

[1] Special Senate Committee on Poverty, *Poverty in Canada*, (Ottawa: Information Canada, 1971), p. 65.

[2] Stephen Leacock, *The Social Criticism of Stephen Leacock*, edited and introduced by A. Bowker, 1973, p. 60 as quoted in V. Strong-Boag, "Wages for Housework: Mothers' Allowances and the Beginnings of Social Security in Canada", *Journal of Canadian Studies*, Vol. 14, No. 1, (Spring 1979).

Social Services and Women

Muriel Duckworth

As you know, the themes of the Decade for Women are Equality, Development and Peace. At two recent international conferences which I have attended I have been struck by a profound sense among women delegates that war and the threat of war, the enormous cost of arms, the devastation of land and the human suffering sabotage our attempts to make a good society for ourselves and our sisters. Under any constitution, war, armies, armaments and sales of arms abroad will remain the responsibility of the federal (i.e. national) government and one of our biggest tasks as caring women, who have a vision of a caring society, is to see this for what it is: the gravest threat to the achievement of that society. One of my favourite posters, a child's drawing of a warship with the caption: "What if day care centres and schools had all the money they need and the airforce had to hold bake sales to buy a bomber?", could be the theme of this paper.

For example, the Stockholm International Peace Research Institute recently reported that:

> Since 1945 there have been 133 wars involving the territory of more than seventy countries and the armed forces of more than eighty states . . . Almost all of these wars took place in the Third World. The bulk of the weapons used in them have been supplied — through the arms trade — by the industrialized countries.

And yet, the plea of one of our Third World sisters, an African woman speaking at an International Conference of Women for Peace in Montreal in 1967 was: "Don't send us arms to kill each other."

We all know from our own experience, from our community involvement and from research that governments are slow to respond to the legal, political and social needs of women. We know how it is. We have a vision of how it should be. We see specific needs to be met. But what happens when we try to meet them? One of our chief objectives should be to change the system possibly through constitutional and electoral reform to ensure that the voice of women will be heard wherever laws are made and policies determined.

Social services, the basis of a caring society, have low priority in the current constitutional debate. Limited efforts have been made by government to hear from women. Natural resources are high on the agenda of constitutional conferences. The debate is about power, control and income, largely in relation to natural resources. The debate is about how these factors will be balanced between the levels of government. The debate cannot be seen to be about what distribution of power, control and money will be in the best interests of the people of Canada, of the families of Canada, of the women of Canada. Women have until now had no part in the debate. Decisions are, as usual, being made for us.

Let me give you a few examples of the disheartening process women must go through when they attempt to establish a service which is absolutely necessary in our society, but which is seen as peripheral by men in power.

Bryony House in Halifax, a much-needed centre for battered wives and children, was opened in 1978. This was after four years of volunteer work by women who knew the need and had to prove to the men in government that such a need existed. Such invisible work of women is demanding and time-consuming and often, as in this case, should be unnecessary. How many times over must women prove in our society the need for such a service? The need was already established in other provinces. Let me say, in parenthesis, that possibly a new constitution and/or guarantee of human rights could make this kind of duplication of effort unnecessary and could speed the transfer of information and good programs from one province to another.

One of the biggest problems now is that grants to Bryony House are based on "settlement," which means that the municipality in which the family has been living must pay the per diem cost and then collect 75 per cent from the provincial government, which in turn collects two-thirds of that from the federal government. What is the Centre supposed to do when a municipality refuses to pay, refuses to recognize that this is, indeed, a battered family? In Nova Scotia, the "settlement" qualification is met when the husband has lived for 12 months in that municipality. Hence, it can happen that no municipality will take responsibility.

For many months, the Board and staff of Bryony House have been trying to negotiate grant funds to supersede "settlement" funding. Meantime, Halifax, Dartmouth and Halifax County, from whom 90 per cent of the families come, pay 90 per cent of the cost. A great deal of staff time must be spent in chasing up reluctant municipalities, even ones which are quite well-to-do according to Nova Scotia standards.

Funding is, characteristically, always retroactive, thus Bryony House is always in a deficit position. In March they almost went under. They could borrow no more from the bank. Is this the way to run an essential service? As long as we have a violent society, most of whose victims are women and children, there will be this need. Surely governments can be expected to organize their budgets cooperatively to meet it and to make possible a reliable income, year in and year out.

By the way, the provincial government's response so far to the request for grant funds to replace "settlement" funds has been to raise the per diem to $26.50 — 50 per cent higher than it was; great for the Centre, but not conducive to better response from the municipalities. What Bryony House really wants is a yearly income paid to it in monthly instalments.

Another unpleasant aspect of funding of Bryony House is that women who come there in urgent need must be totally destitute in order to be totally funded. Of course, they often are totally destitute, having fled their homes. Then, when a woman is lucky enough to get a job, she must immediately begin to contribute to the House which shelters her and her children. She should be free to use that money to re-establish herself and her family. Since women's incomes, especially those of female heads of one parent families, are notoriously and disgracefully low, the services of Bryony House should be offered freely, as an established community service as long as they are needed.

This could be done with a different base of funding. The per diem rate is based on occupancy of a certain percentage of rooms. The resulting fall in income, if there happen to be fewer women in the house, is disconcerting, to say the least. There must be a steady yearly income. It should be possible under the Canada Assistance Plan.

To place the responsibility on municipal governments to support Bryony House, and then to seek reimbursement from the provinces, which will collect funds through CAP from the federal government, almost guarantees a sluggish, long-delayed, unsatisfactory response to a need. It is obvious that change is necessary and that different standards must be set. It is not so obvious that constitutional reform or patriating the constitution even with an enshrined *Bill of Rights* will effect that change.

A final word about Bryony House. This service is obviously

needed 24 hours a day and seven days a week. It requires a staff of seven women. The budget on its per diem basis will pay for only six. They work long hours, on deficit funding, and spend an enormous amount of time struggling for necessary funding.

Let me give you an example of a proposal for funding by the federal government which was inappropriate in at least one province, New Brunswick. The program was designed to work in relation to "existing services," which that province did not have. It was meant to provide a minimum wage to women who would work with these non-existent services. Madeleine LeBlanc, President of the New Brunswick Status of Women Council, has told me that it was difficult and time-consuming to gain federal government approval of an alternative proposal which they devised and which they felt would be useful to women in her province. This was an assertiveness training program which seemed basic, if they were ever to get the "essential services" which the federal government seemed to assume they already had. They began their negotiations in April 1978 and the program finally got under way in September and October. Through contacts established with 6,000 women, a six-month assertiveness training course was taken by 600 women. Seven women worked on this throughout the province. In March 1980 the program was dropped. What remains? Cassette tapes in English and French — but cassettes alone are hardly enough to accomplish both consciousness-raising and action.

There are three main questions to be raised here:
- One would wish that government departments would have readily available information that would indicate whether or not a particular program is appropriate for a given area. How would they not have had this information about the lack of services to the women of New Brunswick?
- Having had the necessity for a more basic program pointed out, why was it "difficult and time-consuming" to get a highly-imaginative, exciting and useful alternative program accepted? Six months is a long time to spend on such an exercise. It is an exasperating use of one's time. It, in fact, indicates a low opinion of the value of a woman's time, or of the time spent by a whole group of women. The acquisition of the skill of "grantsmanship" is a hollow reward.
- Why could the program not have continued for more than six months? It should be made easy to extend such a program of affirmative action for women.

There have been some results — some local groups have been organized and have endured; 350 women came to a productive conference in May of this year; homes for battered wives and children are being established in New Brunswick, with the usual resistance and time-consuming seeking for funds.

Now I wish to turn to another community service essential to families in our present society, dependent on funding from all levels of government as well as from ''bake-sale'' types of money-raising for support, and on workers who have to be very good at their job and have to expect a very low salary scale. I am talking about child care services.

It is 40 years since I was first involved in setting up a play school for pre-school children of mothers who were not working for pay outside the home, though I must add they were working long hours without pay both at home and in the community. At the same time, day care centres were set up for the children of women working in the munitions factories. These, as everyone knows, had a tendency to disappear after the war. But women who realized the benefits to both children and their parents continued to organize play schools, nursery schools, day care centres and early childhood associations. We worked for and got legislation setting standards to apply wherever people cared for little children in groups. The Royal Commission on the Status of Women gave high priority to day care in its report, and Grace MacInnis, M.P., tried to mobilize women to see to it that the day care recommendations would be carried out.

In Nova Scotia, there are increasing numbers of dedicated people employed in child care and working for extremely low salaries. In this province, the average salary for a day care worker is less than $8,000. This is almost unbelievable. Moreover, the rate for salary increases is linked to that of a group of civil servants with higher salaries. This is a clear instance of the unacceptable practise of percentage salary raises with the inevitable consequence of an ever-increasing gap between higher and lower salaries. As usual, the workers involved are mostly women.

Another aspect of the day care program in Nova Scotia which works a hardship on the families needing it is that parents, even single parents, above the social assistance level, pay too high a proportion of the fees. For example, if the baseline were $110 a week for social assistance, and the family's net income were $160 a week, they would be required to pay $25 a week for day care. The formula is 50 per cent of income above the baseline until the full fees are met.

I should point out that there is a serious difference in approach among provinces. In Ontario, for instance, day care fees are set according to family *needs*, not family *income*. This means that such items as mortgage payments and other responsibilities are taken into consideration when determining a family's ability to pay for day care. This would appear to be an area where there could usefully be some federal guidelines.

Many women have had the experience of initiating programs, and either finding that there were no funds to continue, or receiving short-term funding, at the end of which they are supposed to find "other sources" which were never there in the first place. They have found it extremely difficult to meet standards which, desirable as they may be, are beyond their meagre income. Pre-school, voluntary, organized child care is a case in point. Groups of women have set up pre-school care for their children on a cooperative basis in church basements, community halls, and comparable facilities, only to find that they cannnot meet health standards required for funding. Yet they cannot meet health standards precisely *because* of lack of funding. This vicious cycle must be broken.

I would like also to comment on one other program and how it affected women. The Local Initiatives Program was designed to employ the unemployed, on the assumption that these were men. As it turned out, thousands of women flocked to make use of the grants and the LIP resulted in expanding the labour market in a way not anticipated by its initiators. It revealed the concealed number of women wanting paid employment, even at minimum wages. But it did not last. It has been replaced by other programs which are purportedly open to both men and women. It remains to be seen whether, in actual fact, women will have equal employment opportunities under these new programs.

It does not seem to me to be possible to show that patriating the Canadian Constitution, amending the Constitution, adjusting or eliminating overlapping jurisdictions, even entrenching the *Bill of Rights* as it now reads, will guarantee the kind of caring society for which women are striving. The priorities of government and the social, political and economic climate are such that the services women need will be provided only if women continue to initiate them and to give an inordinate amount of time to nurturing them. The evidence is all around us that governments, which spend billions on potential violence, destruction and repression cannot at the same time meet basic human needs. The one militates against the other, and the word "militates" is exactly right. It is essential that Canadian women get into the decision-making process in which our representation now is little more than tokenism.

Berit Ås, alternate member of the Parliament of Norway, spoke recently at the Dalhousie Law School on "Women in Politics." According to the report in the Dalhousie *Gazette*, she said: "The only way to get parliament to respond to the needs of women is to get more women involved in the decision-making process." After describing how women increased their percentage of representation from five per cent in 1963 to 22.5 per cent in 1979, she said: "Parties that set a quota for women will attract more women voters and more women members. Their platforms do not necessarily reflect the interests of women at first, but as more and more women join, more women's issues are addressed."

Now, finally, who *is* to set the standards for social services? And where are the women in this process? I am very pessimistic about getting away from the "bake-sale" mentality, a role assigned to women by the macho-male/dependent-female view of the world. I propose that the men working on our Constitution set up a task force, composed of a membership of at least 40 per cent men and 40 per cent women to work out a new system — a system that would guarantee that all elected governments (federal, provincial, municipal) be composed of at least 40 per cent women and 40 per cent men. Furthermore, that all appointed bodies, the Supreme Court, the Senate (if we continue to have one), other courts, school boards, task forces, etc. have the same composition formula applied. I make an exception for the Canadian Advisory Council on the Status of Women and the High Command of the Military, which are, I hope, two different worlds.

As women, then, we no longer set as our goal acceptance into the macho-male world. Rather, we will develop a world of caring, cooperation and nurture and invite men into *our* world — the good society. Together, and only together, and on what I call feminist terms, can we achieve it. *Then* we will have the money to do what needs to be done. How absurd that we don't.

V. Economic and Social Issues Facing Women

Women's Rights and "National Interests"

Micheline Carrier

For some time now politicians have been preoccupied with matters which they consider to be of the utmost importance — the constitutional discussions — but they have excluded the women of the country from them. This year, next year, or even later, they will decide on a new constitution and perhaps a changed society. They will establish what they believe to be the best way or protecting human rights, including the rights of women, but they have not asked women for their advice, except in outside discussions. Still they claim to be treating women as full citizens.

Time for Bold Action

The time is right to take the kind of forceful stand that has characterized the women's movement for the past 10 years, but it must go beyond the exchange of pleasantries. Strong action is required if federal and provincial politicians are going to pay serious attention to the claims and legitimate needs of women.

Public opinion is sharply focused on the "constitutional train" but women have been slow to get on board. The constitutional discussions have still not concluded, and this gives women time to better explain their position on the future of Canada and the provinces, and on the best way of obtaining the guarantee that their rights will be respected.

We are trapped if we depend too much on the constitutional context to get across the message of women. Simply granting them explicit guarantees will not mean that their rights will be respected in practice. But this is a good opportunity to draw attention to the problems that women have encountered, and still encounter, because they are inadequately represented and because governments and judicial authorities do not recognize that they have the same rights as men. This is precisely the topic that was suggested to me. Thus, if I appear to be down-to-earth and far removed from the lofty considerations of a purely constitutional nature, which have greatly interested some people, it should be realized that I have not been asked to decide on a division of powers between the provincial governments and the federal government.

Our Similarities not our Differences

Before showing how the existing rights of women are limited in comparison with those of men or outlining the grievances of Canadian women, I will discuss the conditions necessary for our attempts to be heard successfully.

Like Canadian men, Canadian women have varied socio-economic interests and belong to various groups. Therefore, they have diverse political and constitutional opinions, and it would be improbable and unhealthy if it were otherwise. But they are not interested in constitutional reform just to display their partisan positions, however legitimate they may be. On the other hand, women cannot ignore that governments hide behind overlapping jurisdictions in order to justify the *status quo* in several fields when they could act now by using their respective powers. Women are too often taken in by excuses of this kind.

I do not see what we can expect to obtain from political leaders if we do not put ourselves above partisan interests, the "national interests" that are always considered superior to others, and that too many men and women in politics tend to confuse with their own interests. By uniting with the leading proponents of various constitutional options and, it must be underlined because we cannot escape the "roots of our origin," we could be tempted to soft-pedal our legitimate demands when male politicians warn us of the presumed dangers that threaten "the nation." This is all the more likely because women traditionally have been self-sacrificing. Throughout history, women have often been asked to subordinate their rights and aspirations to the interests of the family, society, the economy, the nation and other ones that would better serve male politicians than the population as a whole. I will give a few examples: It was only in 1929 that women were recognized as having the status of persons, and even then it was necessary to have the matter settled by Britain. Fifty years later it is still not certain whether women are always treated as persons in the same way as men.

The majority of Canadian women obtained the right to vote after men and in Quebec, it was obtained after a bitter struggle. But that has not prompted political leaders to consider women full citizens. They grant them political importance at election time and when "national interests" call for it. Therefore, during each of the two world wars, "national interests" required that women replace men on the labour market. When the wartime economy no longer needed them, they were sent back to the kitchen and the cradle. As we approach the end of the twentieth century, the right to paid employment for women in this country is still not recognized. They are tolerated in the labour market, but if they can be excluded from it, unjust measures are readily used to do so. What have the women of this country gained by serving the common interest at the expense of their own interests? Certainly not recognition. Are some of them who lived through difficult times in the war factories among our poorer citizens today?

Women are at fault for being passive in their demands, and for giving way too quickly before "national interests" when these same interests assume that they will sacrifice themselves over and over again. We must destroy forever this stereotype of "saviours" of the nation or "redeemers". There are limits to assigning special missions to us when we are taken for a ride and power is used at our expense.

Some Examples in Other Countries

To be sure the lot of Canadian women is better than that of Iranian women. Our male politicians, however, are not discussing a new constitution in Iran but in Canada. We want them to recognize the rights of Canadian women, not the rights of Iranian women, although they might be more concerned about the latter in international fora.

Since I place much emphasis on the sacrifices required of women in the service of their country and the small amount of recognition these sacrifices have afforded them, let us look at Iran further. Iranian women have received the *tchador* in return for their contribution to a revolution which they believed would bring liberation. They have become the victims of a repression that ought to be denounced by all citizens in the world, and first and foremost by our governments. Farrokhru Parsa, the first Iranian woman to sit in parliament and occupy a position within the government as Minister of National Education (1968 to 1974) was also the first to be executed by Islamic revolutionaries last May, presumably for political reasons that were never explained. "Her case is all the more serious because she is a women," the judge stated at Parsa's trial. The reason was understood. All things considered, the men of this country, and legislators in particular, are also of the opinion that in Canada everything is more serious when it is a woman.

If I were asked to recall other examples of women too generous to their country and deceived by the powers they believed in, I would mention Cuban women. They are the ones who constitute a majority among the refugees and who are abused, sexually or otherwise, by receiving countries because they are destitute. The women of Nicaragua played a very important role in the insurrection that liberated their country from the dictator Somoza. Today, they are still demanding, from the new regime, the abolition of all discriminatory laws; the participation of women in the drafting of new legislation; precise statements of policy on health, education, employment, wages; and in vain, for training programs for women. They took part in armed revolution; now the most qualified, as volunteers, take care of the social services in the country. Russian women, who took part in all the revolutions, were deported as soon as they denounced the inequalities between men and women in their writings. This denunciation was perceived as being just as serious as if they had opposed the political regime in power, if not more so.

Americans have hoped from decade to decade, from government to government, from president to president, from state governors to state governors, that the new leaders will agree to entrench their rights in the constitution. The Equal Rights Amendment, which prohibits discrimination based on sex, was passed by Congress in 1972 and ratified by the legislatures of 35 of the 50 states. Three more states must approve it before June 30, 1982 if this amendment is to be included in the constitution. The Republican Party, which had been in favour of it for 40 years, changed its position this year. Compared with the political interests of leaders, and aspiring leaders, the rights of women do not carry any weight.

Women should realize that the same scenario is repeated everywhere and they should begin to change their strategy, if they ever had one. There is a fundamental conflict between the objective of the women's movement — the recognition of equal rights — and the partisan interests and struggles of political powers. It is precisely these powers and interests that hinder equality because in reality they owe their survival to the existence of subordinate classes, including women and other socio-economic groups. Women have never really united to question these powers. They accept half-measures too easily, and this is why they are hardly ever taken seriously. They retreat too rapidly when challenged or slighted, and they hide behind both men and women politicians too quickly. They are too open to the flattery of politicians who have a thousand and one ways of "pacifying them into silence."

Every Canadian Woman is an Indian Woman

Next to "higher national interests" and purely partisan interests, respect for customs and traditions is often used as a pretext for denying women their basic rights. Women make themselves the staunch guardians of the ways and customs that oppress them;

conditioning for dependence is often the only form of "security" they know. It is not by chance that customs and traditions are always more oppressive for women. They are the instruments of patriarchal power that organizations supposedly based on peace and justice dare not denounce because they share the same power.

Why not point out the cowardice of the World Health Organization and the United Nations which say nothing about the mutilations (excisions, infibulations, clitoridectomies, etc.) involving millions of young girls and women victims throughout the world? Denunciation of these atrocities need not wait until all the women in countries where they are committed have learned to read, are getting three meals a day or are members of their government. Canada has never taken a stand on the issue of mutilated women, some of whom die and all of whom have had their physical being impaired.

There is certainly no need to wander through Asia or Africa seeking examples of rights which are sacrificed for traditions or for other motives disguised as traditions and customs. Look at Canada where the status of Indian women, who are the most exploited among the exploited, clearly illustrates how the political and economic interests of men are protected by their traditions and customs. In my opinion, this is typical of the way all women in Canada are treated.

Indian women are caught between the interests of both Indian men and the Canadian government; both treat them as hostages. The first women inhabitants of this country have been deprived of their property, their status and, when they marry a non-Indian, the right to belong to the band into which they were born. The same does not hold true for an Indian man who marries a non-Indian woman. The children of non-status Indian women also lose their rights, in particular the right to inherit from their grandparents. The Indian woman who marries a man from another band automatically becomes part of her husband's band. If she belongs to a wealthier band, her economic situation may change overnight from one extreme to the other. The child of an unmarried Indian women may lose his or her status if it can be proven that the child's father is a non-Indian.[1]

The Canadian government claims it has suspended the section of the *Indian Act* that imposes this fate on native women. Women members of the Senate and the House of Commons maintain that their pressure and their petition are responsible for this moratorium. But this is not the case. Indian women are not asking for a *circumstantial* recognition of their rights, a recognition that is likely to be taken away from them as circumstances vary. They want to exercise all the rights of full citizens. But there is more to it. The claimed moratorium announced by the federal government is not really one. It is a simple reaffirmation, under more favorable political circumstances, of a particular stance which was revealed by the Honourable Jeanne Sauvé in July 1979. Madame Sauvé said, in effect, that she and her female colleagues in the Cabinet had been refusing, since 1976, to sign departmental orders that would have deprived native women of their rights and their status. They were, in effect, blocking the application of the *Indian Act*. Today, what is presented to us as a victory for women politicians is only a partisan resurrection of a subject already debated in advance of the Copenhagen conference. The real motive behind this gesture on the part of the women in the Commons and Senate is political — it enhances the reputation of Canada abroad, as the preamble to the text of the petition indicates.

Incidentally, the women politicians did not consider claiming, for native women, the recovery of rights and status lost before the legislation was blocked. The Minister of Indian Affairs, Mr. John Munroe, stated that he was inclined to suspend this section of the law which deals harshly with native women if the National Indian Brotherhood asked him to do so. And if the Brotherhood does not ask it, will he respect the *status quo*? Men negotiate among themselves the rights of Indian women. It is understood that masculine privileges will be preserved, because that is what it is really all about, certainly not the customs and traditions to which they are supposed to be so attached. Agreements between the government and the National Indian Brotherhood offer significant financial or other rewards. Therefore, it is better that men remain owners of these assets. When it is a question of property rights, men understand one another.

To ensure the effectiveness of the trusteeship principle, the Canadian government has introduced into the *Human Rights Act* article 63(2) which exempts the *Indian Act* from the terms of the Charter of Rights. Thus, it deprives native women of any legal recourse. We must question whether the draft presented by the federal government protects the rights of Indian women. I have insisted on tackling the subject in this introduction because, in comparison, all Canadian women are like Indian women to a degree. In several areas their rights are sacrificed to supposed customs and traditions. Since 1869 Indian women have been victims of federal policies aimed at rapidly assimilating natives and taking their reserves away from them.

As for Canadian women in general, patriarchal customs, politico-economic interests and attitudes have almost the force of law. The rights of Canadian women are not in so satisfactory a state as our leaders would like to have believed when they are travelling abroad. The picture that follows below offers nothing to cheer about. It shows that women's rights are limited and circumstantial, in other words they are recognized or suspended as circumstances vary. To a degree, it is a portrait of the status of women throughout the world, seen in the Canadian context.

The Status of Women, a Three-Sided Cage: Economic Dependence (Poverty), Sexual Exploitation, and Physical and Moral Violence

From birth to death, women have to fight for their rights one by one, with the possible exception of reproduction, although reproduction is more of an obligation than a right. The women of Canada share with women throughout the world a status which is bound by a permanent three-sided cage — the base of it is economic dependence leading to poverty and the two other sides are sexual exploitation and violence. Most laws keep women in the cage and any examination of the problems which confront women citizens makes this obvious. Equality before the law is a delusion. It is this kind of equality that the first draft of the federal proposal would attempt to guarantee.

Economic Dependence

The majority of women interested in these debates undoubtedly do not see themselves in the description of caged women. Certainly very few of them are forced to "scrape together" 10 or 20 dollars to cover their weekly personal expenses or stick to a very strict budget. I am concerned about those who are less well off; the others have enough people to speak for them, although in varying degrees the majority of Canadian women become aware, sooner or later, that rights are different or recognized differently according to whether a person is born a woman or a man. The report on *Women and Poverty,* published in October 1979 by the National Council on Welfare, will help me to illustrate the economic dependence of women. It must be remembered that this report excludes native women and bases its case on statistics that are several years old. Reality is always some distance ahead of the statisticians.

The National Council on Welfare informs us that 16 per cent of adult Canadian women live in poverty, that is one in six or 1,219,000 (one out of nine men is poor, or 851,000). It estimates that the majority of Canadian women are faced with poverty at one time or another during their lives and that this situation is the logical outcome of their social role of being essentially subordinate to the family. The economic situation of women is thus a function of their family or marriage status. More than two-thirds of those women who are well-off economically live with their spouse or father, while this holds true for only one-fifth of poor women. Poverty occurs when women cease to depend economically on men.[2]

According to their family or marriage status, the 1,219,000 women are divided in the following way: 17 per cent of them belong to single-parent families (as heads of families, adult children or mothers); 39 per cent live in two-spouse families including wives, adult children and mothers; 40 per cent live alone or with non-relatives (in a boarding-house, for example). If married women run less risk of being poor, they still make up the most important group of poor women — because the great majority of Canadian women are married a small percentage of wives actually adds up to more women than a larger percentage of any other group.

Widows and other women who were previously married (divorced, separated or abandoned) run the greatest risk of being poor: 54 per cent of them have incomes below the poverty line defined by Statistics Canada in 1978: this amounts to from $3,520 to $4,844 for a single person, depending on the area in which the person resides. (Remember that these women are often responsible for one or more individuals and that the 54 per cent figure would be much higher if it included Indian women abandoned with their children.) Some 44 per cent of women who are heads of families and 34 per cent of the unmarried women are poor. Finally, only nine per cent of married women still living with their husbands are in a precarious economic situation.

Older women live in even more drastic economic circumstances. In 1978, in Canada, there were 140 women for every 100 men over 70 years of age, and it is anticipated that before the year 2000 this figure will be 165 women for every 100 men.[3] Therefore it must be underlined that women constitute the greater percentage in the socio-economic group known as senior citizens. According to the report of the special Senate committee on policies related to retirement age, 48 per cent of the single women over the age of 65 were living on an income of less than $3,000 in 1977.[4] In 1978, 200,000 men and 500,000 women, who were over 65, and living alone, had incomes below $96 a week. Of this group, 200,000 — again the majority were women — had weekly incomes below $57.[5]

Social programs for senior citizens are similar in nature to those reserved for women in this country; they are "women's programs" — just enough to exist on and less than what is really needed. In Canada there are 2.2 million people who receive the Old Age Pension and half of them or 1.1 million, are eligible for the Guaranteed Income Supplement. The pension was set at $191.18

per month and the supplement is $192.03. Since then the supplement has been increased by $35. But because this increase is granted to the *household,* and not the *individual*, the eligible single recipient has benefited while married couples have had to share this amount. If the spouses live apart, each of them receives this increase. Social programs, more than anything else, illustrate that marriage and living together do not pay. Under most of these programs the rate of benefits is based on the couple or the family, which is unfair to one of the two spouses. Usually the woman is the loser.

Included in the pension and supplements program are other unsuitable aspects. If a woman between the ages of 60 and 65 is married to a man, 65 or over, and thereby eligible for a pension, she receives a spouses' allowance of $339.35. If unmarried or married to a man of 63 or 64 years, she has no right to this income. The same goes for unmarried men under 65. This is discrimination based on marriage status and it would be interesting to know whether the Canadian Human Rights Commission has already taken up this matter.

The chance of being poor is 20 per cent less likely among married women 65 years and over than among widows and unmarried women of the same age. Two out of three widows have incomes below the poverty level.[6] Widows between 50 and 65 years of age are in a particularly difficult situation: they have not reached the required age to be eligible for pensions and income supplements intended for senior citizens. They live on a meagre widow's pension or social assistance. In 1974, 40 per cent of all wage-earners participated in private pension plans, but more than half of them belonged to ones that fail to provide a pension for the surviving spouse.[7]

Widows also do not benefit from the annuity and pension plans of their spouses, because the annuities and pensions only belong to the one who pays for them. Life insurance plans provide little to the surviving spouse and at times, she has to fight to have her rights recognized. In 1978, the number of women in their fifties who had already been married (widowed, divorced, separated, abandoned) was 500,000.[8] A guaranteed annual income plan, adapted to the real needs of the recipients, could help these poor women who have almost no chance of entering or re-entering a labour market where discrimination, based on age and flagrant sexism, prevent women from achieving economic independence.

Women in the Labour Market

Our society still does not recognize the right of women to paid employment. All kinds of experts and ordinary citizens continually assign responsibility for the unemployment rate to women and keep alive the false notion that women work, not out of necessity, but to keep themselves in luxuries. However, the unemployment rate has reached 9.6 per cent for women and 7.6 per cent for men.[9] And so few Canadian families are living in luxury that the number of poor two-spouse families would increase by 51 per cent if the wives left the labour market.[10] In 1976, 46.9 per cent of all married couples, both husband and wife, were employed and 46.3 per cent of all married women worked outside the home or were looking for work.[11]

The labour market does little to make women rich. Instead it helps to keep them in the three-sided cage which I spoke of earlier. The laws connected with it have the same effect. Salaries of women with equivalent training and experience are always less than those of men. The Canadian Advisory Council on the Status of Women has shown that 87.1 per cent of the women who hold paid positions, and are included by Statistics Canada in the labour force (as if workers at home performed no labour) have high-school education or better. This figure is only 79.6 per cent for men who perform similar functions. That still does not prevent women from getting about 60 per cent of the wages received by men. Women must work for eight days to earn the wages that a man earns in five. In 1977, a nurse with 14 years of education earned less than a deliveryman; a female nursing aide earned $184 a week and a non-registered male medical attendant, $195. An inexperienced saleslady earned 39.2 per cent less than a salesman in the same type of position.[12]

The federal public service is a centre of sex discrimination: 1.3 per cent of the women and 11.7 per cent of the men who occupy full-time positions in it earn $25,000 and over.[13] Last May the Human Rights Commission revealed that 3,000 women employed with the federal government were treated less fairly than men in the same or equivalent employment categories. Wage adjustments and back pay could cost up to $7,000,000 and even more, if the labour union carries out a careful review of collective bargaining agreements. But it seems that the government is not obligated to pay the extorted amounts.[14] This is the way women of this country are robbed and obliged to support the economy. It is not surprising that there are always more poor women than men.

Part-time work — a real employment ghetto offering poor pay and no protection — is almost the preserve of women who are said to be earning extra money: 71.6 per cent of part-time workers are women.[15] If part-time work is suited to some people, then it should be made available to men as well as women.

Fringe benefits, in proportion to the hours of work, should be added and it should be regulated in such a way that it does not become a means to exploit underpaid workers who must accept any condition just to survive. Incidentally, women occupy the majority of non-union jobs and this adds to the inferior treatment and little protection they receive. Some 27.4 per cent of the women wage-earners are unionized compared with 41.6 per cent of the men.[16]

Legislation governing the labour market affect women more harshly than men. In the eyes of legislators and administrators, women are suspected, more than men, of cheating on unemployment insurance. The unemployment insurance legislation demands more of women than men: for example, it requires a mother claiming benefits to prove she has a guardian for her children and is therefore in a position to hold a job. Workers who re-enter the labour market after a two-year absence are required to work 20 weeks before again being eligible for benefits. This aspect of the legislation is particularly hard on women who must be absent from the labour market more often than men in order to give birth to children or to take care of them.

Tying unemployment insurance benefits to family income or the number of the claimant's dependants is also being considered. This would be extremely discriminatory; it would further limit the rights of women within the family and persuade some to leave the labour market. Day care services are inadequate and governments are not considering improvements. About 625,000 children (under 7 years of age) with working mothers cannot be placed in day-nurseries approved by the government.[17] Safety on the job is not a recognized right, since a woman is sometimes left with the choice of either compromising her health and that of her child or quitting her job. Then, too, the health risks that are part of a job are sometimes used as a pretext to dismiss a woman and take away the benefits that belong to her job. Finally, the Quebec charter of social rights allows for sex discrimination in retirement and insurance plans and in the social benefits area.

New Canadians: the Women Workers

Among new Canadians, women workers are exploited both as women and as foreign nationals; they are very vulnerable in the economic system. A large number of them constitute a slave class over which the federal government and its provincial counterparts have complete control. I want now to discuss the domestic workers brought in as cheap labor to serve the well-to-do of Canada. These workers are the victims of unjust legislation and in particular, the

Immigration Act. They are granted work permits which are valid for two or three years, and can be cancelled at any time. They are seldom renewed. The workers are simply sent back to their country of origin and the supply of slaves is renewed. These domestic servants cannot change jobs without government approval and are not granted landed immigrant status. Therefore, they do not have the right to social benefits, social assistance payments, unemployment insurance, health insurance, and pensions. In other words they receive no benefits. Their wages range from $50 to $75 a week for 50 to 60 hours of work.[18]

The disgraceful laws that allow exploitation of this kind should be contested before the Human Rights Commission, and if necessary before international courts. Other countries take officials hostage; in Canada, the government itself makes hostages of men and women workers who have left their homelands for political and economic reasons and who often have to earn enough here to support children or parents left behind. It is not surprising that during the past five years many women from the Third World have found little more freedom in Canada than they had in their own country. Above all, these women provide cheap labour.

In addition to these foreign domestic workers, who are exploited in our capitalist system which is too cheap and chauvinistic to recognize domestic work at its fair price and to attract Canadian men and women to the positions available in this sector, other women who have recently become Canadians are not really treated as full citizens. These women workers experience the same difficult conditions as other women in the least rewarding categories of employment (domestic work, hotels, restaurants, the clothing and textile industry). Their situation is made worse because they often are not familiar with either official language; they have very little schooling and, therefore, access to a limited choice of jobs; and they do not know how to defend themselves. For example, legislation governing minimum labour standards requires that workers with grievances bring action themselves, something not easily done by people who are ignorant of the law, the language and the customs of the country. In bringing action they run the risk of losing their jobs which they need very much.

Because of certain aspects of the *Immigration Act,* revised in 1978, and in particular the undefined clause on subversive activity, these women live in terror or being deported. They would rather give in to discrimination in all its forms than complain. The *Act* stipulates that the landed immigrant "may be deported not only for having committed a crime, but also if there are reasons to believe that he or she could have committed it." Such a measure can be used as a weapon for all sorts of reasons against new Canadian workers, both men and women.

When people from other countries are granted entry, they should be guaranteed the same rights as other Canadians. It is difficult to take the legislators seriously, both men and women politicians, who give their blessing to such discrimination and then claim that all citizens enjoy equal rights in this "multicultural" country.

Women Working in the Home

Now, I will deal with the rights granted to unpaid women workers or "housewives" and to women who are heads of families. Women who are single parents and housewives make up the majority of Canadian women. They are treated as though giving birth to children and bringing them up is a vocation that does not afford the right to social recognition. Too often they are forced to assume, on their own, the socio-economic costs of motherhood. Since family law and matrimonial legislation are dealt with by others in this publication I will consider only the practical results of the unequal recognition of family rights.

There are more than five million unpaid women workers in the home. So far no study has estimated accurately the value of their work and its importance to the national economy although it is roughly estimated to be several billion dollars. Studies by Statistics Canada set it at about 40 per cent of the Gross National Product between 1961 and 1971.[19] If this work were calculated as part of the GNP, perhaps it would be realized that women in the home support the economy of the country and that they do not receive their fair share of the common wealth, either in the family or in society.

Recently, women who work with their husbands in family businesses were granted employee status as long as they remained with the business. Some of them are the real managers of the enterprise; their husbands play only a secondary role that allows them to be paid wages. Other homemakers still lack personal income, pensions or other revenue, and often various forms of insurance. The *Income Tax Act* considers the homemaker a "dependent" of the wage-earning spouse and allows an exemption on that basis. The "housewife" is also one of the few workers with no protection against work-related accidents or sickness. Women working in the home do not contribute to any benefit or pension plans; as a result they do not receive disability benefits when needed or leave any benefits to their husbands and children when they die. Nor do they accumulate any for their retirement. The wife of a contributor has a right to only half of her husband's retirement pension, although her work in the home allowed him to accumulate pension benefits based on his paid employment. In Quebec, until recently, a divorced homemaker had no right to share the retirement pension of her husband, even if she had served the family and husband for 30 or 40 years. The wife has no right to part of the retirement pension in a private plan when the marriage is dissolved. The widow who remarries loses her retirement pension because she is then considered the responsibility of another man. The majority of plans for supplementary payments do not include the payment of benefits to the widow of a contributer.

Most women do not have the means to contribute to registered retirement savings plans and registered home ownership savings plans. At home they have no income, pay no taxes and therefore do not benefit from these fiscal advantages. In the labour market, they are confined to the lowest-paid sectors and are certainly not affected to any great extent by the federal tax relief on dividends and the deduction for income earned in the form of interest and dividends.

To illustrate how women, and particularly housewives, are at a disadvantage in financial terms, we should mention deductions under a progressive fiscal plan that benefits the very rich. Of the 7.1 billion dollars allowed in 1976 for about 20 exemptions, deductions and credits of various kinds, 53 per cent of it went to 20 per cent of the taxpayers in the highest income brackets. Obviously very few women are among this privileged group. Middle-income taxpayers saved $400, while the five per cent of taxpayers whose income was the highest saved an average of $2,662. The 77,400 taxpayers whose income was over $50,000 saved $4,781, which was 12 times more than middle-income taxpayers.[20] Are there many Canadian women whose incomes exceed $50,000? Low-income taxpayers cannot take advantage of all these exemptions because their incomes are too small; the same thing is true for those who have no income, or incomes too low to be taxable. The majority of these are housewives.

Women who marry without ensuring that they have a measure of economic security are gambling with their future just as if they were playing poker. As long as things are going smoothly for the household, most of them probably do not lack the necessities. But when the marriage breaks up, everything goes wrong for these women.

Matrimonial Regimes and Property Rights

Matrimonial regimes are drawn up to protect the priority given to the property rights of men and to keep women in their place, i.e. in their role of wife and mother. It is not surprising that they provide a smaller share for women when a marriage breaks up.

In 1970, the Royal Commission on the Status of Women called on provincial governments to pass legislation governing matrimonial assets and to recognize the principle of equal association in marriage, which takes into consideration the contribution of both spouses. The Commission demanded that marriage systems grant former spouses equal rights to the assets acquired through their work and personal savings during the time they were together. Since then, provincial councils on the status of women, and six out of seven provincial law reform commissions, have demanded similar changes. And the Canadian Advisory Council on the Status of Women has supported these claims. It has demanded that the law recognize marriage as an association of equals and that the work of the spouse at home is just as valuable as the one outside the home.[21] New legislative measures adopted by some provinces and draft legislation not yet adopted by others still do not recognize the "equality of spouses" principle. This is the case with Bill 89 passed by the Quebec government. It states the principle of the legal equality of spouses but does not provide the practical means to achieve it.

There are great differences among provincial marriage systems and because of this, family law will likely be an area in which consensus will be most difficult to achieve. The federal government had proposed to transfer complete legislative jurisdiction in the field of marriage and divorce to the provinces. The provincial premiers have examined several possible solutions but none of these has been firmly agreed upon, even though one formula has been accepted by the majority. (See text by Nicole Bénard).

Whatever may be decided, the provinces must come to an agreement on this matter so that citizens in all areas of the country will be treated fairly. Here for example, I am thinking about the practical consequences that the absence of an effective agreement on alimony would have: the debtor who moves a few kilometres beyond the boundary of a province has a good chance of escaping prosecution even if he deprives his ex-wife and children of a subsistence allowance or alimony to which they have a right. Should the provinces obtain full legislative jurisdiction over marriage and divorce and not work out agreements to administer these laws more effectively than at present, then we can imagine what would happen. For example, Alberta might grant a divorce by mutual consent and Ontario might refuse it; British Columbia could establish a plan for the universal and automatic payment of alimony and Nova Scotia, no such plan. Women and children bear the costs of political differences in this field because all legislation gives priority to the man as owner of the household assets.

One-parent Families

The economic dependence of women is clearly revealed when they become widows or their marriage breaks down. We can see accurately the fate that this country reserves for its female citizens by examining the problems of women who are single parents or heads of one-parent families.

In Canada, in 1974, there were more than 300,000 one-parent families which were responsible for at least one child under 18 years of age. Altogether in these families there were 631,360 children; 85.5 per cent of the families were headed by single women.[22] And these figures are out-of-date. In Quebec alone it is estimated there are close to 200,000 one-parent families, with 300,000 children belonging to them. It appears now that this number will continue to increase during the coming years if the divorce rate (one in every three marriages) remains constant; if common-law marriages with children break down at the same rate as traditional marriages; and if adolescents, who assume sole responsibility for their children, continue to contribute to the birth-rate in growing numbers. Children are still almost exclusively the concern of women and are also economically dependent on them.

According to the National Council on Welfare, one quarter of those receiving social assistance in Canada are heads of one-parent families and half the mothers receive some form of welfare; 53.2 per cent of the one-parent families live below the poverty line as defined by Statistics Canada.[23] In Quebec, in 1976, 70 per cent of the divorced women (not counting widows, women legally separated, and those separated in fact or abandoned) were living on welfare.[24] A certain number of ex-spouses, particularly among those on low and medium incomes, are probably not able to contribute financially to the maintenance of their children, but is this really the majority? The federal Law Reform Commission estimated that 75 per cent of court-ordered alimony payments were not made or were made for a short period of time.[25] It is not a question of depriving ex-husbands and preventing them from starting a new family, if they want to do so, but the protection of the rights of women and children — who often find themselves from one day and the next on social welfare — that is essential.

Governments should also be forced to distinguish between the rights of children and women in legislation. This would end the injustices perpetrated against women who would no longer have children in their care and who are often denied a pension which they should have in return for 30 or 40 years spent in the home with no personal income. They are not likely to enter the labour market and have no other recourse but social welfare. It would be more just to children if their rights were no longer placed in the same category as those of their mother and if they were given a separate subsistence allowance, as is done in some European countries.

In 1975 the National Council on Social Welfare indicated that 21.2 per cent of Canadian children living with two parents were poor. It also discovered that 33.7 per cent of the children who lived with their father and 69.1 per cent who lived with their mother were also poor. Thus, one-parent families headed by women are the most deprived.[26] The National Council on Social Welfare pointed out in 1979 that a one-parent family with two children had to live on an income from 17 to 40 per cent below the poverty line, according to the province in which the family lived. (In 1978, Statistics Canada established that the low-income level for a family of three persons was between $6,516 and $8,957, according to the region and the population in the area of residence.)[27]

The labour market is less accessible to female heads of families then to other women, and this is no small matter when we realize the situation of most paid working women. Women who are family heads often need job retraining and cannot obtain it. They are restricted to the lowest paying jobs in the restaurant and hotel field, for example, and to those jobs that are least suited to the single parent (transportation difficulties, absence of day care services, shift work, and so on). Imagine a 30-year old woman who must take the subway in one direction to bring her two children to the babysitter's house before taking the subway and bus in the opposite direction to get to the factory. Imagine also, women between the ages of 45 and 50 who still have to support adolescents and are told to go out and earn their living instead of claiming alimony payments, when they have only worked in the home during their entire lifetime. Even feminists, when they have attained a certain level of comfort, are quick to forget those who have not had their opportunities. Economic dependence is the lot of the majority of Canadian women and official spokesmen must, under no circumstances, forget it.

Sexual Exploitation and Violence:
Criminal Law Serves the Aggressor

I think I have provided enough of the background, now to explain how the economic situation of women renders them vulnerable to all forms of abuse, particularly sexual exploitation and physical violence. These forms of abuse and the economic situation of women are so closely linked that one wonders whether women are deliberately kept in economic dependence so that they will not react to physical and sexual oppression. If a single guarantee of rights should be entrenched in the constitution, it would be the guarantee of rights to physical and moral integrity, to safety and protection under the law. I would like to see that entrenched. Physical and moral integrity is a condition *sine qua non* for the exercise of all rights.

Before speaking of the treatment that the law inflicts on women who are the victims of rape, beating, prostitution, pornography and harassment, I should like to explain why defending the rights of women in these fields, to me, seems to be of primary importance. I doubt very much whether a woman who has suffered from violence and sexual subjugation can find the motivation and the strength to claim a right to occupy a paid position, the right to suitable day care services, the right to a share of her husband's income when she works in the home, the right to equal wages for equivalent work, the right to a fair share of the marriage assets in the case of a break-up, the right to be treated as a full citizen. In other words, this woman is trapped in a vicious circle, hence my analogy of the cage. Because she is economically dependent, she finds herself out on the street if she leaves the house to escape the violence of her husband. Is violence not a means of dissuading her from leaving the home, or claiming a scrap of independence?

I will not expose in detail the inconsistencies of the criminal laws now in force. By definition, the laws are supposed to protect citizens but, in the cases that concern us criminal laws seem to protect the aggressors. They incriminate the victims. Above all, this is the case with laws that are supposed to protect the victims of rape.

Woman as Rape Victims

A judgment of the Supreme Court of Canada has just reminded us that the present legislation is based on the presumed consent of the victim and, more generally, on the recognition that men have ownership rights over the bodies of women. Every victim of rape is therefore suspected, *a priori*, of having consented to aggression which, in the view of legislators, is not really a crime to be included with acts of violence. It is not a crime against the individual but, a sexual act. Since all women are suspected of provocation and men are not presumed to be responsible for their impulses — impulses that we are led to believe are uncontrollable in order to provide them with an alibi — in the view of legislators and a great many people, rape is a rare occurrence. What does it matter that statistics indicate that a rape takes place every 17 minutes in the United States (and there is no reason to believe that things are very different in Canada); what does it matter that the assaults and beatings associated with numerous rapes leave permanent reminders and that things (sticks, bottles, and other objects) are inserted into the vagina; what does it matter that gang rapes are frequent and that victims are forced to consent to sexual acts at knife-point or after being beaten; what does it matter that some young victims are killed after being raped; what does all that matter? The leading citizens of this self-righteous society, who claim to be rational beings, continue to support the view, either openly or in private, that rape is a rare act, that women run after men and that they consent to violence. In short, they grant a permit to rapists to abuse women of any age or class.

Certainly, rapists will have more difficulty getting away with it if they have attacked a woman under the protection of her father or her husband, or a woman who is economically comfortable in a high social position. And here we can see the close ties between the socio-economic status of women and their right to physical and moral integrity, the ties between their economic dependence, and the violence (including that supported by the law) to which they are subjected.

When the victims are questioned about their sexual past, and the Supreme Court confirmed the legitimacy of such questioning in the spring of 1980, it signifies that women do not own their bodies and sex life. When preserving "peace in the household" is used in refusing to include the excuse of any recourse for women abused by their husbands, in the draft legislation, it is recognized implicitly that women are the property of men. When a victim is subjected to five or six interrogations under the pretext of verifying whether she has a record of good sexual behaviour or not, the women of this country are denied the right to ownership of their own bodies and to the most fundamental justice. If legislators persist in maintaining these iniquities, it will be essential to demand that the sex life of the aggressor also be exposed, if necessary, in a public place. Perhaps then the powers-that-be will change their minds. Courageous victims, supported by groups of women, must come out of hiding and show the whole country the stupidity of the laws and of those who administer them.

Battered Wives

The same ties between economic dependence and family violence are apparent in the case of battered wives. The Canadian Advisory Council on the Status of Women has proven that one Canadian woman in 10 is beaten regularly by her husband, and this is only the known cases.[29] The police are reluctant to interfere when battered wives complain or when neighbours do on their behalf; no doubt they also fear disturbing the "peace in the household", which is so dear to those who consider a woman private property. The police could lose all motivation when they see how magistrates dispose of cases that police officers have carefully prepared. For example, isn't it discouraging to see a judge decide, out of kindness, to send a man home to sleep after he has beaten his wife? This case again illustrates that violence suffered by women is not considered a crime against the person or an act of violence. It is recognized as a husband's right.

Women should start demanding transition houses for aggressors. There are limitations on victims leaving home to take shelter elsewhere but aggressors are neither helped nor disciplined and believe they are within their rights. The right of women to be safe in their own homes is certainly not respected in the case of battered wives who must escape them. They could receive help from outside agencies if provincial governments provided sufficient funds in their budgets to cover adequate services for all battered individuals. Unfortunately, the federal Department of Welfare does not seem worried about this problem.

Women as Victims of Prostitution and Pornography

Prostitution, in my opinion, is a form of violence and much needs to be said on this subject. The present law condemns solicitation by both women and men. In practice, it is not the solicitation that is checked but individuals of the female sex who are considered "guilty" of solicitation. In other words, prostitutes. It seems that asking a man for money in return for sexual favours is frowned upon more than harassing women in the street, at the office, or anywhere else to obtain these favours free-of-charge.

Prostitutes are sexually exploited and violated women; they suffer from difficult socio-economic and "emotional" conditions, and the clients and procurers exploit their situation. But I am not asking that such a form of exploitation be legalized. I would prefer an attack on the causes of prostitution which, apart from the aforementioned conditions, are greed of the procurers and the socially influenced immaturity of men who are incapable of relationships, among equals, with women. Again, we are back to the three-sided cage in which women are imprisoned. The women, and the male or female children, who prostitute themselves do not usually come from favoured socio-economic backgrounds and those from middle class backgrounds do it for reasons of an economic nature as well. By studying prostitution from an economic standpoint, the complex moral judgments that always fall upon women can be avoided and, prostitution defined as it should be. In effect, it is an economic enterprise in which the users are precisely those who hold economic power in all sectors. (I do not know whether male prostitution serves women in the way it does homosexuals. But if women want to use male prostitutes, they must also meet the economic criteria because prostitutes cannot "work" for nothing.)

Public and judicial authorities know that procurers and the underworld control the prostitution industry. I am beginning to think that they are interested in dealing with them at the expense of women. In other places, they are beginning to aim at the procurers rather than the prostitutes. At Grenoble, last July, a judge decided to take seriously the prostitutes who complained about violence and torture at the hands of procurers; he put about a dozen pimps behind bars for two to 10 years. Prostitutes are rarely listened to by magistrates, who are responsible for dispensing justice. But the presiding judge in the Grenoble case was not intimidated by threats. He was convinced of the guilt of the accused and was less prejudiced against prostitutes than the average magistrate, both in Canada and elsewhere.

In Canada, the laws are questionable: there is no desire to stop prostitution yet prostitutes are kept under control as though they could carry on this occupation without clients. The federal Minister of Justice, who says he intends to carry out a "big cleanup" in the streets, should "aim his broom" in the right direction, that is, at the procurers and the clients who are often not touched. If he directs it against prostitutes, he will be giving meaning to the absurdities of this society which treats women as objects, exploits them in all sectors of the pornographic industry, and, forces them at the same time, to sell sexual favours.

It follows that the criminal laws on pornography (which a Swedish commission of inquiry calls the beginnings of prostitution) protect neither women nor children. Everyone can interpret them in his or her own way and the courts are reluctant to have these laws respected even when the police decide it's time to act. Most often the police wait for citizens to file complaints and, when they do, the complaints are rarely taken seriously. The laws are such that soon citizens will have to carry out police inquiries, collect the facts and gather the evidence, while policemen wait in their offices or hand out traffic tickets. The police are granted limited powers, or they misinterpret them; in any event, they are not well equipped to prevent crimes against the individual and to protect women and children who are victims of sexual abuse.

Tavern owners are allowed to carry on a form of procuring when they require that women, seeking work, not only serve beer but dance in the nude or be "available" to clients. This requirement has become a condition of employment in many places, but none of the provincial councils on the status of women have reacted. They are probably afraid of being called censors and moralizers. Their lack of concern for women and children, who are the victims of violence in places where prostitution is carried on openly, casts doubt on their real objectives. Are they seeking the advancement of all women and defending the rights of all women or only those of particular groups of women? Out of necessity our priorities reflect the spirit and purposes that keep us going. As with some women, are the official agencies that are supposed to represent women, using the consent of workers in the pornography and prostitution industry to justify their indifference or fear? If this is the case, they are in a poor position to lecture those who use the consent of the victim argument in cases of rape or, in a completely different area, the consent of workers employed in the garment industry under unhealthy and discriminatory conditions. In this latter case they do denouce the living conditions of the workers. They do not seem to be aware that the right to physical and moral integrity is threatened by prostitution and pornography.

I am convinced that it serves no useful purpose to attempt to have public officials limit prostitution and pornography as long as women have a morbid fear that they will be accused of being puritanical and remain silent when they are confronted by arguments no matter how far-fetched they may be. The ambivalent attitude of women and their fear of speaking-up are the greatest stumbling-blocks to the protection of women in those areas where high finance and political interests are linked. Women pretend not to know what is going on and perhaps maintain a "peaceful household" in this way; afterall, it is essential that their husbands or their friends be the consumer so the pornography and the prostitution industry can flourish. And it does, more and more.

Sexual Harassment

When we tolerate the marketing of women's bodies in public establishments and the control of women's bodies by procurers, when it seems to go without saying that the body of a woman is a capital asset, then rape, incest and other aggressive behaviour are also tolerated. This spirit of tolerance, which always benefits the exploiters and seldom the victims, has serious consequences for the daily life of women and in yet other area that is barely touched by the law. I am referring to sexual harassment — at work, on the streets, in public places, everywhere — which increasingly involves women as the victims.

Did not the federal Public Service Alliance sound the alarm in the spring of 1980 by making public some facts and figures on the subject? The Canadian Human Rights Commission had already deplored the fact that harassed women have practically no legal recourse and it had just lost the first case prosecuted in this area. Women are suspect if they complain. There is room to question a charter that does not protect the right of individuals to physical and moral integrity. Can we wait for changes in this area when we know that the harassers are often those who have the power to make employees lose their jobs; or those who make the laws and can change them?

Rape, pornography, prostitution, harassment, other bodily assaults, all these crimes and abuses of the individual are considered mild by a society that thinks women, to be "liberated," must remain at the disposal of all men. It seems to me that sexual exploitation and violence are the means of preventing women from achieving independence or resisting the powers that threaten them.[30] Sexual exploitation and violence involve women and men from all walks of life, but they have more serious consequences for the victims who are economically dependent on their aggressors.

I would like to see family law revised, recognition of the rights of women to paid employment and to freely-chosen motherhood, and removal of abortion from the Criminal Code. I would like to see women guaranteed health and safety at work; families provided with adequate day care services; changes in fiscal plans to which women contribute; a guaranteed minimum income, in any form whatever, for workers in the home; an end to the scandalous treatment of immigrant workers; and assurance of economic security for aging women, female heads of families, and others. I would like very much to see equality of women and men entrenched in the constitution. But all that is in vain if those most affected cannot benefit from these measures because they are subjected to sexual violence and exploitation. Obviously the first rights for which we must obtain guarantees are those of physical and moral integrity, of safety for everyone, everywhere. The criminal laws now in force do not protect women at all. Pressure must be exerted to change them and the first right to be entrenched in the constitution must be the right to physical safety, the right of every person living in this country to physical and moral integrity.

Women Have the Solutions

I have just painted a rather bleak picture of the status of women. Although incomplete, it does reflect reality. I should conclude my paper by proposing some solutions which better protect the rights of women. But, are there any? It would be disappointing to have to answer "no" to this question. However, there are solutions, although I do not believe in traditional ones like lobbying; lobbying by women is not effective, and it is the fault of women themselves. That is why the important short-term solutions I envisage, apply directly to women.

Certainly, we can ask that the rights of women be included, explicitly in the constitution. But what will that change if the constitution is not respected any more than the present laws under which all men and women citizens are supposed to be equal? It is always the same people who make, repeal, administer and interpret the laws and they think first about the interests of those who hold power. They are also the ones who carry on the constitutional discussions and who will agree, if necessary, to trade the rights of women for a few oil-wells or hydro-electric power stations.

In that case, should we insist that women participate directly in the constitutional debates by sending delegates to sit beside the cabinet ministers and premiers? It would be a waste of time. The few women involved would be received with polite and courteous ways but they would have no influence on the debates that men continue to conduct among themselves. Canadian women have time to prepare their claims before a new constitution is adopted. There lies the hope of playing a role of some kind in this area but I see this taking place away from the negotiating tables and behind the scenes. I consider the constitutional debates to be one of the best opportunities, but only *one* opportunity, to promote the rights of women. The means of achieving those rights do not consist of sending several representatives to sit at a table where they will soon be neutralized without disturbing the leaders. Because male politicians are sensitive to political questions discussed in public, women should prepare themselves and play their role in public. Then they could demand to be treated as an important part of the debates in progress. But, to begin with, terms will have to be defined.

At the risk of appearing rude, I will simply say that women do not exert any worthwhile influence as long as subjects are dealt with by women who are well-to-do, cultivated and well-educated, as we are doing in this context. If we hope one day to be a driving force, there is a fundamental need to form study committees in all regions, committees that will study thoroughly the important documents dealing with the rights of women. Let us renounce the utopian ideal of unanimity. The women of Alberta will certainly not want to give up their personal opinions on certain matters, nor will the women of Quebec, and the same applies to other Canadian women. Nevertheless, there are ways of reaching agreement on the fundamental documents and joining together to exert pressure. But it is essential to work with those most affected and, if necessary carry out an information campaign among them, so they will commit themselves. We claim to demand for them, a guarantee that their rights will be better protected in a new constitution than in the present one. Women in the mainstream, that is, women who live the daily life I have described, must be closely associated with the discussions that concern them. Our hopes to exert a real influence will be in vain if only a handful debate the question. The AFEAS (Women's Association for Education and Social Action) has made important gains for women who are associated with their husbands in business because they have organized the important people concerned — the women partners. The method used by this organization to organize women for action deserves to be copied.

But who will pay for this organization and the study committees formed across Canada? Quite simply, the federal and provincial governments which spend large amounts for constitutional discussions among men. Just as much could be spent for the participation of women, and these discussions should go beyond "feminine" subjects. However these subjects must be discussed in familiar surroundings in order to make the most of them: the contents of the *British North America Act*, the reforms being advocated, and the place of their rights in these reforms could all be explained to women. All this must be done apart from political parties which, as we know, use good intentions for their own purposes.

Once the committees were formed and the discussions proceeding on schedule, a national conference, of reasonable length, could be planned to determine the priorities and ways of exerting pressure on leaders. Pressures originating from the top of the pyramid are completely ineffectual if they are not supported by the base.

Having said that, there is another condition to be met if women are to be taken seriously. We must speak louder and show that we are not inclined to retreat at the first sign of retaliation or "dirty pool." Male politicians — and women are beginning to copy them — fully exploit the timidity of women in political matters, their fear of confronting officials and unfortunately, their tendency to seek the blessing of those who hold power. It is easy, then, to make women accept many situations in the name of "national interests." Women must show themselves more indifferent to the excessive flattery indulged in by all politicians. It is impossible to serve opposing interests: the interests of political parties and sometimes those of governments, are often contrary to the interests of individuals and even of nations.

It is not just enough to increase the number of women representing us in various decision-making areas. And official organizations, for example the councils on the status of women, must not be the only ones concerned with the interests of women. Their small gains in the past seven years are explained, in all fairness, by the fact that they do not always have the force to drive in the nail once they have delivered the first blow of the hammer. I do not really believe that the Canadian government or the provincial governments want to see women getting involved in constitutional affairs. The good faith of governments could be tested by demanding funds for this purpose.

In a constitutional situation, as in any other political situation, those who speak for women will never play an important role in the debate unless they demonstrate that they can quickly organize strength to fight back when they are attacked. And supporters can be organized when they have participated in all stages — study, consideration and discussion — not when certain priorities or decisions are dropped on them at the last minute.

Even assuming that governments agree to include a guarantee of women's rights in the new text of the constitution, I no longer believe that these rights will necessarily be protected. The present laws are intended to protect the rights of both women and men, but they protect men's rights more than women's. I should like to point out that Canada signed the United Nations Convention on the elimination of all forms of discrimination with respect to women, but it refused to sign the action plan. Canada claims to oppose all forms of discrimination against women, but it upholds discrimination against native women and discriminatory laws toward all Canadian women.

When we speak of policy, there is an enormous gap between theory and practice. That is why all women must constantly stand guard in order to keep a close watch on political powers. All evidence indicates that the majority of women are not ready to play this role at least in the immediate future. We must appeal to women of all socio-economic levels so that they will look after their own interests, in this case, recognition and respect for their fundamental rights. Currently the question of constitutional rights remains a matter for intellectuals. Those at the lowest levels of the female population, for whom we claim to demand justice, will not readily accept decisions made without consulting them. Furthermore, they do not have to accept.

Notes:

[1] K. Jamieson, *Indian Women and the Law in Canada: Citizens Minus*, Ottawa, Canadian Advisory Council on the Status of Women, 1978.

[2] National Council of Welfare, *Women and Poverty*, Ottawa, 1979. Unless otherwise noted, statistical data cited in this text come from this report.

[3] L. Dulude and E. Rosen, *Women and Aging*, Summary, Ottawa. Canadian Advisory Council on the Status of Women, 1978, p. 1.

[4] *Retirement: Policies, Pensions and Proposals*. Highlights of *Retirement Without Tears*, the Report of the Special Senate Committee on Retirement Age Policies, Ottawa, 1979, p. 11.

[5] Statistics Canada, 1978 data cited in *Le Devoir*, February 8, 1980, p. 2.

[6] National Council of Welfare, *op. cit.*, p. 9.

[7] L. Dulude, *op. cit.*, pp. 2-3.

[8] *Ibid.*

[9] P. Dale, *Women and Jobs: The Impact of Federal Government Employment Strategies on Women*. Ottawa, Canadian Advisory Council on the Status of Women, 1980. Also CACSW, *Women and Work*, Fact Sheet: 1, 1979.

[10] National Council of Welfare, *op. cit.*, p. 21.

[11] P. Dale, *loc. cit.*

[12] *Ibid.*

[13] *Ibid.*

[14] *La Presse*, May 31, 1980.

[15] P. Dale, *loc. cit.*

[16] *Ibid.*

[17] *Ibid.*

[18] S. MacLeod Arnopoulos, *Problems of Immigrant Women in the Canadian Labour Force*, Ottawa. CACSW, 1979.

[19] M. Proulx, *Five Million Women: A Study of the Canadian Housewife*, Ottawa, CACSW, 1978, summary, p. 3.

[20] National Council of Welfare, *The Hidden Welfare System Revisited*, Ottawa, 1979, p. 7.

[21] *Statement on Matrimonial Property Laws in Canada*, Ottawa, CACSW, 1979.

[22] National Council of Welfare, *One in a World of Two's*, Ottawa, 1976. Also S. J. Menzies, *New Directions for Public Policy: A Position Paper on the One-Parent Family*, CACSW, Ottawa, 1976.

[23] *One in a World of Two's*, p. 1.

[24] Council on the status of Women, *Pour les Québécoises: égalité et indépendance*, Quebec, 1979, p. 189. English summary, *Québécoises: Egality and Autonomy*.

[25] *New Directions for Public Policy. . .*, *loc. cit.*, p. 3.

[26] National Council of Welfare, *Poor Kids*, Ottawa, 1975, pp. 7-8.

[27] National Council of Welfare, *In the Best Interests of the Child*, Ottawa, 1979, p. 8.

[28] On this subject consult CACSW document: *Background Notes on the Proposed Amendments to the Criminal Code in Respect of Indecent Assault (Bill C-52)*, Marcia H. Rioux and Joanna L. McFadyen, CACSW, Ottawa, 1978. The Honourable Jean Chrétien has tabled a bill which will improve the law. Still the consent of the victim remains the basis of the law and the assaulted individual can be questioned on past sexual behavior. By not going far enough to improve a law we keep the means of maintaining the status quo in practice.

[29] L. MacLeod and A. Cadieux, *Wife Battering in Canada: the Vicious Circle*, CACSW, Ottawa, 1980.

[30] M. Carrier, *La violence: Riposte des pouvoirs menacés*, 1980, available from the author.

Employment and Motherhood

Lucienne Aubert

The never-ending problems that plague women illustrate that governments rarely give priority to matters related to the status of women. They adopt partial solutions after endless delays, and at the cost of slow and expensive mechanisms.

Because women have children, have had them, or are able to have them, they encounter discrimination. Motherhood, the exclusive domain of women, ensures the renewal of the species and is at least as important as national defence and environmental protection. Women with children constitute an important segment of the electorate and the labour force. The most elementary principles of justice dictate that women not be penalized because they are mothers.

However, childbearing is still considered a private activity that is more or less compatible with paid employment. Employers and governments are just beginning to recognize their share of the responsibility in protecting and compensating for motherhood. Ten years after the Bird report recommended that eighteen weeks of maternity leave be granted to all Canadian women, governments have not even recognized the right to maternity leave for all female workers. To receive it, women must be eligible for unemployment insurance benefits. The unemployment insurance system, which equates motherhood with unemployment, favours women working in the best organized and paid sectors and leaves those in the least to take on motherhood as a volunteer activity. Pregnant working women who are entitled to take maternity leave run into numerous difficulties because they have to find their way through the maze of incoherent laws created and administered by two levels of government.

Different Laws

With the exception of Prince Edward Island and the Northwest Territories, all Canadian provinces have passed laws concerning maternity leave, but they are all different and contain restrictive eligibility conditions. They include several categories of working women: those in temporary positions, those who are pregnant at the time they are hired, those who become pregnant before accumulating the prescribed number of work weeks with their employer and, in most cases, those in the domestic and agricultural sectors.

Not only do the eligibility conditions vary among provinces and between levels of government, but different laws also apply to different categories of working women within the same province.[1] For example, to be entitled to maternity leave, women governed by the Canada Labour Code must have worked 12 months for the same employer. Ontario's legislation requires 63 weeks,[2] while in Quebec, the law on minimum work standards requires that women work 20 consecutive weeks in the 12 months preceeding the request for leave. Women working in Quebec in businesses under federal jurisdiction must meet the criteria of the Canada Labour Code; the others are governed by a Quebec act, which has been in effect since April 1980, and which replaced Order No. 17 on maternity leave published in November 1978. As for women employed in the Quebec civil service or the federal public service, the terms of their maternity leave are determined by different collective agreements.

Differences also occur in the maximum length of leave allowed. Only Quebec, Saskatchewan and Alberta have passed legislation allowing for the 18 weeks proposed in 1970 by the Bird Commission.[3] Legislation in the other provinces, and the Canada Labour Code, allow for a maximum of only 17 weeks' leave — the length of time specified in the *Unemployment Insurance Act*.

In Quebec, pregnant women are eligible for maternity benefits if they have held an insurable job during the shorter of the following two time frames: 20 of the 52 weeks preceding the application for benefits, or 20 weeks since the last application for unemployment insurance. They must also have worked or received unemployment insurance benefits for at least 10 weeks between the fiftieth and thirtieth week leading up to child-birth.[4]

Injustices in the Compensation System

Incorporating maternity leave into the *Unemployment Insurance Act* is both senseless and unfair. The pregnant woman is leaving her job temporarily; she is not unemployed. When the unemployment insurance benefit rate dropped from $66^2/_3$ per cent to 60 per cent of insurable income, women on maternity leave suffered the same financial loss as unemployed workers. It is hard to believe that they should be subject to the two-week waiting period prior to receiving the first benefits, since the object of this delay is to encourage job hunting, and they are not available for work. The *Act* only provides for 17 weeks of benefits, but because of the waiting period, pregnant working women only receive benefits for 15 weeks. They receive no income if they take extended leave, and they may be penalized if the period during which they are entitled to take maternity leave is shorter than, or does not coincide with, the one provided for by the *Unemployment Insurance Act*. Finally, in some provinces, pregnant working women are required to terminate their leave six weeks after giving birth.

Legislation in Quebec is more flexible. Since January 1, 1979, working women who are eligible for unemployment insurance benefits and can prove that they have lived in Quebec for one year receive a lump sum payment of $240 to compensate for their financial losses during the waiting period.[5] This is a welcomed initiative, but it only partially compensates for the loss. Furthermore, it complicates and breaks up the compensation process for maternity leave, particularly when supplementary employment benefits are involved. These benefits, which are written into a number of collective agreements and paid by the employer, add to the basic plan in accordance with the regulations of the Employment and Immigration Commission. They may cover up to 95 per cent of the difference between the worker's regular income and the basic benefits. In this respect, collective agreements in the public and related sectors contain generous provisions.

Most working women do not enjoy these benefits because they work in small businesses or in sectors where unions are not sufficiently strong to obtain supplementary benefits. Having employers pay the cost of increased fringe benefits for pregnant women could cause some of them to hire women who are returning to the labour force after raising their families, rather than women of childbearing age.

Identifying motherhood with unemployment leads to other difficulties. Because benefits are based on the claimant's wages, the cost of motherhood is not the same for everyone and for employees with low incomes, the benefits are equally low. In some cases, working women who are normally eligible under the plan are excluded because unemployment or sickness have prevented them from contributing for the required number of weeks. Women who work less than 20 hours a week are not entitled to maternity leave because they are not eligible for unemployment insurance benefits. The consequences are even more considerable, since most part-time workers are women. Maternity leave for all is still a long way off.

For their part, women at home have a right to feel left out because they have no personal income and, therefore, are not entitled to paid maternity leave. Motherhood is a social function common to all women; it is unfair to recognize this essential contribution to society only among women who have paid, permanent, full-time jobs. The economic importance of work done at home and the irregular participation of women in the labour market are known facts.

At present, pregnancy entails loss of income threatened job security and exposure by women to various forms of discrimination. Recognition must be given to the right of women to retain their economic independence while bearing children. Insisting on the right to maternity leave for all Canadian women, a fair benefits system and consistent laws which govern the administration of such a plan, would help them to do so.

Constitutional Guarantees

Because they are able to create life, women will always have a special status in life and, therefore, special rights. Shouldn't these rights be guaranteed in a new or amended constitution? All pregnant women would then be assured of occupational safety and health, adequate compensation during a reasonable period of maternity leave, and the chance to return to their jobs at the end of their leave, with no loss of social benefits.

Maternity benefits should also be given to women leaving the labour market for a limited period of time. And the years they spent at home caring for their children, should be included in calculating their pensions. Women would thus be protected from all discrimination associated with their reproductive function and partially protected from economic dependence and poverty, which are often the lot of women who choose to become mothers.

It does not matter what methods are adopted by governments, so long as they take into account the real needs of the female population, both now and in the future. Recognizing motherhood as an essential social contribution and protecting the right of women to be mothers and workers at the same time, is thinking for today and building the nation of tomorrow.

Notes

[1] Intergovernmental Committee on Women in Employment, Women's Bureau, Labour Canada, *Maternity Leave in Canada*, Ottawa, 1980, pp. 10-13.

[2] *Ibid.*

[3] Canada. Royal commission on the Status of Women, *Report*, Ottawa, 1970, pp. 397-398.

[4] *Maternity Leave in Canada*, p. 36.

[5] Direction des communications, ministère du Travail et de la Main-d'oeuvre, Gouvernement du Québec, *Les allocations de maternité*, dépliant, Québec, 1979.

Other sources

CCH Canadian Limited, Maternity Leaves, *Canadian Labour Law Reporter*, pp. 907-911.

CCH Canadian Limited, *Canadian Unemployment Insurance Legislation*, 1979.

Conseil du statut de la femme, *Pour les Québécoises: Egalité et indépendance*, Québec, 1978, 335 pages.

Labour Canada, *Legislation relating to Working Women*, Ottawa, August 1979, 43 pages.

Labour Canada, *Human Rights in Canada*, Legislation, Ottawa, 1978, 96 pages.

Statements by the Fédération des femmes du Québec

I. WOMEN AND WORK

Women are entering the labour market in increasing numbers. In 1966, 33.6 per cent had salaried jobs or were looking for work. In 1976, this figure had risen to 45 per cent of the 8,570,000 women who were 15 years of age or over.[1]

That same year, 37.4 per cent of the 10,308,000 people who made up Canada's labour force[2] were women. Women accounted for 44.2 per cent of the unemployed and 36.9 per cent of those working. The unemployment rate was 8.4 per cent for women and 6.4 per cent for men. Twenty-one per cent of the women and 5.1 per cent of the men on the labour market were working part time.[3]

There are a number of questions worth studying in relation to the work world. However, given the lack of time and resources, we will limit our remarks to two specific areas: labour legislation and the programs and services provided by the various levels of government. The garment, knitting, textile and footwear industries, which have a high concentration of female manpower, will serve as examples.

Laws and the Example of Professional Training

The garment, knitting, textile and footwear sectors, in which a majority of women work, have recorded disturbing decreases in profitability and number of available jobs (see table in the appendix). As a solution, some have suggested closing the factories and transferring this manpower to other industrial sectors. Others feel it would be more useful to modernize the equipment, introduce a more logical form of management, and adopt a protectionist policy in order to reduce the number of bankruptcies and factory closings. None of these proposals have been implemented to date. Training programs in these manufacturing sectors are not easily accessible to workers and we are especially concerned with the problems faced by women.

The federal government is responsible for accepting applications from businesses and assuming the cost of industrial retraining and development programs. It alone establishes the standards and priorities to be met by employers. "Soft industries" or those which do not generate employment, are not included in training program priorities. Canada employment centres disregard applications from the garment, knitting, textile and footwear sectors. The reasons given are budgetary constraints and the lack of complex tasks. Women employed in these industries are therefore denied access to training programs because the companies for which they work do not meet federal government standards. A basic training program may occasionally be provided for a company's new female employees. However, unlike their larger counterparts, small businesses employing large numbers of women usually cannot afford the cost of such training programs.

Employment centres sometimes assist businesses in these sectors to train managers or individuals chosen to receive specialized training, but this is usually the only aid provided. Just the same the problems persist: program content, choice of instructors, teaching material, administrative controls and program duration must all receive provincial approval, which leads to further delays.

Because women working in the textile, garment, knitting and footwear industries perform repetitive tasks, they are not eligible for development or retraining programs that would prepare them for other duties. As such these employees are the victims of two levels of jurisdiction. The federal and Quebec governments have different priorities and ways of interpreting industrial needs. Both government officials and employers do not see training in terms of the workers' needs. In fact, employers often join programs only to receive short-term financial benefits. Makeshift training programs are set up to solve problems of motivation and productivity when they would be more cost-effective if they were aimed at developing industries and benefitting the various worker groups. When an agreement is reached, there is still a delay of five to eight weeks before the enployees begin to receive training, and even then the programs lack both continuity and the means to evaluate results.

Women employed in the service sectors (insurance, banking, appliance, agriculture and food, commerce, and the laundry business) encounter the same difficulties if they wish to take training programs. Small businesses cannot afford to provide such programs and large businesses allow too much room for arbitrary decisions. In the technical and management categories, in particular, female employees fail to meet the admission standards for what are, in effect, very restrictive programs.

Placement Programs and Government Services

Job security depends on the profitability, vitality and management of businesses, and, of course, on the skills of the employees. Small and medium-sized businesses do not always possess the essentials of good management. Numerous bankruptcies, factory closings and layoffs indicate that workers suffer the consequences of poor management and backward policies in various employment sectors. Since women have less seniority and perform unskilled work, they are the first to be affected, especially in the garment, knitting, textile, footwear and retail industries. Placement programs, institutional training, counselling, manpower training, job protection and aid to private industry all have an effect on working women. The division of responsibilities between levels of government adds to the problems encountered.

Women who are looking for work can go to two placement offices: the Canada Employment Centre or the Quebec Manpower Centre. They must often use the two of them because they offer both special and common services. Applicants meet with counsellors in both offices and pay regular visits to these centres in order to check the job offers posted. The Canada Employment Centre deals with placement, mobility, training, vocational counselling and other services to employers and workers. For its part, the Quebec Manpower Centre deals with qualifications, equivalences and competency cards but also provides counselling and other services for employers and employees. One of the criticisms levelled against these centres is that they do not pay sufficient attention to the employer's specific needs or job security when making placements.

Institutional Training

The number of women who register for courses offered by the two levels of government is constantly increasing and a number of factors explain why women need training. Many of them have become the family's sole means of support, others have been recently divorced and want to enter the labour market and still others wish to re-enter the work force after raising their children. These women encounter many difficulties, especially if they live in rural areas. And those who are dismissed or laid-off do not always receive the services they need.

Since courses are offered only in certain cities, many women are unable to apply because of their schedules and the transportation costs. Some courses are offered on an irregular basis making it necessary to wait up to a year before being admitted. Courses are often spread out over a period of two, three or four years, or more, depending on the number of applicants and the human and financial resources. Despite repeated protests from women's associations, experience acquired in the home or through volunteer work is still not recognized. As such, many women are at a disadvantage when applying for certain training programs. To date, attempts to eliminate discrimination in the area of choosing courses have brought few results. Some women are still dissuaded by guidance counsellors from pursuing studies they prefer and pressured into taking courses which are traditionally open to them. These courses do not always prepare them to re-enter the labour market within reasonable periods of time.

There are some obvious differences between the kind of training provided and the jobs available. For example, the committee for manpower requirements in the aerospace industry has identified the need to fill 4,000 positions within four years. Recently companies in this sector had to import foreign workers because Canadian colleges and universities do not train a sufficient number of people. Training officers in Quebec could propose such programs but as long as such disparities between training and jobs exist, employers will complain about the lack of qualified workers and lower productivity, and unions will continue to demand seniority clauses in their collective agreements. Unions will also reject technological changes in order to protect the workers, although plant shut-downs and layoffs inevitably lead to unemployment.

Manpower Requirements and Job Protection

Institutional manpower training and placement services fail to meet all the needs of unemployed women since many of them are laid off shortly after beginning their new jobs. They are then forced to start job hunting all over again. Employer and employee assistance programs have been provided by both levels of government for a number of years. The Quebec Department of Labour and Manpower and the Canada Manpower Consultative Service assist both sides in industry in order to prevent massive layoffs. When this cannot be avoided, they help workers find new jobs. This program is important and innovative because, the two levels of government provide financial, technical and human resources to assist employers and employees, and they try to bring both sides together to find solutions to their problems and ways of maintaining a fixed number of jobs in the company.

However, the manpower evaluation and other services provided leave something to be desired. The federal Department of Regional Economic Expansion and the Department of Industry, Trade and Commerce exclude the textile, garment and knitting industries in the Montreal area from employer assistance programs because they do not generate employment. On the other hand, the Quebec government has allocated $80 million to these sectors to encourage companies to modernize their equipment, become more competitive and increase their profits. As well, growth in these areas is influenced by diverse factors, such as the GATT negotiations being undertaken by the federal government.

Women, who make up the bulk of workers in the textile, garment and knitting sectors, know about difficult conditions. They are practically defenceless against arbitrary decisions of certain administrators and managers of government programs. The everyday life of these employees is like a puppet show — they are pushed and pulled in every direction. At best it is a trying experience for those involved. Most of them are trapped in a vicious circle of job hunting, layoffs, unemployment insurance and welfare. A more even distribution of economic power is urgently needed.

The Future of Working Women

What does the future hold for women employed in the more unstable sectors? The actions of the federal and Quebec governments, in their respective areas of jurisdiction, have been unintelligent and ineffective, primarily because of their different economic policies. Improving the quality of life in the work world and the economic situation of workers is an issue that should receive special attention during the constitutional talks. The right to work of all Canadians, women and men alike, should be recognized in practice, not just in theory.

Moreover, the policies affecting each citizen would be more understandable if only one government had jurisdiction in the labour field. The one that administers the programs and services should also control the social, technical and financial activities in such a way that results can be evaluated for employers and employees.

The government responsible for employment should make industrial assistance one of its priorities, especially as it relates to research and development, and have employee and employer representatives participate in industrial assistance programs. This would ensure that programs are better adapted to the real needs of the various industrial sectors. It would also lead to greater management stability, provide job security, and promote the development of human resources. The first steps would thus be taken toward improving the quality of work life.

Since its formation, the Fédération des femmes du Québec has always demanded that women be given the same rights and opportunities as men and attain the status of full citizens. However, we know we have to walk before we run. We feel it would be advisable and realistic, then, to identify the goals and principles which guide those involved in working out constitutional reforms. In the employment area, it is essential that the roles of the two levels of government be clearly defined.

If the architects of the new constitution wish to respond in an appropriate way to the needs of women, they should consider the injustices and inequalities suffered by thousands of Canadian women and adapt the constitution to the social and economic realities of today. Much needs to be done before the final goal of providing the country with a new constitution can be accomplished. The elected representatives will no doubt meet this challenge, but they should do it on terms which are decided upon by all citizens.

Appendix
Decrease in employment in the garment and knitting industries

	1961	1973	1974	1976	1977
Garments and Knitting					
Jobs in '000s					
Quebec	71.9	84.2	83.1	82.6	75.5
Canada	116.0	130.6	127.2	129.6	119.9
Quebec/Canada					
percentage	62.0	64.5	65.3	63.7	62.7
Primary textiles					
Jobs in '000s					
Quebec	39.8	40.0	39.0	33.8	29.9
Canada	64.9	76.9	75.6	63.8	58.1
Quebec/Canada					
percentage	61.3	52.0	51.6	53.0	51.5
Footwear					
Jobs in '000s					
Quebec	11.9	8.9	8.1	7.5	—
Canada	20.9	17.6	16.4	15.9	—
Quebec/Canada					
percentage	56.9	50.6	49.4	47.2	—

Sources:

Le textile primaire et le vêtement. Pour des politiques et des mesures de stabilisation de l'industrie. From the social and economic conferences held at Quebec City and Drummondville on September 6, 1977 and Montreal on September 8, 1977.

La chaussure. Pour des politiques et des mesures de stabilisation de l'industrie. From the social and economic conference held at Quebec City on September 9, 1977.

Notes

[1] *Women in the Labour Force: Facts and Figures,* 1977 Edition, Part I, *Labour Force Activity,* Women's Bureau, Conditions of Work, Labour Canada, Ottawa, 1977.

[2] Statistics Canada uses the term "labour force" to refer to individuals who occupy paid positions in the work world or those looking for work, whether unemployed or not.

[3] Women in the Labour Force, 1977.

II. Women and Work

The fundamental rights of Quebec citizens, in particular those rights relating to work, are protected by two pieces of legislation: the Quebec *Charter of Human Rights and Freedoms*, and the federal *Human Rights Act*. The latter aims to perfect Canadian legislation as it relates to discrimination and the protection of an individual's lifestyle. It covers areas under federal jurisdiction, such as communications, banks, Crown corporations, federal departments, broadcasting and television.

Since these laws protect against different kinds of discrimination, and apply to different sectors of employment, it follows that they do not afford the same type of protection to all women workers in Quebec. Both the federal *Act* and the Quebec *Charter* prohibit discrimination based on race, national or ethnic origin, colour, religion, sex and civil status (Quebec) or marital status (federal).

As for the differences between the two laws, the Quebec *Charter* protects the physically or mentally handicapped, ex-alcoholics and former psychiatric patients, but the federal *Act* protects only the physically handicapped, and then only where employment is concerned. The Quebec *Charter of Human Rights and Freedoms*, alone prohibits discrimination based on social condition, thus protecting ex-inmates, unemployed persons and welfare recipients, among others. The federal *Act*, however, does protect the rights of a person who has received a pardon. Only the Quebec *Charter* provides protection from discrimination based on political convictions, sexual orientation and language. However, age is not cited as it is in the federal *Act*. These disparities cause women to find themselves in discriminatory situations, as the following examples show.

Two Neighbours, not Necessarily the Same Rights

Marie works at a radio station and is dismissed on the basis of her political convictions. She has no recourse against her employer. The Quebec Human Rights Commission cannot deal with her complaint because broadcasting is under federal jurisdiction. Nor can the Canadian Human Rights Commission take action on Marie's behalf, because the federal *Act* does not recognize discrimination based on political convictions as grounds for prosecution. Had Marie's neighbour, a cashier in a store, found herself in a similar situation, she could have appealed to the Quebec Human Rights Commission.

A second example has to do with age: Madeleine applies for a job in a drugstore but her application is refused because she is 45 years old. The Quebec *Charter* does not recognize discrimination based on age, and therefore Madeleine has no recourse. Pierrette, who was refused a job with a bank because of her age, will obtain the support of the Canadian Human Rights Commission.

There are other major differences between the two pieces of legislation. Special programs designed to correct imbalances in the case of disadvantaged groups, such as women in the work force, are prohibited by the Quebec *Charter of Human Rights and Freedoms* but permitted in section 15 of the federal *Act*. In the case of pension and insurance plans, an employer coming under federal jurisdiction is obliged to offer men and women the same enrollment opportunities. The same does not apply to those areas under Quebec's jurisdiction. Section 97 of the Quebec *Charter* allows discriminatory practices in pension and insurance plans, based on civil status, sex, sexual orientation and handicaps. On the other hand, both federal and Quebec legislation protect the right to equal pay for work of equal value, while other Canadian provinces still only guarantee respect for the rule of "equal pay for equal work."

An Uncertain Right

Women also suffer because the means of recourse vary. In the event that mediation fails, the Canadian Human Rights Commission can establish a tribunal with members appointed by the Governor-in-Council. In Quebec, under identical circumstances, the Commission asks for a court injunction against the offender. Both men and women may also apply to the court directly, without going through the Commission, when they wish to protect a right that has been infringed.

The existence of different laws administered by various levels of government leads inevitably to differences in the way women are treated. Women suffer the consequences of these inconsistencies, and it is sometimes difficult for them to obtain relevant information because of the duplication of services. At the very least, the protection of one's right to work is uncertain.

Postscript

The thirty-second Parliament of Canada was recalled early and began sitting on October 6, 1980 to deal with an urgent and pressing matter. On October 2, 1980, the Government of Canada had released a document containing a "Proposed Resolution respecting the Constitution of Canada." The constitutional talks among federal and provincial First Ministers held in Ottawa, September 8 to 13, had ended in disagreement. To move the process along, the federal government decided on unilateral action to patriate the *British North America Act* and to entrench a charter of rights in the Constitution. The proposal was tabled in both the House and the Senate and debate began immediately.

The substantive proposals were set out in the *Constitution Act* portion of the resolution. The first part of this bill outlined a Canadian Charter of Rights and Freedoms to include: fundamental freedoms; democratic rights; mobility rights; legal rights; non-discrimination rights; official language rights; minority language educational rights; and, a guarantee of existing rights. The second part of the bill dealt with equalization and regional disparities. The third part dealt with the role of constitutional conferences. The fourth and fifth parts were directed to delineating an amendment procedure. Three means of bringing the search for consensus on an amending formula to a conclusion were proposed.

As the debate in Parliament got underway, six of the provinces announced their intention to challenge the legality of the resolution in the courts. Native peoples organized and took their case for inclusion of aboriginal rights directly to London. In Parliament itself, the Government had to invoke closure to move the debate from the House to joint committee stage. The establishment of the joint parliamentary committee on the Constitution of Canada sparked a high degree of interest among groups and individuals. The original deadline of December 9, 1980 for committee hearings had to be extended to allow for the presentation of briefs.

In the midst of these several activities and responses to the federal initiative, the question of human rights for women has become a visible issue. Section 15(1) of the Charter respecting non-discrimination was questioned on the grounds offered by Eberts and Baines and other experts. On October 8, 1980, the Canadian Advisory Council on the Status of Women made public its position that: "Unless the wording of the Charter is revised to guarantee fundamental rights for women, they will continue to risk the kind of discrimination so often experienced in the past." The Council had previously advised the Government of its position and set out to prepare a formal brief for presentation to the joint parliamentary committee when it was announced. It also set about to inform the public and solicit feedback through a questionnaire mailed to women's groups across the country. Support for the position has been growing. At least one female member of Parliament spoke in favour of the Council's position during debate in the House of Commons and others, such as the federal Human Rights Commissioner, have expressed concern publicly about the inadequacy of the provision.

If there is to be an entrenched Charter of Rights and Freedoms in a new constitution, the guarantee of fundamental rights for women is a central issue. It constitutes a necessary first step in improving women's status in Canada. However, there are many other issues which will also need to be addressed if this issue is resolved. Family law, provision of social services, the creation of economic and employment opportunities, and the representation of women in governmental institutions are matters which will still need to be examined and positions developed. The process of constitutional reform and renewal will thus be with us for a long time. Hopefully, it will provide an opportunity for women to assert themselves and learn how to bring influence to bear on the decisions of governments.

Contributors

Lucienne Aubert, lawyer, Hydro-Québec, Montreal, Quebec

Beverley Baines, Assistant Professor, Faculty of Law, Queen's University, Kingston, Ontario

Nicole Bénard, lawyer, Aide juridique de Longeuil, Longeuil, Quebec

Myrna Bowman, lawyer, firm of Bowman, Bound and Hirsch, Winnipeg, Manitoba

Micheline Carrier, journalist, Quebec, Quebec

Audrey Doerr, Associate Professor, Department of Political Science, Simon Fraser University, Burnaby, British Columbia

Muriel Duckworth, President, Canadian Research Institute for the Advancement of Women, Halifax, Nova Scotia

Louise Dulude, freelance researcher and writer, Ottawa, Ontario

Mary Eberts, lawyer, firm of Tory, Tory, Deslauriers and Binnington, Toronto, Ontario

Fédération des femmes du Québec

Carol Mahood Huddart, lawyer, firm of Buckler, Fast and Brown, Victoria, British Columbia

National Action Committee on the Status of Women

Native Women's Association of Canada